CARNIVAL IN ALABAMA

CARNIVAL in ALABAMA

Marked Bodies and Invented Traditions in Mobile

ISABEL MACHADO

University Press of Mississippi / Jackson

Publication of this book was supported in part by the UPM First Author's Fund.

The University Press of Mississippi is the scholarly publishing agency of the Mississippi Institutions of Higher Learning: Alcorn State University, Delta State University, Jackson State University, Mississippi State University, Mississippi University for Women, Mississippi Valley State University, University of Mississippi, and University of Southern Mississippi.

www.upress.state.ms.us

The University Press of Mississippi is a member of the Association of University Presses.

Any discriminatory or derogatory language or hate speech regarding race, ethnicity, religion, sex, gender, class, national origin, age, or disability that has been retained or appears in elided form is in no way an endorsement of the use of such language outside a scholarly context.

An earlier version of chapter 5 was published as "Never Too Big, Never Too Much: How the Order of Osiris Helped Build a Visible LGBTQ Community in Mobile, Alabama," in *Oral History*, vol. 46, no. 1, March 2018.

Copyright © 2023 by University Press of Mississippi
All rights reserved

First printing 2023
∞

Library of Congress Cataloging-in-Publication Data

Names: Machado, Isabel (Cultural historian), author.
Title: Carnival in Alabama : marked bodies and invented traditions in Mobile / Isabel Machado.
Description: Jackson : University Press of Mississippi, [2023] | Includes bibliographical references and index.
Identifiers: LCCN 2022047047 (print) | LCCN 2022047048 (ebook) | ISBN 9781496842589 (hardback) | ISBN 9781496842596 (trade paperback) | ISBN 9781496842602 (epub) | ISBN 9781496842619 (epub) | ISBN 9781496842626 (pdf) | ISBN 9781496842633 (pdf)
Subjects: LCSH: Carnival—Alabama—Mobile. | Mobile (Ala.)—History. | Mobile (Ala.)—Social life and customs.
Classification: LCC GT4211.M6 M33 2023 (print) | LCC GT4211.M6 (ebook) | DDC 394.2509761—dc23/eng/20221110
LC record available at https://lccn.loc.gov/2022047047
LC ebook record available at https://lccn.loc.gov/2022047048

British Library Cataloging-in-Publication Data available

Para Ieda

To accept one's past—one's history—is not the same thing as drowning in it; it is learning how to use it. An invented past can never be used; it cracks and crumbles under pressure like clay in a season of drought.

—JAMES BALDWIN[1]

Memory is life, borne by living societies founded in its name. It remains in permanent evolution, open to the dialectic of remembering and forgetting, unconscious of its successive deformations, vulnerable to manipulation and appropriation, susceptible to being dormant and periodically revived. History, on the other hand, is the reconstruction, always problematic and incomplete, of what is no longer.

—PIERRE NORA[2]

CONTENTS

Acknowledgments ix

List of Abbreviations xv

Preface: On Carnival Cities and Language Choices xvii

Introduction 3

PART I: INVENTED TRADITIONS

Chapter 1. Official Narratives, Origin Myths,
and Tradition Invention 17

Chapter 2. Regulating, Controlling, and Sanctioning Revelry 31

Chapter 3. Downtown: Mobile's "Negro Main Street"
and the Emergence of the "Fruit Loop" 50

PART II: MARKED BODIES

Chapter 4. Official "Colored" Mardi Gras and Mobile's
Black Liberation Struggle 75

Chapter 5. Queering Mobile's Mardi Gras.................................100

Chapter 6. Carnivalesque Bodies:
Defying the White Gaze and Respectability Politics 127

Chapter 7. Plus Ça Change? 149

Conclusion: Now You Do Watcha Wanna 166

Appendix: Narrators Index 177

Notes...183

Bibliography...215

Index..231

ACKNOWLEDGMENTS

We often talk about research and writing processes as journeys. In this particular case, that is quite appropriate. I lived in eight different homes, in three different countries, while researching and writing this book. Along the way, I counted on indescribable love and support from friends, colleagues, compañerxs, and family (as well as with the kindness of strangers). So many people helped me along the way that I offer my sincerest apologies in advance if I forget to mention anyone here.

As this project began at the University of Memphis, I would like to acknowledge the guidance and support of Michele Coffey, Sarah Potter, and especially Aram Goudsouzian. At a moment of self-doubt, when I was not sure that I was capable of going through with this, W. Chris Johnson told me I could not give up, because he had to read this book. Here it is, Chris! I am also grateful to the Department of History and Karen Bradley and Karen Jackett for their assistance. The Department's Writing Fellowship Award, the Ruth and Harry Woodbury Graduate Fellowship in Southern History, and the Dr. William R. and Helen Lucille Gillaspie Scholarship in Latin American History, as well as the College of Arts & Sciences' Summer Travel Enrichment Award made it possible for me not only to conduct my research in Mobile but also to present and discuss it in the United States, Mexico, Northern Ireland, and Canada. Due to the interdisciplinary nature of this project, I knocked on the door of a good part of the Department's faculty at some point or another seeking references and advice. So thank you, Amanda Lee Savage, Andrew Daily, Beverly Bond, Chrystal Goudsouzian,

Dennis Laumann, Guiomar Dueñas Vargas, Peter Brand, Scott P. Marler, and Susan E. O'Donovan. I would like to recognize chair Daniel Unowsky for his efforts to make the best out of a difficult situation as I arrived for a postdoc a few months before a global pandemic wreaked havoc on my plans. I was also lucky to study there with inspiring colleagues such as Andrea Ringer, Le'Trice Donaldson, and Rebekkah Mulholland. My comrade Troy Hallsell not only read many drafts of different incarnations of this project but also visited me during fieldwork in Mobile.

But I could trace the origin story of this project further, to the time I spent as an MA student at the University of South Alabama. There, Clarence Mohr reminded me that I am a historian and guided my first steps into US southern studies. In the USA I had the privilege of auditing Frye Gaillard's class on the history of the US civil rights movement, which helped this foreigner have a better grasp of the complicated dynamics of Alabama's race relations. As a fellow outsider-insider historian living in Mobile, Martha Jane Brazy provided invaluable feedback on different versions of this manuscript. Our Zoom conversations, her unwavering support, and the corrections she sent me days before I submitted the final draft were a life (and book) saver. At South I also had the honor of meeting Kern Jackson, whose pioneering investigation of Black Mobile Mardi Gras laid the foundation for anyone who follows. His embracing me as a fellow Mardi Gras scholar provided me a much-needed sense of belonging and community.

Perhaps I could dig even deeper and take this narrative further back to my youth as an undergraduate in the Carnival City I was born in, Salvador, Bahia, Brazil at the Universidade Federal da Bahia. (Viva São Lázaro!) Being João José Reis's student and advisee showed me that it is possible to be generous, accessible, committed to one's principles, and a stellar scholar and writer at the same time. Those are goals I try to live up to as a historian and as a human. So it is hard to explain how exhilarating it was, after all these years, to still count on his precise critique and encouragement as I navigated the daunting process of writing my first book.

The months I spent as a Research Associate with the SARChI Chair in South African Art and Visual Culture at the University of Johannesburg in 2021 allowed me to concentrate on my writing without having to worry about teaching responsibilities. For that I am grateful to Brenda Schmahmann.

I thank my fellow Carnival/celebration/festivity studies folks, Howard Philips Smith, Jack Santino, Miguel Valerio, and Rebecca Dirksen, for their fellowship and words of encouragement. Collaborating with the *Journal of Festive Studies* team for two years on a special issue, "The Materiality of Festivity," greatly influenced this book. I am grateful to Aurélie Godet, Ellen Litwicki, Cora Gaebles, and Yelena Kalinsky for their support and patience throughout that process. I am also indebted to Aurélie for sharing her knowledge and sources, and providing feedback on my work. Other scholars and independent researchers graciously shared their (sometimes unpublished) writings, sources, and advice with me: Amy L. Stone, Ann J. Pond, Bruce Brasell, Gill Frank, James Ito-Adler, Jerry T. Watkins III, Joshua Burford, Lauren Gutterman, Paulo Miguez, Scotty Kirkland, Slade Watson, Steve Joynt, and Wayne Dean.

Thanks to my now-colleagues at the *Oral History* journal, I was able to share a part of this research in 2018 in an article that would serve as an early abridged draft of chapter 5. That experience reassured me that it was possible to tell a local story that was relatable to folks in other parts of the globe.

One of the highlights of this process was collaborating with two amazing academics and friends: Katerina Sergidou and Emily Ruth Allen. My *compañera carnavalera* Katerina has been a source of inspiration for her scholarship and activism since our first encounter at the 2018 ESSHC meeting in Belfast. She is a constant reminder of the hypocrisy of theory without praxis. Seguimos juntas, hermana! During the times that I was working on this book without institutional support and, more importantly, without access to an academic library, Emily had my back. I lost count of the books, articles, clippings, and documents she sent me via email and Facebook Messenger.

I also appreciate the University Press of Mississippi, and especially my editor Emily Bandy, for their interest in and support for this project. I am grateful for the readers whose critiques helped me materialize the ideas that, at first, made sense in my head but not necessarily to others. My gratitude goes as well to the marketing/publicity folks, Joey Brown and Courtney McCreary, to copy editor Lisa Williams, and to designer Jennifer Mixon.

Of course, no research is possible without the collaboration of librarians and archivists. So, my most heartfelt thank-you to everyone who assisted me in the archives I visited and to those who provided support remotely: Carol Ellis (The Doy Leale McCall Rare Book and Manuscript Library), Phillip Cunningham (The Amistad Research Center), Valerie Ellis (Local History and Genealogy—Mobile Public Library), and Zennia Calhoun (Mobile Municipal Archives). This project would not have taken off if Charles Torrey had not taken me under his wing. Aside from being a narrator and a dear friend, he patiently walked me through the labyrinth of Mardi Gras sources at the Jack Friend Research Library. Without Deborah Gurt's support and dedication, The Mardi Gras and Social Change Oral Histories collection would not exist.

One of the main goals of this project has always been to introduce new stories and characters to this historical narrative, and I knew that it would take a lot of images to accomplish that. It was important to me that readers not only read about the people and places that are being introduced here. They also had to see them. Many of the images included in this book have never been published before, and it took years of research to compile them. It also took a lot of help. So, I am extremely grateful for the University Press of Mississippi not only for accommodating my request to add so many illustrations to the book but also for making that possible through the UPM First Author's Fund, which covered most of the permission and digitizing expenses. I would also like to thank again Deborah Gurt, who provided invaluable assistance with the amazing photos from the Doy Leale McCall Rare Book and Manuscript Library collections, along with Michael A. Campbell and Kristina Polizzi. My gratitude also goes to Meredith McDonough and Amelia H. Chase from the Alabama Department of Archives and History, who helped me with the Claire Matturro photographs; and Sharon Steinmann, Lawrence Specter, and Sydney Batten for their support with the Prancing Elites photo. And, of course, everyone who entrusted me with their personal archives: Al Vaughan, Domingo Soto, Joey Potter, Julie Dunlap, Kathie Hiers, King Lawrence XV, Miss Cie, Queen Danielle II, Richard Rain Perez, Sheila Hagler, Sherry Odom, Suzanne Cleveland.

Family and friends lifted me up and helped me maintain my sanity through this demanding process. Antonino and Ieda gave me régua e compasso (salud y vida por nuestros muertos!). Angela and Sérgio help me carry their legacy. Olga delivered our future into this world in the shapes of Clara and Jorge. Jorge, my godson and friend who encourages his godmother to pursue her dreams. I can't wait to see Clara fulfill hers. Mara, Emilio, and Marcos, the family I gained when I met my life partner. The sisters I chose, the amazing women who, for almost three decades, fill me with pride and grant me a safe port: Caroline, Fabiane, Giovana, Janaína, Lorena, Maira, Taíse, Tenille, Vanessa. My thanks also to everyone who helped me fill and empty our backyard beer buckets in Mobile, Memphis, Salvador, and Monterrey. Your companionship provided the much-needed moments of levity and joy through some of the most stressful periods of my life.

But this project does not exist without the generosity and trust of the people in Mobile who opened their hearts, and their homes, and shared their stories with me. All the folks who provided information, on and off the record, who fed and housed me, who gave me rides and ball tickets. I will never be able to thank Kim McKeand and Cari Searcy enough. There was a time when they even had a room named after me in their house, and Cari also helped me conduct some of the oral history interviews. Gideon Carson Kennedy gave me shelter and visited archives for me when I was not able to. Thank you also, Claire Melanson, Cristine Rivas Bramlet, Heather Rowell, Jonathan Campbell, Keia Martin, Leah Odeneal, and Patrick Odeneal for always making me feel at home in the US Gulf Coast. Others who I did not have a chance to interview but still provided contacts, photos, documents, and information: Becky Hier, Bunnie Hopson, Carl Eccles, Charlie Smoke, David Hardee, Donna Hall Foster, Harry Tarver, Howie Cuevas, Jack Rupert, Jamie Middlebrooks, Judi Gulledge, Katherine March, Ken Mauldin, Kevin Lee, Leigh Jones, Miss Cie, Renita Mason Tonder, Tim Wolff, Tom Perez, Tom Mason, Tyra Barry Lancaster, and Vonnie McMillan Jamison. And, of course, the narrators who helped me believe again in the power of connections and stories. I hope you know that I will be forever grateful for your kindness and trust: Bobby Dennison, Domingo Soto, Eric Franklin Finley, George Moore, Homer McClure, Hosea London, Jack Bishop, Joey Potter, Al Vaughan, Julie Dunlap/Queen Julie III, Juanita Richardson, Kathie Hiers, King Charles XXIV/Charles Torrey, King Lawrence XV, L. Craig Roberts, Linda Dennison, Nick Shantazio, Palmer Richardson, Pam Richardson Moore, Queen Danielle II, Queen Janette XII/Janette Curry, Queen Richard IV/Richard Rain Perez, Queen Vickie V/John G. Uptagrafft, Ron Barret, Sherry Odom, Stephen Gaudet, Suzanne Cleveland.

The only constant in this eventful and uncertain journey was Daniel Wildberger's support and companionship. With our depaisé family (which includes cats from Alabama and Nuevo León) I am always home. Obrigada por tudo, companheiro!

For the last year of writing this book I was close to the beaches of Bahia. That may sound like a privilege, but it is actually a birthright. I am Soteropolitana. When I was born, Ieda Machado asked a wise person to consult the cowry shells to find out who would share with her the responsibility of looking over me. Turns out, I am also the daughter of the Queen of the Seas. Something Ieda always reminded me not to forget. While I did not remain as close to the religion she raised me in after her death, that doesn't mean that I stopped feeling their nurturing presence every time I see and hear the ocean. Thank you, mothers! Odoyá!

LIST OF ABBREVIATIONS

CMMA = City of Mobile Municipal Archives
DLM = The Doy Leale McCall Rare Book and Manuscript Library
JFRL = The Jack Friend Research Library
LHGL = The Local History & Genealogy Library
MAMGA = Mobile Area Mardi Gras Association
MCA = Mobile Carnival Association
MCCA = Mobile Colored Carnival Association
MGSCOH = Mardi Gras and Social Change Oral Histories
NAACP = The National Association for the Advancement of Colored People
NOW = Neighborhood Organized Workers
NPVL = Non-Partisan Voters' League of Mobile
OOM = Order of Myths
OOO = Order of Osiris
SCLC = The Southern Christian Leadership Conference
UKA = United Klans of America

PREFACE
On Carnival Cities and Language Choices

Most cities have some sort of public festival or celebration. But that does not make them a Carnival City. As I articulate elsewhere, in Carnival Cities, "whether you participate in the revelry or not, like it or not, your daily life is deeply affected by it. Your most mundane decisions have to take into consideration an unusual and sometimes inconvenient calendar. In a Carnival City, the year does not start until the partying ends and it is all but impossible to avoid the sounds, the smell, and the euphoria surrounding you."[1] As Mikhail Bakhtin put it: "While carnival lasts, there is no other life outside it."[2] Although I do not consider myself a *folia*, I was born and raised in a Carnival City: Salvador (Brazil).[3] Hence, it is not surprising that I wanted to understand and write about another Carnival City dear to my heart: Mobile (USA), where I lived for four years (2008–12). As some of the narrators whose stories helped me write this book noted, it is hard to explain to "outsiders" what that means and feels like.

While conducting the research for this book, I attended Mardi Gras balls from eight different organizations (Black, white, and interracial, LGBTQIA+ and straight) and watched countless parades. On Joe Cain Day, 2016, I joined a second line to attend my friends' joyful wedding ceremony in front of the Church Street Cemetery, a celebration that would not have been possible a year earlier, since they are both women. From there I ran to Down the Bay's "Mardi Gras Central" to visit with the Richardsons and enjoy delicious gumbo, red beans and rice, fried fish, and other delicacies they were so generous in sharing with me. We talked and watched parades on TV, and then it was time to run back to the Fruit Loop to catch B-Bob's special Mardi Gras drag show featuring local legends such as Miss Cie and Venus Shante DaVis. The following year I marched with the Secret Misters inside the Joe Cain procession. In that one day, which surpasses Fat Tuesday in importance for Mobilian revelers, I crossed several invisible physical, social, and emotional barriers that divide the city. This book investigates how these barriers came about and what they mean for Mobilians who have been othered by the "traditional" narrative about their city's Mardi Gras history.

When I set out to investigate how Mardi Gras, an institution created for and by rich white men as a heteronormative tool of white supremacy, became an important mechanism of identity building, social ascension, and acceptance for African Americans and LGBTQIA+ people in Mobile, I knew I would have to rely on oral history, as the stories and experiences I was searching for were not available in archives. In an attempt to capture the complexity of Mobile's recent sociocultural history, I spoke with twenty-six narrators from across spectrums of race, gender, class, and sexuality between 2014 and 2017. Most of these conversations were recorded oral history interviews, others were more-informal phone conversations or messages exchanged via email and social media. The project resulted in the Mardi Gras and Social Change Oral Histories (MGSCOH) collection currently available at the University of South Alabama's Doy Leale McCall Library archives.[4] (There is an Appendix at the end of this book for anyone interested in more information about the people mentioned and/or quoted).

By putting disparate voices and identities in conversation, I sought to create a more complex image of the city and its annual celebration, rather than uncovering any particular group's experiences. I am aware that this approach (seeking the broader rather than the deeper picture) means that this book provides a surface-level texture of the city rather than a profound investigation and analysis of any particular experience. This was a necessary and deliberate choice. Since not much has been written on the social and cultural history of Mobile and its Carnival celebration, this project was envisioned as a starting point. By putting these disparate memories in conversation, I hope to paint a more nuanced picture of the city's Carnival experiences. At times I introduce the narrators, other times I place different voices together, establishing an artificial dialogue between people who often didn't know of each other. Many times I let the narrators speak for themselves using block quotes rather than paraphrasing them. These decisions reflect this book's goals: to add other voices and actors to the historical narrative of Mobile's Mardi Gras, and to show the interconnectedness of these diverse experiences.

Mobile's racial relations and dynamics are further complicated by the presence of an intermediary group, which, to borrow from US historian Carl Degler, used the "mulatto escape hatch" to elude some of that society's harsher discriminations: Creoles of color.[5] The term Creole has held different meaning in different parts of the Americas in different time periods.[6] In the context of Mobile specifically, Creoles are described as (usually light-skinned) people of mixed African and European descent who speak a dialect of the French or Spanish languages. Late nineteenth-century city directories, which separated people by race, placed Creoles in a different category from "colored" people, while some racially segregated institutions, such as the city's fire forces, presented three separate categories. Yet the city's 1897 Code of Ordinances thus defines its racial terminology: "The term 'negro' within the meaning of this Code includes mulatto. The term 'mulatto' or 'person of color' within the meaning of this Code is a person of mixed blood, descended on the part of the father or mother from negro ancestors to the third generation inclusive, although one ancestor of each generation may have been a white person."[7] Although Creoles retained some social status due to colorism, they lost their special legal status during Reconstruction.[8] I decided not to discuss Creoles as a separate category in this book, understanding that more research needs to be done to capture their peculiar experiences.[9] Furthermore, in several instances, the categories of "colored" and "Creole" were blurred, as Creoles took part in some of the African American organizations discussed here. Hence, I will focus on organizations created by people of African descent in Mobile without making a distinction.

Historians who write about lesbian, gay, bisexual, trans, and otherwise queer people from the past are often confronted with difficult linguistic choices. Should we use the language of the time period even though that might seem inadequate or even offensive to current audiences? Or should we "update" the terminology, running the risk of being anachronistic or ahistorical? Labeling historical actors retroactively is even more complicated. People's identities and desires can be fluid and are not always straightforward. As matthew heinz notes, identity labels are "unstable, conflicted zones of cultural contests" and queer theory and activist critique have shown that "identity practices are not necessarily intentional, tactical, or strategic. While for some, disrupting gender normativity is an explicit political goal, it is a contextual social choice for some, and an artifact of one's physical appearance for others."[10] Some of the men interviewed for the MGSCOH project identified as gay but discussed romantic and/or erotic relations with women. Some people mentioned here identified themselves or were identified by others as heterosexual but had sexual and/or romantic relationships with people of the same sex. To some, cross-dressing during Mardi Gras was a fun experiment, to others a way to publicly embody an identity that had to be hidden. There were also, of course, those to whom cross-dressing served as a means to mock femininity and/or offend people whose sexualities and gender expressions were perceived as deviant. It is not always clear which was which.

Although the acronym LGBTQIA+ was not available for most of the period covered here, it will be used as an umbrella term to refer to folks who somehow did not conform to gender and sexual normativity. For instance, I refer to the Order of Osiris as an LGBTQIA+ organization, which is congruent with its current incarnation but would likely not have made sense to its founders in the early 1980s. When used as an adjective (queer people/queer spaces) and without quotation marks, the term queer is used here in the same capacity.[11] When used as a noun and inside quotation marks ("the queers") it is used as a reference to terminology of the past. I agree that queer is "not just the new gay" and understand the pitfalls of using umbrella terms to refer to a collective that contains people whose experiences can be considerably diverse.[12] Yet I see it as a useful term to refer to a group of people who were marginalized (and who organized) because of what were perceived as deviant sexual orientations and gender identities, despite their individual differences. While contemporary readers might find it excluding, "gay" was also used as an umbrella term (gay Mardi Gas balls, gay pride, gay bars, etc.) in the past and will be used as such here in respect of narrators and historical actors' linguistic choices.

I understand the importance of and have the utmost respect for historically marginalized groups' rights to linguistic self-determination. People of African descent in the US have been referred to, and referred to themselves, using different terms throughout the country's history. Understanding that my terminology will likely be outdated at some point soon, and that there is no clear consensus, I tried to employ here the most currently accepted language when I am referring to US Americans "who trace their ancestry to Africa:" Black (capitalized) and African American.[13] Yet I also use here historically accurate terminology that might be uncomfortable to some readers and kept the wording, spelling, and capitalization (or lack of) in the direct quotes from primary and secondary sources. Again, I do so in order to respect the agency of historical actors. While terms such as "Negro" or "colored" might offend sensibilities in the 2020s, they were used by Black people to identify themselves, forge common identities, and build community in order to fight and survive systemic racism in the past. Hence, "correcting" the terminology would imply ignoring their right to self-identify. While some recent publications refer to Mobile's African American Carnival organization in the past as Mobile Area Mardi Gras Association (MAMGA), I use their original name Mobile Colored Carnival Association (MCCA), when I am referring to the group before they officially changed it in 1972.

The book also contains terminology that is, and has always been, unequivocally violent and offensive. I do not use these words lightly or gratuitously. I believe it is important that, as historians, we register and confront the linguistic violence of the past. In every instance, the words appear here as literal quotes from primary or secondary sources.

The initial (rather ambitious) plan of this project was to analyze the experiences of marked bodies in Mobile in all of their complex intersections. Yet, in six years of research, I failed to record the specific experiences of older Black LGBTQIA+ Mobilians. This is possibly a result of the double-edged nature of marked Mardi Gras experiences. While marking oneself or a group by creating a separate organization for Black or LGBTQIA+ people provided an avenue for marginalized folks to participate in their city's defining festival, it sometimes meant that people had to dissociate the different elements of their intersectional identity. It can also, of course, mean that people who embodied intersectional oppressions were not comfortable sharing their life stories with an outsider.[14]

I recognize the urgency of documenting the specific experiences of queer people of color in Mobile while also accepting the limitations this project. I wanted to understand how historically marginalized groups of people used Mardi Gras as a vehicle to navigate and negotiate their space and place in their city's society. To do so I had to focus on people who organized and participated in Carnival as Black and/or as queer. As far as I can tell, until very recently, there was no organization dedicated to people who identified specifically as both Black and LGBTQIA+ in Mobile. I found a 1992 announcement in a gay publication for the creation of a group "formed in

Mobile to cultivate positive perceptions of lesbians, gay men, and bisexuals of African descent among themselves and those exploring the diversity of sexual orientation and lifestyles" but was unable to track any of its members.[15] It is not the intention of this book to present queer and Black experiences as mutually exclusive, but rather to show how, in a segregated and conservative city, people who embodied intersectional axes of oppression sometimes had to choose between different identity markers to congregate with their peers.[16]

CARNIVAL IN ALABAMA

INTRODUCTION

Born in 1938, Suzanne Cleveland looks back fondly on the history of downtown Mobile, Alabama, to a time when people wore gloves and hats to enjoy the elegant department stores and restaurants. But she eventually realized that there was something wrong with those memories when she recalled that the domestic worker who took her there had to ride in the back of the bus.[1] Eric Finley has a more critical relationship with his downtown memories as he remembered the segregated spaces and facilities that were off-limits to him as an African American child in the late 1950s. He could not enter, for instance, the bathroom located underneath Bienville Square, which Suzanne did not use, because it was not considered clean enough for an affluent white girl. That same bathroom would eventually become a cruising spot for gay men and is also where a white novice police officer, Jack Bishop, encountered one of his first murder victims in the early 1960s: an older man killed by "rough trade" in a practice known as "rolling the queers." As these few examples show, the experience of the same space can be very different depending on different historical actors' perspectives.[2]

On the surface, Mobile, Alabama is a very segregated city where people tend to acknowledge (and stay in) their "place." Mardi Gras organizations seem to perfectly reflect that dynamic. Although there is no official rule segregating them, they are often divided by gender (women's and men's organizations) and across racial lines (Black or white), while "gay" societies tend to encompass a more diverse spectrum of people who identify as LGBTQIA+.[3] Previous works that investigated Mobile Mardi Gras focused on organized Carnival societies and events, reinforcing those separations. This book seeks to explore intersections and interactions by looking at the time (Mardi Gras) and space (downtown) where different groups of people converged in that city, even if at times they were not aware of (or acknowledged) each other's existence.[4]

Mardi Gras plays a crucial role in the construction of Mobile's identity and has a considerable impact on the city's economy and on how its citizens have defined and imagined themselves.[5] Carnival mystic societies, originated in the 1830s, started as extremely exclusive organizations composed by a white male elite seeking to uphold and display their perceived superiority.[6] Their annual pageantry reflected the city's social hierarchies: people of African descent were excluded, white women played an important yet secondary role, and codes of gender and sexuality normativity were imposed (at least in public). At different moments during the twentieth century, however, Mobile's African American Carnival Association, white women's parading groups, and LGBTQIA+ organizations have challenged that tradition.

The equivalent to New Orleans's Carnival krewes, mystic societies are private organizations that throw the balls and parades that happen in Mobile during the pre-Lenten celebrations season. While they are technically secret societies, friends, family members, and even acquaintances usually know about each other's affiliation with particular groups. Hence, membership in a mystic society means a public acknowledgment and display of identity and social hierarchies. It requires setting boundaries for who belongs to (or is excluded from) the group and a declaration of identification with what it represents.

Yet this book not only looks at the people who participated in societies segregated by race, gender, and/or sexual orientation but also investigates the experiences of "marked bodies" outside of these organizations, or people involved in Carnival through their labor or as audiences (or publics) of the spectacle. It also expands the definition of Mobile's Carnival tradition beyond the official pageantry by including street maskers and laborers and neighborhood cookouts. From flambeaux, flare bearers, marching bands, and majorettes in parades, to musicians and serving staff in balls, Black bodies have always been on display in Mobile's white spectacles. African American Mobilians got together downtown to watch the different (Black and white) organized parades, which until 1992 had two separate routes. Queer labor and aesthetics have also hidden in plain sight at Mardi Gras events even before the

1907 White Mardi Gras monarchs King Felix, Thomas Wilkins Sims, and his consort, Virginia A. Lyons, accompanied by their pages, 1907. Erik Overbey Collection, the Doy Leale McCall Rare Book and Manuscript Library, University of South Alabama.

advent of openly gay balls. Gender and sexuality nonconforming people took advantage of sanctioned moments of inversion to express themselves freely in the city's streets, and the Fruit Loop became an important safe space where LGBTQIA+ Mobilians could enjoy the pageantry and create a counterpublic.[7]

Known as the city of six flags (Spanish, French, British, Republic of Alabama, Confederate States, United States), Mobile is simultaneously a typical and unique city in the postwar United States. It was a quintessential boomtown during the WWII years. That prosperity was followed by a period of rapid urban decline and subsequent (and ongoing) attempts at revitalizing (or gentrifying) its downtown area. As in many other US cities, urban renewal, integration, and other socioeconomic developments led to white flight, marginalized the African American population, and set the stage for the development of LGBTQIA+ community building and subculture.[8] Yet these usually segregated segments of the city's society converged once a year to create a common identity, that of a Carnival City. The twentieth century was a period of reinvention for the Mobile Mardi Gras tradition as marked bodies adopted and adapted the rituals and symbols of a white supremacist and heteronormative institution to claim their place in that society.

Mobile is a fascinating city stuck between the "Redneck Riviera" and the "Big Easy," a geographical location that reflects its split personality. It is a port city that identifies with Old South mythology while presenting itself as a Carnival destination. It has been overshadowed by its more exuberant neighbor, New Orleans, ever since it lost to the latter the status as capital of Louisiana, in 1722. The same is true in terms of historiography, especially when it comes to Mardi Gras. Although the Azalea City is credited for having invented the idea of the mystic society, or krewe, more often than not, when researchers publish books about US Carnival, they are referring to the Crescent City. Most of the scarce historiography on Mobile Mardi Gras was not written by historians but by people involved in the festivities, and it concentrates on its origin myths and on the experiences of white elites.[9]

"Southern culture" in the US is often associated with whiteness and heteronormativity. By showing Mardi Gras as an important element in the identity and community formation in Mobile, this book challenges this separation between southern and Black or queer identities.[10] By looking at the roles assigned, inaccessible to, or claimed and appropriated by straight-identified African American men and women and people who defied gender and sexual normativity in the festivities (regardless of their racial identity), it seeks to understand power dynamics through culture and ritual. By looking at Carnival as an invented tradition and as a semiotic system associated with discourses of power, it joins a transnational conversation about the phenomenon.[11]

Performance studies and queer theory provide a template to approach Black and/or queer bodies in Mobile Mardi Gras, showing how normative discourses affect self-expressions, perceptions, and representations of groups of people who have been othered.[12] This scholarship also complicates narratives that perceive Carnival as a vehicle *either* of social oppression or progress by showing that this process does not necessarily entail lack of agency and pleasure. Joseph Roach argues that performance is simultaneously memory, forgetting, and reinvention, noting that when people "search for the purity of origins" they embark on a voyage not of discovery but of erasure.[13] Roach's description of krewe-centered New Orleans Carnival as

"Pavlovian" (a mechanism of social conditioning) rather than "Bakhtinian" (an instance of inversion of social hierarchies) resonates with this book's questions about Mobile's festivities as it investigates if it is possible to be "Pavlovian" *and* "Bakhtinian" at the same time.

Early works that sought to document the history of Mobile's Mardi Gras reinforced the "markedness" of these organizations by telling a story that had white elites as protagonists and that is imbued with Lost Cause nostalgia. People of color and LGBTQIA+ folks, when mentioned at all, were relegated to separate chapters or footnotes.[14] The same can be said of newspaper coverage and museum exhibitions. Yet, as time went by, that narrative (and tradition) was reinvented. The city developed what appears to be a "separate but equal" approach to the Black and white experiences of the festivities. Black Mardi Gras has a larger space in the Carnival Museum, and the newspaper coverage has become more evenhanded. In 2016 members of the city's oldest surviving LGBTQIA+ mystic society paraded publicly for the first time, and their emblem was part of the closing event for the *Art and Design of Mardi Gras* exhibition held at the Mobile Museum of Art.[15]

Recent tourism commercials sell a city too busy celebrating to hate. In one of them, a white man dressed as an Indian chief dances among an interracial crowd to the sound of a Black brass band. Since the city's Carnival is not necessarily known for its integration, this is a clear example of tradition (re)invention in the making.[16] Attempts to appeal to more conservative crowds brand Mobile's Mardi Gras as "family friendly," while painting a picture of racial democracy to attract tourists interested in Old South charm, absent its baggage. Yet Confederate battle flags are often on display on revelers' clothing and personal objects during the festivities, while the whole pageantry is still drenched in Lost Cause mythology. As the city seeks to reinvent itself, in part through Mardi Gras, it is important to understand how it got here.

Dissecting the Title: A Primer on Key Concepts

Carnival is the pre-Lenten festive season leading up to Fat Tuesday (aka Shrove Tuesday or Mardi Gras), a day of unbridled debauchery that precedes Ash Wednesday in the Catholic calendar. It is observed in different parts of the globe but has particular regional characteristics in each place that celebrates it, and it is a defining festivity in different Pan-American cities. In some places, such as the US Gulf Coast, Mardi Gras is a synonym of both the festive season (Carnival) and of the last day of celebrations (Fat/Shrove Tuesday). Discussing the plurality of the many Carnivals (re)invented in the "New World," Fred Góes argues that while they share a common trait of miscegenation and syncretism in their European, African, and Indigenous roots, the combination of these influences takes different shapes in different places.[17]

Markedness

In oversimplified terms, markedness is the asymmetric relationship between words that can be extended to social relations and hierarchies.[18] Morphology recognizes negative and positive word forms showing that whereas the "negative" form is *marked*, the "positive" word is *unmarked* (happy/*un*happy, adequate/*in*adequate, edible/*in*edible, clean/*un*clean, etc.). The same goes for masculine forms, which do not carry affixes (priest/priest*ess*, host/host*ess*, baron/baron*ess*), or for words that can be used as the default form and have generic applications. For instance, while *man*kind usually includes people of all sexes, *woman*kind would be gender specific. Although the concept generates debates in its application to linguistics, it is useful as a theoretical framework to explain sociocultural formations, relations, and hierarchies.[19] Unmarked forms appear to be neutral, normal or natural, reflecting dominant cultural norms while hiding their privileged status. Marked forms, on the other hand, are perceived as derivative, deviant, and subordinate.[20] Grada Kilomba explains how the process of "marking" is related to the establishment of difference:

> For example, as Black people, we are often referred to as different. And I pose the question: different from whom? Who is different? Are you different from me or am I different from you? . . . I only become different if the white person sees themself as a point of reference, as the norm from which I differ. When I place myself as the norm from which others differ from, then others become different from me. So it is necessary to deconstruct what the difference is.[21]

Markedness is a useful concept for analyzing Mobile's Mardi Gras. In publications and museum exhibitions, as well as in informal conversations, while Black or "colored" Carnival, gay balls, and women's organizations are "marked," societies and events created for and by white, straight-identified, men do not need markers. Therefore, what I refer to as marked bodies here are the people who deviated from the (white, male, straight-identified) norm of Mardi Gras's invented tradition.[22]

It should be noted, however, that the concept of womanhood cannot be dissociated from its intersectional relation to other identity markers and mechanisms of oppression.[23] Hence, although I recognize gender as a crucial category of analysis, I will mostly exclude the experiences of white straight-identified women.[24] They have been covered in previous publications that investigate white (or unmarked) Mardi Gras, and this book is interested in how marked bodies used Mardi Gras as a means of resistance, identity formation, and social ascension.[25] Arguably, the white women in "traditional" Carnival associations already enjoyed relative privilege in Mobile's society. Furthermore, this book sees the narrative created by the invented tradition of Mobile's Mardi Gras as an example of "Confederate culture" and, as Karen L. Cox has shown, white southern women played a pivotal role in that process.[26] In other words, they did not represent what Katerina Sergidou articulates as the "embodied feminist counter-hegemony" in the Carnival stage.[27]

Inventing (and Selecting) Traditions

Traditions are created in particular sociohistorical contexts and, as such, are subject to change over time. In order for Black and/or queer people to enter the Mardi Gras timeline and imaginary, a tradition needed to be invented beforehand, one that excluded them. Yet historically marginalized groups of people used that celebration's semiotic system to reinvent (and at times challenge) excluding traditions, while also upholding their basic elements and *signifying upon* it with "repetition and difference."[28] Korbena Mercer notes that "creoles, patois, and Black English, decenter, destabilize and carnivalize the linguistic domination of 'English'—the nation-language of master-discourse—through strategic inflections, re-accentuations and other performative moves in semantic, syntactic, and lexical codes."[29] I argue that queer and/or African American Mobilians did the same with Mardi Gras's *language*.

Hobsbawm defines "invented traditions" as "a set of practices, normally governed by overtly or tacitly accepted rules and of a ritual or symbolic nature, which seek to inculcate certain values and norms of behaviour by repetition, which automatically implies continuity with the past."[30] The invention of Mobile's Mardi Gras "tradition" sustains the notion that the city was the first to celebrate Carnival in the country (and in some bold accounts, in the New World or in the Western Hemisphere), and hence before New Orleans. This book steers away from the heated "who did it first" debate. Instead, it looks at how the narrative of what is Carnival in Mobile was articulated during the twentieth century.

As David Cannadine shows, traditions are often invented in moments of crisis and change.[31] It is probably not a coincidence that, as the story goes, a former Confederate soldier, Joseph Stillwell Cain Jr. (Joe Cain), started Mobile's "modern" Mardi Gras tradition in the aftermath of the Civil War, and the process of the creation (or reinvention) of Joe Cain's mythology was solidified in the 1960s, as the US South contended with its "Second Reconstruction." The official narrative presents Joe Cain as the man who "brought back" Mardi Gras after the Civil War by parading in the streets of Mobile dressed as an "undefeated Chickasaw chief" to defy Union "occupiers," connecting Mardi Gras to the idea of the US South's resistance to Union oppression. This story is heavily infused with Lost Cause ideology, language, and symbolism.[32] Largely excluded from that narrative are the contributions of African Americans before they began to organize in the same model as the white elite organizations.

Maria Isaura Pereira de Queiroz points out the process of "invention of tradition" that established Carnaval as the highest manifestation of Brazilian identity when samba was adopted (or appropriated) by the white Brazilian elites. The author sees this process as a reaction to the late nineteenth-century influx of immigrants that generated a nationalistic fervor and need to assert national identity by commodifying African and Indigenous cultures and iconography.[33] Pereira de Queiroz criticizes the scholarship that concentrates on Carnaval's origins, essence, and authenticity while ignoring its historicity, challenging previous works that situated the inception of the celebration in the distant past in order to establish a long "tradition" of Brazilian Carnaval.[34] Instead, she proposes the use of the sociohistorical approach and methodology to understand the connection between socioeconomic changes and Carnaval, while questioning the origins and context of these myths.[35] By showing that Carnaval "tradition" was invented in the nineteenth century in order to sanitize and contain popular cultural manifestations but was then reinvented in a moment when the country needed to re-create a national identity, Brazilian scholars produced a roadmap for those investigating US Mardi Gras.[36]

In Mobile, according to the official narrative, the invention process begins and ends with the nineteenth-century paradigm. As shown in the Brazilian example above, if traditions can be invented and selected, they can also be reinvented. The second half of the twentieth century brought significant changes to this port city and its Mardi Gras. Yet, as Palmer Richardson and Bobby Dennison noted, in Mobile "the more things change, the more they stay the same."[37] This book investigates how things changed while remaining the same.

The people who generously shared their experiences and memories for the MGSCOH project show that despite the sequined veneer, they suffered discrimination based on race and/or gender identity and sexual orientation. Black people were forbidden from congregating, from having balls, and from frequenting certain spaces in that city in the not-so-distant past. Dressing in clothes of the opposite sex was a punishable offense in Mobile, while homosexuality was still a crime in the state of Alabama until 2013.[38] Although celebrating Mardi Gras is not exactly a form of radical dissent, it was a means of challenging excluding norms, even if folks had to adhere to respectability politics in the process.[39]

By placing the evolution of Mardi Gras "traditions" in the context of the African American civil rights and the gay liberation movements, it becomes easier to understand how the city has simultaneously endorsed diversity and tolerance while reinforcing social hierarchies and separations. When confronted with the reality of their segregated celebration, Mobilians (white and Black) often reply that "birds of a feather flock together" or argue that these are social groups and that it is normal for people to want to be with their peers. The reasons why these groups tend to break along racial lines or why LGBTQIA+ people needed a separate Mardi Gras organization are seldom questioned.[40]

Chapter Breakdown

As established by its title, this book deals with two main themes, which reflect its organization. The first section (chapters 1, 2, and 3) establishes the invented traditions and sociohistorical contexts that marginalized African American and LGBTQIA+ Mobilians not only in relation to the city's Carnival celebrations and historical narrative but also in terms of the spaces and places they could occupy. The second part (chapters 4, 5, 6, and 7) looks at how marked bodies used Mardi Gras to confront that exclusion, erasure, and subordination, even if at times they had to resort to respectability politics and accommodationist tactics.

The first chapter analyzes official narratives, showing how the invention of Mobile's Mardi Gras tradition excluded/erased/subordinated marked bodies from the city's Carnival history. It discusses the narratives that established Mobile as the "birthplace of Mardi Gras" in the US and explains how they inevitably define the festivities as something created for and by white elites. Chapter 2 examines how those in positions of power and privilege tried to regulate, control, and police revelry, and how these decisions restricted the participation of marked bodies in the festivities while establishing "safe" outlets for inversion and nonnormative expressions. The chapter provides three examples of how the celebration was controlled and negotiated by authorities, the press, and concerned citizens, showing how, as Carnival scholars have argued, the carnivalesque also has elements of the ritualesque.[41] Before looking specifically at how marked bodies used Mardi Gras to negotiate their space in a society that marginalized them, chapter 3 shows how they navigated the physical and symbolic space of downtown Mobile. It also problematizes the excuse to the city's segregated Mardi Gras celebrations, that people like to gather with their peers, placing social inequality and separations in a historical context and showing how they generated radically different experiences that are reflected in and reinforced by Mardi Gras festivities.

Chapters 4 and 5 analyze how marginalized groups organized within institutionalized boundaries. The fourth chapter shows racially marked bodies appropriating and adapting normative discourses and rituals. It investigates the role of Mardi Gras in how African Americans negotiated their space in Mobile's society and places their Mardi Gras experiences in the context of the city's Black liberation movement. Chapter 5 examines how people who have been marked because of their gender expression and/or sexual orientation appropriated and adapted normative discourses and rituals to establish their space in a heteronormative society. It also places Mobile's LGBTQIA+ experiences in a broader context of queer world making and activism.

Moving away from official organizations, chapter 6 investigates bottom-up Carnival celebrations in Mobile by discussing Black spectatorship in (Black and white) spectacles and the roles played by Black people in white parades and by disruptive performers in "respectable Colored Carnival." Chapter 7 looks at how Mobile changed in the last quarter of the twentieth century and ponders what is gained and lost when marked bodies' celebrations go mainstream. It also places these developments in the context of the setbacks and tragedy that affected marked communities and bodies in Mobile and discusses a cinematic representation of the city's segregated festivity. The book concludes with a survey of the recent attempts to reinvent Mobile's Mardi Gras traditions in more inclusive terms.

PART I
INVENTED TRADITIONS

CHAPTER 1

OFFICIAL NARRATIVES, ORIGIN MYTHS, AND TRADITION INVENTION

In June 2017 the Alabama Tourism Department set up a Mardi Gras parade in Times Square to "spread the word about the first Mardi Gras in America," which allegedly took place in Mobile in 1703. On a series of Facebook posts in their Sweet Home Alabama page, they shared livestream videos of the parades where an interracial group of revelers marched to the sound of the Jambalaya Brass Band throwing MoonPies and Mardi Gras beads at curious onlookers.[1] During Mardi Gras, Mobilians of different ages and socioeconomic and racial backgrounds can be spotted with T-shirts and other artifacts with some variation of "Mobile: The Birthplace of Mardi Gras" or "Mobile: The Original Mardi Gras." Yet when people outside the city think of US Carnival, they usually have New Orleans in mind.

Government officials and business leaders are aware of that problem and are consciously investing in claiming and promoting the city's place in the festive calendar. In January 2018 the department "trolled" New Orleans by sponsoring a billboard placed on Interstate 10 near Slidell, Louisiana, which read: "YOU ARE 114 MILES FROM AMERICA'S ORIGINAL MARDI GRAS."[2] That same month the Michael Krafft LLC company released the new "Official Mobile Mardi Gras Flag." Bordered by two purple triangles, it has a yellow diagonal stripe, which serves as the background for the redesigned logo: a solid bold "M" topped by a crown, framed by an outline drawing of two tragic/comic jester masks. At the bottom, in smaller type just two words: Mobile 1703. The company's self-proclaimed goal is "to promote Mardi Gras as the premier cultural and tourist event for Mobile and the state of Alabama."[3] The Mobtown Merch website, where the flag is commercialized, explains it "was designed with careful consideration of our great city's history and is intended to serve as the symbol for our annual carnival celebration, the original Mardi Gras!" The text describing the flag also affirms "this couldn't be a more appropriate time for a refresh as we move forward into this new era of growth in Mobile."[4] The OMG1703 website and social media pages also capitalize on the claim, selling all sorts of merchandise promoting the "original Mardi Gras," from T-shirts to coozies.[5]

For decades, Mobilians have tried to claim their space in the popular imaginary of the celebration. Since they cannot compete in terms of extravagance or debauchery—part of it by choice, as they opted to have a more "family friendly" version of the revelry than their neighbor—they went the historical-relevance route. Two origin myths establish Mobile as "the birthplace of Mardi Gras." According to the first one, Mobile, founded in 1702 (sixteen years before New Orleans), held its first Mardi Gras celebration in 1703. The second, more elaborate, narrative claims for Mobile the title of "Mother of Mystics." This version admits that it is likely that New Orleans had some type of pre-Lenten celebration before Mobile. Yet it also presents that true US Carnival only begins with the creation of mystic societies, originated in Mobile in the 1830s and then exported to New Orleans a couple of decades later. These narratives also establish Mardi Gras as a series of parades and balls in which white elites are the original protagonists, and not as spontaneous street revelry as in other Pan-American cities.

The 1703 version is quite beyond the temporal scope of this book and is not concerned with establishing an *identity* for US Carnival. It simply claims that some sort of celebration was enough to establish a "tradition." The 1830s Mother of Mystics version, however, established the norm for what US Carnival is, defining Mardi Gras as a festivity created for and by white elites who generously include (or permit the inclusion of) marked bodies. Mobile Mardi Gras mythology creates a narrative that has white elites as protagonists and has ties to white supremacist ideals, Confederate mythology, and Old South nostalgia.[6]

The goal of this book is not to challenge the claim that Mobile started the US Carnival tradition, but rather to question the notion of tradition itself. Who gets to establish the starting date of a particular celebration? How do we decide how much *celebratin'* is enough to establish a Carnival "tradition?" What criteria are used to establish it? And what are the (intended and unintended) consequences of those decisions? Although sources dealing with subaltern or marked peoples are arguably scarcer and harder to find, it is important to keep in mind that for those writing early books on the history of Mobile's Mardi Gras, affluent white men (and to a certain extent white women) were the default historical agents. Yet these historical discourses are still being repeated in the twenty-first century. While recognizing the importance (and the urgency) of a comprehensive history and historiography of Mobile's early Mardi Gras that looks beyond the obvious sources and usual characters, this chapter concentrates on the literature and events that established and perpetuated the mythology of its invented tradition since the second half of the twentieth century.

Novelist, sculptor, poet, and self-proclaimed folklorist, Julian (Judy) Lee Rayford is perhaps the greatest champion of Mobile Mardi Gras's origin myths. He established Joe Cain as the celebration's main character while playing a crucial role in the festivity's reinvention. Although other authors wrote about the subject before him, with *Chasin' the Devil Round a Stump: The History of Mardi Gras in Mobile from 1704* (1962), Rayford produced the most popular and comprehensive chronicle of Mobile's Mardi Gras.[7] He also created a progress narrative by which non-elite white men, white women, and Black people start accessing Mardi Gras spaces over time. Rayford's narrative simultaneously adheres to Lost Cause nostalgia and celebrates the city's Confederate past, while also reinforcing the notion that, unlike in other Alabama cities, Mobile's race relations were harmonious. As a great storyteller, Rayford engrosses his readers in an engaging narrative with compelling characters and images. He presents Gulf Coast Mardi Gras as the "most magnificent parade in the New World," which to him seems to be limited to the United States and Canada.[8] While he built on mythology that had been proposed beforehand, he created a clear narrative with a compelling set of characters that would, to this day, be celebrated in museums, websites, publications, and memorabilia and would dominate the popular imaginary of Mobile's Mardi Gras.

Establishing Mobile Carnival's Longue Durée: The 1703 Narrative

Throughout Rayford's book, historical timelines are molded, and the nature and meaning of events are adapted to establish the *longue durée* of Mobile's

Mardi Gras history and "tradition." He characterizes the early eighteenth-century La Societé de La [sic] St. Louis as a Mardi Gras association despite the fact that they celebrated during Epiphany. While it can be argued that Epiphany is part of the pre-Lenten *season*, there is no convincing evidence that the association was involved in the celebration of Mardi Gras.

Mobile historian Jay Higginbotham also contributed to this mythmaking, claiming that in February 1703 the area's French colonists "resumed the [Mardi Gras] festivities they carried on in 1700 and 1701 although the merrymaking . . . was nowhere near as elaborate as that which they had enjoyed in France."[9] It is possible, even likely, that there was some sort of acknowledgment of the date, but he cites no evidence of an actual Mardi Gras celebration. Which is not to say there was not one, or that this timid celebration should not be considered "Carnival"; it just signals that, in retelling this story, Mobile chroniclers have selected starting dates and origin myths that seemed to support their stories.

These narratives have also been carried on to more recent publications. Architect and Mardi Gras specialist L. Craig Roberts opens his 2015 *Mardi Gras in Mobile* with important Mardi Gras Facts. The second item in the list states: "MOBILE WAS THE FIRST CITY IN THE WESTERN HEMISPHERE TO CELEBRATE MARDI GRAS." Roberts does not present evidence for this claim but explains that although the French had settled Canada before the Gulf Coast, "it was too cold to have Mardi Gras there." In addition the author contends that mystic societies were first formed in Mobile in the 1700s and were the "first in the world," making Mobile the Mother of Mystics. As evidence Roberts mentions that when Jean-Baptiste Le Moyne de Bienville established Mobile in 1702 by settling the Fort Louis de la Mobile, "They called it Mobile La Mer [sic] Mystique, or the Mother of Mystics, where in 1703 it is believed the first Mardi Gras celebration was held in the New World. Mobile has called itself the Mother of Mystics ever since."[10] It is unclear if it was a problem of translation or a typo, but if that was accurate, it would make the city the mystic sea (*mer*), not mother (*mère*).

Samuel Kinser, whose 1990 *Carnival American Style* is still a reference in the field and one of the only academic explorations of Mobile's Mardi Gras, finds the "idea that Mardi Gras was an eighteenth-century French creation in the Louisiana colony . . . historically absurd." Yet Kinser also points out that it "would be equally absurd . . . to maintain that Mardi Gras was never observed before" a "1781 edict confirms its existence." To the historian, although some sort of celebration might have happened, it did not create a continuous tradition, which would have been incongruous with the tumultuous nature of the colony's history.[11] Kinser characterizes the Gulf Coast as historically a place of liminality, noting that Mardi Gras in the early Spanish era was part of the Northern Hemisphere winter festivities celebrated by elites that included Christmas, New Year's Eve, and Twelfth Night/Epiphany. He also argues that the plantation lifestyle of the US South had already been established earlier in the Caribbean colonies. Hence, it is quite unlikely that Mobile had the first Carnival celebration in the Americas. Nevertheless, it bears repeating that this book is concerned not with whether or not Mobile had the first Mardi Gras celebration, but rather with the discourse created by the affirmation of that idea.

Mobile's Mardi Gras chroniclers combined different origin myths into a continuous tradition created and carried on by elites of European descent. Higginbotham aptly summarizes this impulse, claiming that when "Mobile moved down river," French settlers "started a celebration which they called Boeuf Gras. Taking a huge effigy of a bull's head, they marched up and down Dauphin and Royal streets and stirred up a parade." Later, the Spanish "started their own mystic societies," while the "English didn't get too excited about it." The Americans, however, "added a little ingenuity to the frolicking." He concludes that these antecedents "were rather small and only a few of the most robust citizens participated." To him (and several other commentators), it would take the Philadelphia cotton broker Michael Krafft "to really get the show on the road."[12] Which brings us to the second origin myth.

The "Mother of Mystics" Narrative

The Mother of Mystics narrative presents the creation of the Cowbellion de Rakin Society in the 1830s as the genesis of Mobile's (and North America's) Carnival tradition. As we learn in the Mobile Mardi Gras Museum tour, Krafft was the "founding father" of that tradition. Higginbotham summarizes the Krafft story:

> On the night of December 31, 1830, Krafft was dining with a dozen or so friends in Antoine La Tourette's café at the corner of Water and Conti Streets. Just before midnight, the party left the restaurant and came to Partridge's hardware

store. Feeling chipper after an evening of guzzling the water of life, they seized the hoes, rakes and cowbells that stood in front of the store. Thus armed, they began a parade that lasted until everybody in town was awakened.[13]

The following year, more men joined Krafft and his merry band, and they created an exclusive society called the Midnight Revelers. By 1834 they had further organized and wore masks and costumes, changing the name of the group to the Cowbellion de Rakin Society, presented as the first US mystic society. Higginbotham also mentions other organizations that celebrated in a similar fashion, without bothering to explain that they all celebrated on New Year's Eve. Rayford's portrayal of an 1840 Cowbellion parade is tinged with Old South nostalgia. He describes it as a "decade of unparalleled prosperity, during which the riverboats became floating palaces and cotton ruled the wave as well as the field." There is no mention in this idyllic scenario of the enslaved people who made that "unparalleled prosperity" possible.[14]

A recurring theme in this narrative is the idea that Mobile's aristocratic mystic societies "saved" New Orleans Mardi Gras from the unruly masses, which indicates that there was a popular Carnival celebration in that city beforehand. In 1857 six Mobile men who had been members of their city's elite mystic societies moved to New Orleans and created the Mistick Krewe of Comus, which, to local commentators, attests to the Mobile origins of New Orleans Carnival.[15] The editor of the Mardi Gras guide *Mobile Mask*, Steve Joynt, writes that Comus "presented the first Mardi Gras parades in New Orleans, literally saving the holiday in that city."[16] This statement assumes New Orleans Mardi Gras needed saving, and Mobile's white elites had what it took to rescue it. This fear and necessity of containing marked bodies and the working class is crucial to understanding the process of tradition invention that took place in Mobile.

This dispute has been going on for quite some time. In 1939 an aggrieved Mobile columnist wrote:

> About this time every year New Orleans sticks out her chin and begins boasting about her Mardi Gras celebration. Nineteen thirty-nine being no exception, she's at it again. From the typewriters of her carnival publicists come reams and reams of descriptive adjectives telling of gigantic and colorful parades, of masking and revelry, which according to Louisiana journalists, are unexcelled in any land or city. Mobile cannot dispute the claim that

New Orleans' Mardi Gras celebration is on a larger scale than her's [*sic*]; quite naturally a city with such a great population as that of the Mississippi River metropolis should and does put on a bigger show.

But most spirited and civic minded Mobilians who may become embroiled in an argument over the merits of Mardi Gras here and Mardi Gras at New Orleans usually triumph when they ask: In what city were mystic societies, so necessary to carnival, born? The embattled representative from the Crescent City usually tucks his head and reluctantly admits: "Yes, Mobile is the mother of mystics."

In conceding that point the New Orleans folks virtually admit that Mobilians played a big part in putting together their own carnival into big time.[17]

A good example of how the "Mother of Mystics" narrative has been recently updated is the 2015 book *The Origin of America's Mardi Gras*. In it Mobile historian Ann J. Pond acknowledges Mobile's Mardi Gras origin mythmaking and finds no basis in the idea that there was a celebration in 1699 or 1703.[18] Yet Pond still finds a way to give Mobile its due. The author describes the Cowbellions as "the group that laid the basis for America's Mardi Gras celebration with its unique combination of fraternity, mystery, ritual, and festivity" and repeatedly refers to its members as "respectable young men." Pond explains that early nineteenth-century celebrations "were considered irrational and dangerous to public peace and order," noting that the Cowbellions created "a form of public masking that was accepted and controlled by the social elite, who could be trusted for their restraint."[19] This picture seems to imply that Carnival revelry was accepted and truly "American" only when it was done for/by white elites. The author describes Krafft as "a civil leader, a family man, and a slave trader" without ever problematizing the combination. While Pond mentions the "spread of cultural influences between all of the major ports," she does not acknowledge the possible influence of transnational encounters, or how racial and ethnic barrier crossing might have affected the US version of a festival that is celebrated throughout the Americas.

This raises an important question about the definition of "American." It seems as if for this and other white Mobilian authors, Mardi Gras becomes "American" only when it ceases to be *Bakhtinian* and becomes *Pavlovian*. The need to re-create and contain Carnival can thus be associated with the idea of US American identity and how it is defined and contained, and whom it includes and excludes. Through this framework, marked bodies' Carnival becomes derivative, while the true "American" identity and Carnival are white and upper class. Although Pond explains how the structure of mystic societies heavily borrowed from Freemasonry, with its secrecy, symbols, titles, and themes from "Classic sources," she does not explain if there was any relationship with white supremacist secret societies.[20] Journalist James Gill, however, directly connects early New Orleans Carnival organizations with white supremacist groups, noting that nineteenth-century gentlemen's clubs had a common purpose: to uphold and promote white supremacy.[21]

While in this popular self-published book Pond shied away from thornier issues and reinforced Mobile's Carnival myths, the author had previously provided a more nuanced analysis almost a decade earlier in a PhD dissertation. There, Pond argues that as the new influx of money and people during the 1830s and '40s created new social hierarchies in Mobile, cotton merchants and other businessmen established fraternal societies to strengthen social connections on which their livelihood depended. These exclusive organizations conferred on them social acceptance and mobility, power, and status. Yet the stagnant economy of the post–Civil War period generated a necessity of "reliance on ritual as a means to construct and maintain social status." Therefore, in the years following the Civil War the parades of the elite fraternal societies took on new social significance, embodying the "traditions and values" of the Old South and using public rituals and spectacles to communicate the survival of white supremacy and masculinity.[22] According to Mobile's Mardi Gras mythology, in the immediate aftermath of the "War of Northern Aggression," the celebration was resurrected by defiant Confederate soldiers (most likely in blackface) led by a man who would become one of the city's most emblematic figures.

The Confederate Rebirth Narrative

Arguably, Rayford's main contribution to this mythology is the enshrinement of the most important character and iconic image in Mobile's Mardi Gras celebrations: Joe Cain. To Rayford, no "private citizen anywhere in the United States since 1600 has had more of an impact on a community—or left a more enduring impression of his personality."[23] While the retelling of Cain's story has changed over time, most Mobilians are aware of the Confederate soldier who, costumed as "an undefeated Chickasaw chief," brought back Mardi Gras to taunt the Union troops, accompanied by a band of fellow "veterans who called themselves the Lost Cause Minstrels."[24]

Jay Higginbotham opens the Mardi Gras chapter in his 1968 overview of Mobile's history with an imaginative depiction of Joe Cain's origin story. He writes of a "dismal day in February in the year 1866," when a "blanket of gloom . . . hung heavy in the air over Mobile." Although it had been almost a year since the end of the conflict, "Mobilians were still lost in self-pity." Startled by the sound of a drumbeat, a Union soldier turned around and was surprised by the image of an "Indian chief outfitted in all his trimmings . . . sitting on top of a charcoal wagon, yelling and waving a pair of drumsticks," accompanied by "six more Indians." He feared a "Confederate plot to seize the city," but when he asked what they were doing, the "chief" replied: "Just raisin' hell."[25] It bears stressing that this was published in a popular Mobile history book as fact, not as lore, even though there is no evidence that this event actually happened when and how it is recounted. Rayford's description of Joe Cain's last photograph as an old man is quite telling of the type of the nostalgia invoked: "He looks like the summation of the whole Civil War age, and that character is remarkably emphasized in his resemblance to Raphael Semmes—to all Confederate veterans," his face conveying "nobility and honor, an open code." Similarly, his explanation of Joe Cain's symbolism is heavily tinged with Lost Cause fantasy:

> Joe Cain sitting there in his charcoal wagon, in that year of doom for his Southland, when all his region had been defeated and were being ground under by Reconstruction—Joe Cain in his poverty-stricken wagon, a symbol of the South, dressed as a Chickasaw—and the Chickasaws were never defeated. And Joe Cain could not wave the Confederate Banner in the face of the Union authority. It was a delicate twist of irony, a delicious bit of symbolism. It meant more than a masquerade, more than simple Mardi Gras. It meant a whole people could still look up—look up in pride—and still keep going on.[26]

Chroniclers managed to retain the "birthplace of Mardi Gras" and "Mother of Mystics" mythologies while also claiming that Joe Cain began the tradition of Mardi Gras parading in the city by saying that he only "brought back" Mardi Gras after the war made people forget it. Arguably, four years would not have been enough to erase from the collective memory an entrenched

Photograph of Joseph Stillwell Cain Jr./Joe Cain in Native American costume. This image led to the often-mentioned notion that Cain was dressed as an "undefeated Chickasaw Chief" when he "brought back" Mardi Gras after the Civil War. So far I have not been able to locate any credible sources to confirm this story, and other researchers have challenged it. The image was possibly taken in Henry Hughes's studio circa 1866. It has inspired subsequent iconography and representations of the character, including a statue located in Mardi Gras Park. Caldwell Delaney Papers, the Doy Leale McCall Rare Book and Manuscript Library, University of South Alabama.

"tradition." Higginbotham, for instance, insisted that Mobilians "hadn't seen a Mardi Gras parade in so long they had almost forgotten such a thing existed," while explaining that "Joe Cain didn't originate Mardi Gras; he only revived it," bringing "the Boeuf Gras back to the minds of the public."[27]

Recent works have contested this narrative, claiming that a more accurate date for the beginning of organized Mardi Gras day parading in Mobile would be 1868.[28] Yet, while they address some of the historical inaccuracies in the timeline of Joe Cain's invented tradition, they do not acknowledge its connection with Reconstruction resentment. The earliest newspaper account of a Mardi Gras parade in Mobile describing Cain's Lost Cause Minstrels' performance provides a clue for early Mardi Gras pageantry's racialized subtexts and seems to indicate that they were not dressed up as "Indians," as Higginbotham suggests, but rather were in blackface: "the Minstrels, who were gotten up as monkeys, were mounted upon a dilapidated wagon and discoursed wild and, we must say, most discordant music."[29] The monkey was an image commonly used to dehumanize and offend African Americans and would be used in that capacity by subsequent Mardi Gras pageantry.

Chief Slacabamarinico (Joe Cain) Statue. Mardi Gras Park. Mobile, Alabama, March 12, 2020. Photo by the author.

Excluding Marked Bodies from the Center of the Narrative

Mobile Carnival mythology is devised of white supremacist archetypes such as an enslaver and a Confederate soldier, and racist themes were common in Gulf Coast Mardi Gras parades and balls. In 1861 New Orleans's Comus paraded in Mardi Gras "with a group of krewmen in blackface carrying an effigy of Abraham Lincoln riding a split rail."[30] In 1873 their "The Missing Links to Darwin's Origin of Species" presented "caricatures of Reconstruction Era politicians such as General Grant" and associated Black people with apes. An illustration for the Comus Ball portrays a Black man as a gorilla "bearing a crown as to indicate his usurpation."[31] In 1877 their parade and ball were "dedicated to the 'Aryan Race' and its responsibility for all the achievements of civilization."[32] In Mobile nineteenth-century Cowbellion parade themes also had racist motifs, such as the 1873 "Science of Phrenology, or, Bumpological Researches."[33] In 1888 the Comic Cowboys paraded the "Dream of a Mobile Coon" float, which depicted a sleeping Black man: "At the foot of the bed was a huge open razor with the inscription 'Bad Man.'"[34]

While Rayford recognizes mystic societies' gender segregation, he does not discuss their racial segregation. In his narrative Black people are still not a part of the history; they either are an appendix or feature as supporting or utilitarian characters. Never protagonists. Despite his efforts to praise Mobile's "respectable" Colored Carnival and a few race men such as Colored Carnival Association founder Dr. W. L. Russell, when Rayford describes a Mardi Gras parade scene, mules and Black men have the same standing: they perform the same function and are both nameless subjects.[35]

> The night, the purple, the purple and red night, the flaring flames of orange torchlight wavering hippity-humpity hippity-humpity through the exciting, magic realm of Mardi Gras by night. The great polychromatic floats glittering in gold leaf and silver leaf, the tinsel scintillation of the floats rocking along beside the white-robed Negroes toting their white metal boards against which the yellow torch-flames dance. The white-robed mules pulling the floats, and on the floats, the symbols that spell out a complete fairy legend or a tale from classic Greek.[36]

Aside from the utilitarian and mostly nameless African Americans mentioned throughout his book, Rayford dedicates only a five-page chapter at the end of *Chasin' the Devil* to Black Mardi Gras. But a 1935 letter he wrote to Mobile mayor Cecil F. Bates provides an insight into this white Mobilian's perception of the city's Black citizens and the role they should play (and place they should occupy) in the city's defining celebration. Encouraged by Congressman Frank Boykin, Rayford decided to outline his "plan for a new style of Mardi Gras carnival for Mobile" so that they would be better equipped to compete with New Orleans. He began the letter by expressing his fears that "someone might just take the idea and use it to their own advantage" without giving him proper credit, and establishing that if the project were to be implemented, he wanted to "take a leading part in planning and directing it." He also solicited an "emergency relief" to sponsor his relocation to the city and "some salary for living expense."[37] This is an important detail, as it indicates that he intended to profit from a project that would further stigmatize African Americans and reinforce the celebration's segregation. He declared that he saw "no reason why" the new attitude toward Mardi Gras outlined in his proposal "should not serve to create a great deal of tolerance between white and black" and wanted to "utilize colored children as well as the white children" in the elaborate "children's dances" he envisioned opening the parades. Yet the document displays condescending attitudes and assumptions toward African American Mobilians and makes it very clear that Mardi Gras was understood as a "tradition" invented by and for white people, where marked bodies' celebrations were something derivative and marginal.

His plan included the creation of "a Mardi Gras for the negroes" which he described as follows:

> The negroes will carry out jungle motifs. There will be a chief and his harem, with warriors. The great parade float for the chief will be a war canoe pulled by decrepit mules. This negro parade will develop great humor. It will traverse the length of Davis Avenue and follow eventually the Comic Cow Boys' parade. The negroes will have several great balls of their own. I do not see why the white people should object to the negroes having a carnival of their own, for their festival will not interfere with the white activities. New Orleans has had a great negro carnival for years, and it is one of most famous parts of their Mardi Gras. It is time we did likewise.

On the following point, he continued: "This negro carnival is merely a part of the whole plan I am considering. Now, for the rest of the carnival, I mean for the white people: There will be a night of revelry on Dauphin Island." He described the arrival of "the negroes' chief" in the city on a schooner or "some kind of boat" as an event that would "add a great deal of humor to the occasion."[38] As shown in chapter 4, although some Black Mobilians rejected what they perceived as the "more burlesque aspects" delineated here, they did organize a few years later and created their own mystic societies, parades, and balls.

Reinventing Cain

The final step in the invention of tradition of Mobile's Mardi Gras occurred in 1966 with the commemoration of the Joe Cain Centennial. As the country, and the US South in particular, was grappling with its "Second Reconstruction," it seems fitting that white Mobilians would literally disinter a man who they believed openly defied occupying Union troops. After publishing his defining Mardi Gras mythmaking book, Rayford continued his efforts to give Joe Cain what he considered his rightful place in the city's Mardi Gras tradition and public imaginary. Part of that effort meant removing the remains of Joe and his wife, Elizabeth Rabby Cain, from the Independent Order of Odd Fellows cemetery in Bayou La Batre and reburying them in downtown Mobile's historic Church Street Graveyard, where no one had been buried since 1898.[39]

On February 5, 1967, Rayford inaugurated the tradition of dressing as Chief Slacabamarinico (Joe Cain's Indian chief character) to lead Joe Cain's funeral procession. He would embody the character until 1970, when he "passed the feathers" to fireman J. B. "Red" Foster, who then passed them along to Mobile independent historian, pastor, and actor Bennet Wayne Dean Sr. (Wayne Dean), who still embodies the character in 2022.

Cain's "homecoming" procession marked the beginning of the People's Parade, which has served as an important time and space for Mobilians of different identities and backgrounds to defy and reinvent tradition, and actively participate in the city's otherwise closed public revelry. The event represents a shift in the type of public performance presented in Mobile's carnival from "presentational" to "participatory." As Andrew Snyder (borrowing from Thomas Turino) explains, while "presentational performance makes a clear distinction between the roles of performers and spectators," in participatory performances that line is blurred, as anyone can be a part of the spectacle.[40]

Although there is still debate over whether or not Joseph Stillwell Cain actually paraded or even was in Mobile in 1866, that has not stopped Mobilians from celebrating this annual tradition. Regardless, this book is concerned not with what happened in the nineteenth century, but rather with how this alleged event has been enshrined as a *lieu de memoire* in Mobilians' collective memory.[41] The establishment of the Joe Cain Day People's Parade was an attempt to rearticulate Mobile's Mardi Gras as a more popular and democratic celebration. As Emily Ruth Allen and I discuss, although the event as imagined and developed by its official organizers was imbued with Lost Cause nostalgia and Confederate mythology, it is constantly "adopted and adapted" by marked people "as a time and space to perform resistance and exercise difference."[42] Yet some of the more conservative members of Mobile's society were not happy with the popularization of the festivities.

CHAPTER 2

REGULATING, CONTROLLING, AND SANCTIONING REVELRY

> Somewhere along the way the Joe Cain Procession has gotten beyond the bounds of decency and control. We have no suggestion as to what can be done, but we strongly urge you before the next year that decisions be made to eliminate the objectionable and offensive features of the Joe Cain Procession.
> —CHAIRMAN OF DEACONS S. S. COOKSEY AND PASTOR M. P. HARRISSON, First Baptist Church of Mobile[1]

In Mobile the carnivalesque was controlled and negotiated by authorities, the press, and concerned citizens. As those in positions of power and privilege tried to contain and police revelry in Mobile, their decisions often limited the participation of marked bodies in the festivities but also established "safe" outlets for inversion. While city ordinances regulated marked bodies' celebrations and expressions, costuming contests served as safe outlets for public self-expression but also as a practice that reinforced social hierarchies when people in privileged social positions wore marked identities as costumes. Controversy over the future of the Joe Cain Procession in the late 1970s led to different reactions from different segments of the population.

In a comprehensive survey of carnival studies scholarship, Aurélie Godet reminds us that "not every carnivalesque act is emancipatory" and advises us "to distinguish between 'true' transgressions and those which redirect the carnivalesque toward a system's own reproduction." Godet uses New Orleans white elites' krewes as examples of how satire can actually "reproduce dominant structures," arguing that while these public performances "may mimic 'true' carnival in their excess and expressiveness . . . they ultimately preserve the hegemony of the in-group through transgressions which reinforce their privilege at the expense of an out-group." Hence, to assess "the concrete social impact of carnival," we need to "compare the effects of two types of symbolic disruption: the imitation of the powerless by the powerful, and the reverse."[2] This is a useful framework to keep in mind for understanding the sanctioned public revelry discussed in this chapter.

As Jack Santino notes, "the paradox of festive license . . . is that it is sanctioned by the entrenched authorities."[3] Santino discusses the differences and overlaps between the carnivalesque and the ritualesque, explaining that while Carnival celebrations signify "great abandon, social inversion, public excess, sensuality, and the temporary establishment of an alternate society . . . free of or even in opposition to the norm," ritual "constructs and validates the very categories it deals in," serving as a "means for creating and reinforcing power structures."[4] Yet he also explains that Carnival and ritual are "idealized constructions" and that the difference between them is "blurred and porous."[5] By looking at how public performances and revelry were regulated, promoted, and negotiated by people who held privileged positions in Mobile's society, we can better understand how marked bodies used these norms by aligning with, reacting to, or *disidentifying* with normative structures and rules.[6]

Ordinances: Regulating and Policing Public Revelry

City ordinances served as a means for authorities to regulate actions and interactions in Mobile. A brief survey of the evolution of these documents from the 1830s to the 1960s reveals how marked bodies' ability to celebrate and even exist and express themselves in the city was controlled and policed.

The 1835 Collection of City Ordinances declared that "no ball, dance, or assemblage of people of color" would be permitted in the city unless the owner of the establishment where the event would be held secured a license. Furthermore, even with the license, the event could not "extend beyond the hour of one o'clock at night," and the Watchman was encumbered with enforcing the policy, requiring "such persons, at that hour, to retire to their dwellings." Those who refused could "be taken into custody as disorderly persons; and the person at whose house they have assembled, [would] be deemed to have kept a disorderly house and be liable to the penalties in such cases provided."[7] In 1889 the prohibition of masked and public balls or parties was applied to anyone conducting them "where licentious or disorderly persons may congregate within the city" unless they secured "the consent of the Mayor in writing." That same code prohibited any drum beating not related to "military, fireman and society parades" and established that people who appeared "in any public place in a state of nudity, or in a dress not belonging to his or her sex" would be punished with a fine.[8]

In 1907, for the first time, the Mobile Code of Ordinances dedicated a whole section to Mardi Gras. The section contains a masking ordinance stipulating that:

> All persons shall have the privilege of appearing in mask, in the streets in the city of Mobile on Mardi Gras; provided, that no person, appearing in mask, shall wear gloves, or have his, or her, hands otherwise covered, and that no masking should be allowed after nine o'clock p.m., of said day except of persons who are members of, and take part in the parading of the following associations, to wit: Comic Cow Boys, Knights of Revelry, Krew of Cyreniacs, Infant Mystics, Order of Myths, Emperor Felix and his escort, or any other regularly organized Mardi Gras Society.[9]

These were, of course, all elite-white-male organizations.

By 1934 the code's language regarding "Disorderly or Malicious Conduct" had changed slightly. The specific cross-dressing prohibition was replaced by a fine ministered to "whoever shall appear in any public space in a state of nudity, or in an indecent, or lewd, dress, or shall make an indecent exposure of his, or her, person, or to be guilty of any indecent act, or behavior."[10] The reasons for the update are unclear, but the broader terminology gave law enforcers more room to decide what was "appropriate" attire and "indecent" or "lewd" dress. The new code presented a larger Mardi Gras section that reiterated the masking ban, declaring it "unlawful for any person to appear in mask in any street. Or other public place within the police jurisdiction of the City of Mobile." Again, members of societies or associations "regularly organized solely for participation in said Mardi Gras or Carnival Celebration" were exempt from the rule during the festivities (from Friday before Mardi Gras/Fat Tuesday until Mardi Gras day midnight) but had to file written applications for permit with the mayor at least five days in advance and provide specific information about those involved, dates of the parades, and routes. No one could appear or parade in masks without that approval and written permit. Once again, a masker could not "wear gloves or have his or her hands otherwise concealed or covered."[11] The 1960 code declared that any "individual appearing in mask" was required to remove the mask "on demand from any police officer of the city" and provide the "officer his name, place of employment, if any [. . .] place of residence, and [. . .] any document which will establish his identity."[12]

The regulation of masking is intriguing. Yet the accompanying gloves prohibition makes it clear that city officials were concerned with Carnival's opportunity for inversion, or for people to temporarily inhabit other identities occupying a place they did not belong to. These ordinances raise questions that previous works that contributed to Mobile's Mardi Gras mythmaking never bothered (or did not want) to ask. Were masking ordinances trying to keep Black and/or gender-nonconforming people from hiding in plain sight? Was banning public drumming and policing gatherings by people of color a way to keep the city's cultural matrix European? A reflection of white fears of Black insurrection?[13]

Julian Rayford (as well as subsequent authors and commentators) dressed up possibly problematic elements of Mobile Mardi Gras in whimsy in his explanation for the demise of the custom of masking in Mobile. He begins by recalling a time "when many many people felt impelled to put on a mask and walk around the streets in a goofy spirit of masquerade." Yet, he laments, as time went by, the city's revelers began to reject the practice of street masking, accepting it only on official floats, because "television, movies, radio, have conditioned us to professional comedians, and the old amateur spirit of masking just for the hell of it is gone."[14] This assessment ignores the mechanisms of repression and regulation manifested in official prohibitions such as these city ordinances that policed street revelry throughout the decades.

Contemporary explanations for Mobile's masking ban, provided by locals, tourist guides, and museum tours, range from fear of masked bandits to the rise of the KKK. Mobile architect and Mardi Gras Museum guide L. Craig Roberts, for instance, explains the reason for the 1902 prohibition of masks in Mobile:

Unknown to most of us today, historians reflect on the early 1900s as a time when crime was as bad as it has ever been in America, and at that time, criminals were known for wearing masks—hence the term "masked bandit." At that time, the public often dressed in costumes with masks during Carnival, just as maskers did on floats. Local authorities were concerned criminals dressed up with masks could take advantage of the situation in downtown Mobile.[15]

Contrary to what Mobile chroniclers like Rayford and Roberts have asserted, masking legislation in the US Gulf Coast is likely connected to anxieties over racial mixing and possibly a mechanism for policing gender nonconformance. According to Kinser, since the Spanish period, masking prohibitions served as a means to control enslaved and free Black people in public spaces during Carnival in New Orleans.[16] In the late eighteenth century, the Spanish *cabildo* outlawed masking for "colored people" and expressed concerns about the possibility of racial mixing in the festivities and about the danger presented by people of color attending balls disguised behind masks. As noted by Gill, by 1806, "all masking and disguises ... were prohibited in the streets and public spaces" in the Crescent City, while accounts of street revelry in 1827 also reveal concerns that masks allowed "people of different classes and even races to mingle."[17] Mobile lacks such studies, so it is hard to have a clear picture of how or why masking prohibitions were enforced there. We do know, however, that Black people's celebrations and cultural expressions were monitored, regulated, and policed. And, as we will see in chapter 5, the first person arrested because of the city's 1902 masking ban was a person who tried to enjoy the festivities in drag.

Ordinances served as mechanisms to control and curtail interactions and keep people "in their place." They also transformed city officials into the gatekeepers of public performances. While these regulations restricted popular revelry, city authorities and businesspeople understood the financial potential in street merrymaking. Organized costume contests served as a means to encourage (controlled) popular participation.

Costuming Contests: Promoting Sanctioned Public Revelry

A defining feature of Carnival worldwide, public costuming has been a contested terrain in Mobile. It seems as if Mobilians are always longing for the "return" of the long-lost good ol' days of street revelry, while also trying to contain and control popular participation. City authorities recurrently tried to expand popular participation in the celebrations through costuming contests. Considering the legislation that prohibited masking and determined "proper" attire, it appears as though only sanctioned and controlled instances of inversion were encouraged.

Fat Tuesday, March 4, 1930, was designated "Masking Day" in Mobile. In hopes "of stimulating and adding color to the festive Mardi Gras ceremonies," the *Mobile Press* offered cash prizes totaling $80 to the best costumes in several categories, and a secret committee of three judges would select the winners. The article announcing the prizes did not miss the opportunity to convey some Mardi Gras mythology:

> Crowds already mull about on Mobile streets. Balloon hawkers maintain a steady cry. Streets have put on their carnival dress. Drapes of purple, red, yellow, and every color of the spectrum flutter above thoroughfares and upon the face of buildings. Bicycles whir by, spokes entwined with gaily colored crepe paper. Mobile is donning her harlequin suit and cap and bells. Mobile originated Mardi Gras. Mardi Gras forms an integral part in the history of social tradition of Mobile, and has, ever since Michael Kraft [sic] led his youngblood companions in the raid on a local hardware store to obtain rakes and cowbells for a celebration. The Mobile Press believes Mobile should adhere to mystic tradition in observance of the carnival season. Masking should be encouraged to bear out this observance.[18]

Competing as an "East Side peddler," Louis Diemert won the best individual masker category and claimed his disguise was so good that "many persons approached him seeking to buy shoelaces and other goods which were displayed on his tray."[19] This was neither his first nor his last award. Known as "The Man of Many Faces," he received the individual masker prize in 1921, when the Mobile Carnival Association first offered it, and continued dominating the category until he died three decades later, winning that competition seventeen times in twenty-five years.

The Man of Many Faces was proud of never having to wear a mask, composing his characters using "his own formula for makeup" and "proper attire," completing "his costume with grease paints, spirit gum and crepe hair," a process similar to the one employed by some drag performers. To accomplish the precise likeness, he scanned "newspaper pictures of [the] subject closely so as to reproduce as accurately as possible his wearing attire." Diemert appeared as different political and historical figures, in blackface, and in drag. Among his many characters were: Scotch Golfer, Old Black Joe, Scarlett O'Hara, the Queen of England, Wallis Simpson (the Duchess of Windsor), Mayor Pom Pom, an Old Witch, Jiggs, Haile Selassie, Abraham Lincoln, Neville Chamberlain, Adolf Hitler, and Santa Claus. He claimed he didn't do it for the prizes, but rather to "make people happy."[20]

Diemert brought the custom of masking from his native city, New Orleans, which he left for Mobile in 1912 to work as office manager for the Crescent News & Hotel, located in the Mobile, New Orleans and Chicago Railroad Company (later known as the Gulf, Mobile and Ohio Railroad/GM&O). His first experience embodying someone else was when, at eleven years old, he and a friend "masked as a couple of girls in military uniform."[21]

In 1946 the *Mobile Press Register* claimed he was "probably the most photographed man of the past quarter century of Mobile's Mardi Gras" and a "choice subject" of newsreel cameramen covering the celebration. He also posed for pictures for "hundreds of tourists and visitors" and marched in front of the Knights of Revelry Parade on Mardi Gras Day. The article was an homage to then-sixty-nine-year-old Diemert and his many award-winning costumes. The piece relays anticipation for Diemert's next production, noting the character he embodied each year was a "closely guarded secret" kept even from his family and revealed only on Mardi Gras Day.[22]

Two years later the periodical warned that Diemert would face stiff competition due to the "added incentive" given by the Carnival Association encouraging Mobilians to make bold attempts at the top costuming prizes. Carnival officials expected "upwards of several thousands of individual maskers" on Fat Tuesday. The article invoked the city's tradition of popular revelry:

> Mardi Gras has always been a "smash day" for the greater portion of Mobilians. Starting early in the morning and continuing until sundown, persons dressed as clowns, black-face characters, comic strip characters, political leaders and world figures and just plain homely characters romp through the streets of the "Mother of Mystics" turning it into a gigantic circus hippodrome runway crammed with clowns.[23]

Louis Diemert as Princess Elizabeth II as a bride, for the 1948 Mardi Gras. Erik Overbey Collection, the Doy Leale McCall Rare Book and Manuscript Library, University of South Alabama.

A few days later, Diemert, then working as a haberdashery salesman, broke his customary suspense by announcing his character for that Mardi Gras: Princess Elizabeth "dressed in a wedding gown with a veil and all the pompous trimmings of a regal bride."[24] In the year of his death, 1951, seventy-four-year-old Diemert had planned on dressing as Miss America, with a dress borrowed from a former winner of the pageant, Mobile native Yolande Betbeze. Unfortunately, he did not make it.

While we cannot speculate what drag *did* for Diemert, people who openly discussed their sexual orientation and/or nonnormative gender expression in interviews for the MGSCOH project explained that costuming during these moments of sanctioned inversion, such as Halloween, Mardi Gras Day, and later Joe Cain Day, was a way of "living their truth" or defying normativity in public. In the words of the *Alabama Forum*'s Libertee Belle, Mardi Gras was "another reason for every queen in Mobile to strut her stuff in public, sans fear de police."[25] King Lawrence XV, born in Mobile County in 1943, explains:

> I was in my first Halloween in New Orleans, it was in a bar called The Parade [. . .] this guy said to me [. . .] he was going down the street, he looked and said "Damn, I gotta hurry." He said: "I gotta get to my apartment within ten minutes." Somebody said: "What's the matter, you gotta go to the bathroom or what? Are you expecting somebody?" He said: "No." He said: "If the cops catch me in the street after midnight, they will arrest me for female impersonation." [. . .] It just slapped me in the face, but it was a true statement. He said the only two times that a man can get in drag legally is Halloween and Mardi Gras. Think about that. That's the only time you can do that legally in two 24-hour periods. And there's nothing the damn police can do about it. Not a thing. And the only other time they can do it is if they get a cabaret license and work in a bar as a female impersonator or they are in Mardi Gras organizations. [. . .] It was worse here [in Mobile]. But that's the only two times it would stand up in court. If you dressed as a female for Halloween, you could stay in a dress or whatever you wanted from midnight to midnight and there wasn't a damn thing they could do about it. Nothing. It's legal. It was the same thing with Mardi Gras. Mardi Gras Day they encouraged people to put [on] costumes. Ok? You could get in a costume at midnight and stay till midnight, the next midnight. And you were legal.[26]

City officials and businesspeople continued their efforts to promote popular participation after Diemert's death. Three weeks before the 1953 Mardi Gras Day, the *Mobile Press Register* announced the "greatest amount of cash prize money in history . . . offered to maskers," a total of $1,000. The chairman of the masking committee, Cameron Plummer, encouraged the revelers: "Masking and costuming is traditionally one of the outstanding features of the celebration. We would like to see any and every Mobilian come out in a mask or costume on Mardi Gras Day."[27] That people needed incentives, and that each decade authorities evoked a past "tradition" of street masking, indicates that independent, spontaneous popular participation was not as pervasive in Mobile as it was in other Pan-American cities.

These contests and the celebration of Diemert's talents show how inversion (or perceived deviance) was accepted as long as it was controlled and performed by unmarked bodies. Just as Black participation was also celebrated as long as it was done under the watchful eyes of the white elites or at the service of white pageantry. Diemert, as well as other costumers, could perform in blackface and drag at the same time that Blackness and gender nonconformance were being policed and criminalized.

Blackface, brownface, yellowface, redface, and all sorts of exoticizing orientalist performances of otherness (or "ethnic drag") were common in Mobile Mardi Gras pageantry.[28] The theme of the Infant Mystics 1947 parade was "Minstrel Memories," an homage to "the famous end men and burnt cork comedians of yesteryear." The third float in the procession, "dedicated to four of the greatest blackface comedians that ever graced the end seat of a stage, 'Honey Boy' Evans, 'Sugar Foots' Gaffney, Neil O'Brien, and Lew Docksteader," was adorned with "smiling black faces" and had "the laughing words 'Har Har' spelled out in the center." Yet, according to the newspaper coverage of the event, the "most picturesque" float in the procession was "Ballad Singers," decorated with "huge slices of watermelon with a masked blackface dancer on the center slice," dressed in "the traditional garb of roustabouts and cotton pickers."[29]

While it was considered appropriate for white people to perform (and ridicule) Blackness in blackface characters, Black people could participate in the downtown pageantry only as laborers and performers. Yet they created their own separate version of the festivity in Black neighborhoods, especially on Davis Avenue. Some African Americans used Carnival as a moment to subvert the boundaries of proper Blackness in spontaneous instances of "ritualistic play" in Black neighborhoods.[30] One space where spontaneous masking, costuming, and inversion happened (and still happens) in downtown Mobile is the Joe Cain Day procession, where, in theory, anyone can march, unlike in other events reserved for organizations and that sometimes cost hefty membership fees. The Joe Cain Procession's trajectory, the backstage negotiations, and the fight to define its essence and logistics in the late 1970s illustrate well how the process of reinventing tradition has to contend with opposing ideals, competing interests, and different visions for the city's future.

Joe Cain Day in the Late 1970s: Negotiating Public Revelry

The Joe Cain Day festivities grew yearly after the centennial "homecoming" procession, leading to a process of negotiation between those involved with the festivities and city authorities to formalize the invented tradition. In the aftermath of the 1977 celebrations, concerned citizens and organizations complained to the city commissioners about the chaos and destruction revelers were reportedly inflicting upon Church Street Cemetery. Margaret Arnold Schwarz wrote a letter to the *Mobile Press* editor (with copies to the Historic Mobile Preservation Society and to the Mobile City Commission) to express objection to the Joe Cain celebrations taking place in the cemetery. Speaking "as a Mobilian whose great-grandparents are buried in the Church Street Graveyard," Schwarz argued that the "fact that the people in this cemetery have been dead for a long time does not give the public the right to dance on their graves and use their tombstones for frolicking and picnicking."[31] She was not alone. Several other Mobilians wrote the commissioners, calling the use of the cemetery "disturbing for those . . . who respect the dead," "deplorable," "a repugnant revelry," and "blatant desecration." The Mobile Historic Development Commission as well as the Historic Mobile Preservation Society also wrote the city officials. Although the development commission recognized the Joe Cain celebration's importance for providing "an opportunity for direct individual participation in the true spirit of Mardi Gras," the institution complained about the damage caused to the historical site.[32]

On March 18, 1977, the Mobile City Commission created an ad hoc Mardi Gras Special Events Committee to review "public Mardi Gras functions and make recommendations for improving public participation" while developing "exciting attractions to out-of-town visitors and events [they could] all be proud to hold."[33] The provisional committee was chaired by retired police chief Ed J. McLean and had among its members the three men who have embodied Chief Slacabamorinico: Julian Rayford, James B. "Red" Foster, and Wayne Dean. It held its first meeting on April 4, 1977.

Meanwhile, letters kept pouring in to the city commissioners' office.[34] On March 19, 1977, Robert O. Harris III made a case for the celebration remaining where it was, noting it was "the most rapidly growing and popular aspect of Mardi Gras in Mobile" and "an area of citizen participation, spontaneous expression of mirth and a touch of sentimentality." Hence, it would be "truly

Joe Cain Day in the 1970s. Photo courtesy of Suzanne Cleveland.

fitting" to conclude the event at the cemetery "with a program honoring the founder of Mardi Gras." Harris explained he was a recurring participant in the processions, which he assured were attended by a crowd "made up largely of the more responsible citizens of Mobile, particularly those who are interested in the historical preservation of the City and its customs."[35] City Clerk Richard L. Smith forwarded the concerned citizens' letters to the Mardi Gras Special Events Committee. James B. "Red" Foster, who then served as Chief Slacabamorinico, declared in a public statement that, considering the large crowds attracted by the event, they were contemplating changing the route to begin the celebration in the cemetery and end in a larger space.[36]

On July 1, 1977, Foster, Rayford, Dean, and Mrs. Jimmy McWhorter signed a report addressing the "pros and cons" of the Joe Cain celebration and providing "important recommendations" for improving the event. It included practical suggestions such as an increase in strategically located "portable privies" and "litter drums," the blocking of Scott Street at Government Street, and the presence of the police or National Guardsmen "to preserve law and order." It also suggested the appointment of a committee to inspect the graveyard before and after the event and that the procession should "be led by the Indian 'Chief Slacabamorinico,' followed by the City Celebrities and members of the society, the Excelsior Band and others to follow accordingly."[37]

A few days later, the Mardi Gras Committee published an interim report recommending the establishment of a permanent committee formed by members "selected from organizations and citizens that have shown a desire to promote Mardi Gras as a public function." They called for the establishment of "permanent funding for public Mardi Gras activities by increasing permit fees for those commercial activities that take advantage of the carnival season." More importantly, they made suggestions that would push Mobile's Mardi Gras festivities toward "bottom-up playing," proposing a marching band competition; the encouragement of family participation "by having small amusement areas for younger children," and "that the City of Mobile participate and foster the decoration of the City during the carnival season." Finally, they recommended "that the City of Mobile promote increasing masking and costuming on Mardi Gras Day" and asked for a revision of the public masking ordinance.[38] In a meeting between members of the Mardi Gras Special Events Committee and the city's commissioners, Chief McLean argued that since more people wore masks and costumes on Joe Cain Day than on Mardi Gras Day, even though it was still illegal to mask on Sunday, the city should revise the prohibition or at least make an exception for children. The city commissioners replied that they would take the matter to the city attorney and the Mobile Police Department.

In a meeting on August 18, 1977, the Mardi Gras Special Events Committee and the city's board of commissioners came to an agreement that if the public's behavior did not improve in 1978, they would change the event's location. Chief McLean reassured those present "that the establishment of the new committee [was] not intended to take anything away from the Mardi Gras Association," signaling that the new invented tradition (and the folks involved in its creation and implementation) would not encroach on the territory of the custodians of the old invented tradition.[39]

The following year, however, the dispute continued. While some saw Mardi Gras as a promising capitalist enterprise, others were concerned about how the celebration was affecting the city's mores, character, and traditions. Only three days after Ash Wednesday, Sidney J. Gerhardt (of Gerhardt Investment Group Mortgage Bankers) complained about the lack of national awareness of Mobile's "major Mardi Gras event." He was disappointed that when his "filled to capacity" airplane landed in Mobile, the attendant missed the valuable public relations opportunity to wish the passengers a "fabulous Mardi Gras!" He further complained about the lack of banners in the airport "proclaiming the rule of joy and mirth," arguing that more "concerted publicity" to promote Mardi Gras would "help bring millions of dollars into Mobile annually." If Mobilians followed the lead of other cities that "found how profitable tourism can be," he argued, coins would "jingle in everybody's pockets."[40]

Most of the letters received by the mayor and city commissioners, however, were less concerned with promoting tourism and jingling coins than with preserving the city's institutions and traditions. D. H. W. Eddins wrote that the "situation [he] witnessed" in Church Street Cemetery on Mardi Gras Day, 1978, was "intolerable to those who really care about that place and many of those who have ancestors buried there." He vowed not to rest until he did "everything humanly and legally possible to have that destructive mob of thousands of Mardi Gras revelers excluded from it." Eddins enumerated the damages caused by the celebration, which ranged from broken tombstones, to sauce-stained slabs, to litter, to "the urine . . . poured over some old tombstones by uninhibited revelers." He could not properly assess his wounded feelings for such desecration, as "words for that would be unprintable" in an official letter, but resorted to the old city rivalry to taunt the authorities: "You can bet that New Orleans would never allow such a thing. They know how to have a Mardi Gras and preserve their history too. And furthermore, they have people who have interest enough to see that it is done." Most of the "unruly mob," he explained, "was not from Mobile but rather from "North Florida, other parts of Alabama, and Southern Mississippi." Eddins concluded that if the celebration needed to take place by Cain's grave, then the grave itself should be moved, reminding the addressees that he had only recently been interred there.[41] His statement reinforces the classist sentiment that those taking part in "bottom up" revelry are outsiders and do not represent the city's "true" Mardi Gras tradition. The day after Eddins sent his letter, the "shimmering controversy" of the Joe Cain celebrations was the topic of a city commission meeting. The commissioners forwarded the complaints to the Society for the Restoration and Beautification of Church Street Graveyard Inc. (also known as the Joe Cain Society) and hinted at their willingness to change the event's location. Eddins's letter and report of the destruction were read at the meeting, and Ed Stone, another passionate opponent of the cemetery revelry, made a "lengthy presentation" on the matter. Stone returned to a meeting in November and insinuated that Cain's disinterring and reburial was illegal and against the deceased, while communicating "that he [had] received an offer . . . to have the remains relocated at no cost to the City."[42]

Mrs. Redmond, who identified as a "direct descendant" of former city treasurer Don Miguel Eslava I, expressed her resentment for the "invasion," everyone's apparent lack of sensibilities, and her disgust at the commissioners' omission. She explained that if the opposition to the event seemed weak, it was "perhaps because there are not too many native Mobilians with relatives in the Church St. Cemetery," but assured the commissioners that it existed. Her letter reflects the sentiment of more-conservative (or "traditional") members of Mobile's society reacting to the popularization of an event and a space that was supposed to be occupied and controlled by the elites.[43] The Mobile Historical Development Commission manifested its support for the decision of moving Joe Cain's remains along with "his annual celebration to a more suitable location" to avoid further damage to "one of the few graveyards that is on the National Register of Historic Places."[44]

To prove to Mayor Mims that the objection to the Joe Cain cemetery celebration was not "feeble," Mrs. Mary Louise sent him a petition "secured in just a few days from friends and acquaintances all of whom were shocked and horrified that the City fathers had allowed" such a thing to happen. The list had about forty names, almost all of which were preceded by the honorific "Mrs." A month later, however, a new petition with hundreds of signatures was sent to the commissioners. The document asked that Joe Cain's remains be moved "to a more appropriate place where he [could] be honored without further destruction of the historic Church Street Cemetery."[45] The Christian Life and Public Affairs Community also sent a statement, which they asked to be read at a Mobile City Commission meeting, berating the behavior of the crowd during Mardi Gras and asking the commissioners and the sheriff "to give advance notice that all laws will be enforced during Mardi gras [sic] the same as any other time of the year and make sure that they are enforced."[46]

After the uproar of these concerned citizens and organizations, the commissioners decided to make changes to the celebration. In January 1979, the spokesmen for the Society for the Restoration and Beautification of the Church Street Graveyard Inc./Joe Cain Society announced that the following year's procession would begin at the intersection of Broad and Government Streets and end in Bienville Square. Their advisory committee wrote the chairman of the Mardi Gras Special Events Committee, Martin Johnson, noting that "in the spirit of cooperation," they would move the celebrations to Bienville Square in 1979.[47] It should be noted that several members of the Special Events Committee were also in the Joe Cain Society. Their statement, which creatively employed the past to create a new "tradition," read:

> In observance of the 275th Anniversary of the founding in 1704, of the Society of Saint Louis by Nicholas L'Anglois and his more famous uncle, Jean Baptiste Le Moye Sieur de Bienville, at the little colony of Mobile located at Twenty-Seven Mile Bluff, the 1979 Joe Cain Procession has tentatively arranged for those three giants of Mardi Gras history, Cain, Bienville and L'Anglois, to meet on Shrove Sunday in the historic Square, honoring the city's French heritage, that bears the name Bienville.[48]

A fascinating pastiche of Mobile Mardi Gras mythology, the document evokes the "first 'mystic' society in the new world," allegedly formed in 1704, as well as "the very first Mardi Gras . . . observed in the new world" in 1703, and the new (at this point thirteen-year-old) invented tradition of Joe Cain's procession. The event, they announced, would count on the "historic meeting" between the "Old King of Carnival" and the city's founder.[49]

Not everyone was happy with the changes. "Leading critic of graveyard frolicking" Ed Stone was not satisfied with the new arrangements, as they offered no provision for preventing revelers from entering the cemetery where Cain's grave remained. He demanded, "Further consideration should be given to the desires of descendants of individuals buried there."[50] The Francis Street United Methodist Church complained the relocation affected their regular Sunday worship schedule.[51] Despite all the polemic, on September 12, 1978, segregationist governor George Wallace officially proclaimed February 25, 1979, Joe Cain Day in Mobile. Foster (dressed as the "chief"), and Wayne Dean presented him with a plaque of honorary membership in the Joe Cain Society.[52]

Despite these attempts to curtail the celebration, by the mid-1980s Joe Cain Day had been established as an important democratizing space in Mobile's Carnival celebration. The event is currently held in the cemetery and open to the general public, while the procession makes its way through the streets of downtown Mobile.

The different reactions to Joe Cain Day's evolution are quite telling of the tensions between Dionysian and Apollonian, or Bakhtininan and Pavlovian Carnival. How people see the rise in popular participation in street revelry

Photograph of J. B. "Red" Foster, Governor George C. Wallace, and Bennett Wayne Dean Sr. holding the honorary plaque, September 12, 1978. Courtesy of the Mobile Municipal Archives.

says as much about how they perceive the democratization of a closed and stratified society as it does about their commitment to maintaining an invented tradition. Joe Cain Day became the most important and anticipated event of the celebration, overshadowing even Fat Tuesday in Mobilians' Mardi Gras festivities. As new residents move into the city, and younger people start getting involved in Mardi Gras, they devise traditions of their own. Although Joe Cain Day was conceived in Lost Cause lore, it has been reappropriated by "marked" groups in a variety of ways. Even the process of retelling Cain's story has gone through changes recently. Especially since the emergence of the Black Lives Matter Movement, and the call for the toppling of Confederate symbols, the Lost Cause elements of the narrative have become less appealing. On May 11, 2021, the Visit Mobile website published a "Mobile Mardi Gras Fun Facts" list. Predictably, the list begins claiming,

"Lee Simmons and friends," Joe Cain Day in the 1980s. ©Sheila Hagler

"Originated in 1703, Mobile is THE birthplace of America's original Mardi Gras." But here is how they describe Joe Cain's "facts:"

> Joe Cain is the man. He brought Mardi Gras back to life after the Civil War by leading an impromptu parade down the streets of Mobile and we've been doing it ever since. He has a whole day dedicated to him during Mardi Gras. . . Joe Cain Day is when Mobilians come alive in a way you need to

see to believe. It's a day where families, friends and everyone in between, are downtown to celebrate what our hero, Joe Cain started all those years ago. Mobilians feel incredibly lucky to have Mardi Gras and on Joe Cain Sunday, you can feel it in your bones.[53]

Gone from this version are any traces of Cain's relation to the Confederacy and the Lost Cause dog whistles of the past. The celebration is reconfigured here to emphasize its communal aspects and importance, while Cain's heroism is divorced from Reconstruction resentment. Also conspicuously absent are his companions (the Lost Cause Minstrels) and any reference to his redface character.

CHAPTER 3

DOWNTOWN

Mobile's "Negro Main Street"
and the Emergence of the "Fruit Loop"

A 2017 promo entitled "This Is Mobile," produced by Alex Kiker for the *This Is Alabama* website, introduces the Azalea City to prospective visitors. The opening images, underlain by poetic background music, suggest that three things define the city: the port, downtown, and Mardi Gras. The first shot captures a boat slowly floating up the Mobile Bay while a flock of birds flies toward and past the camera. That is followed by Mardi Gras scenes: a masked white woman throwing beads at the crowds, and a little white girl cheerfully holding up her MoonPie. Then there are scenes of downtown Mobile: a white waitress setting the table at a local café; a tracking shot of Dauphin Street bars; an African American man riding by in a Pedicab; a close-up of a Black trumpet player; and a white man shooting pool. Then a soothing male voice introduces the "city of six flags" that "introduced Carnival to a new land" and its peculiar trajectory to the viewers. The accompanying images show an *insouciant* city where a diverse population enjoys its beautiful urban landscapes and rich traditions. Although the narrator mentions other areas and events, the choice of images indicates that downtown is Mobile, and Mardi Gras plays an important role in how the city defines itself.[1]

Downtown: Mobile's "Negro Main Street," Emergence of the "Fruit Loop"

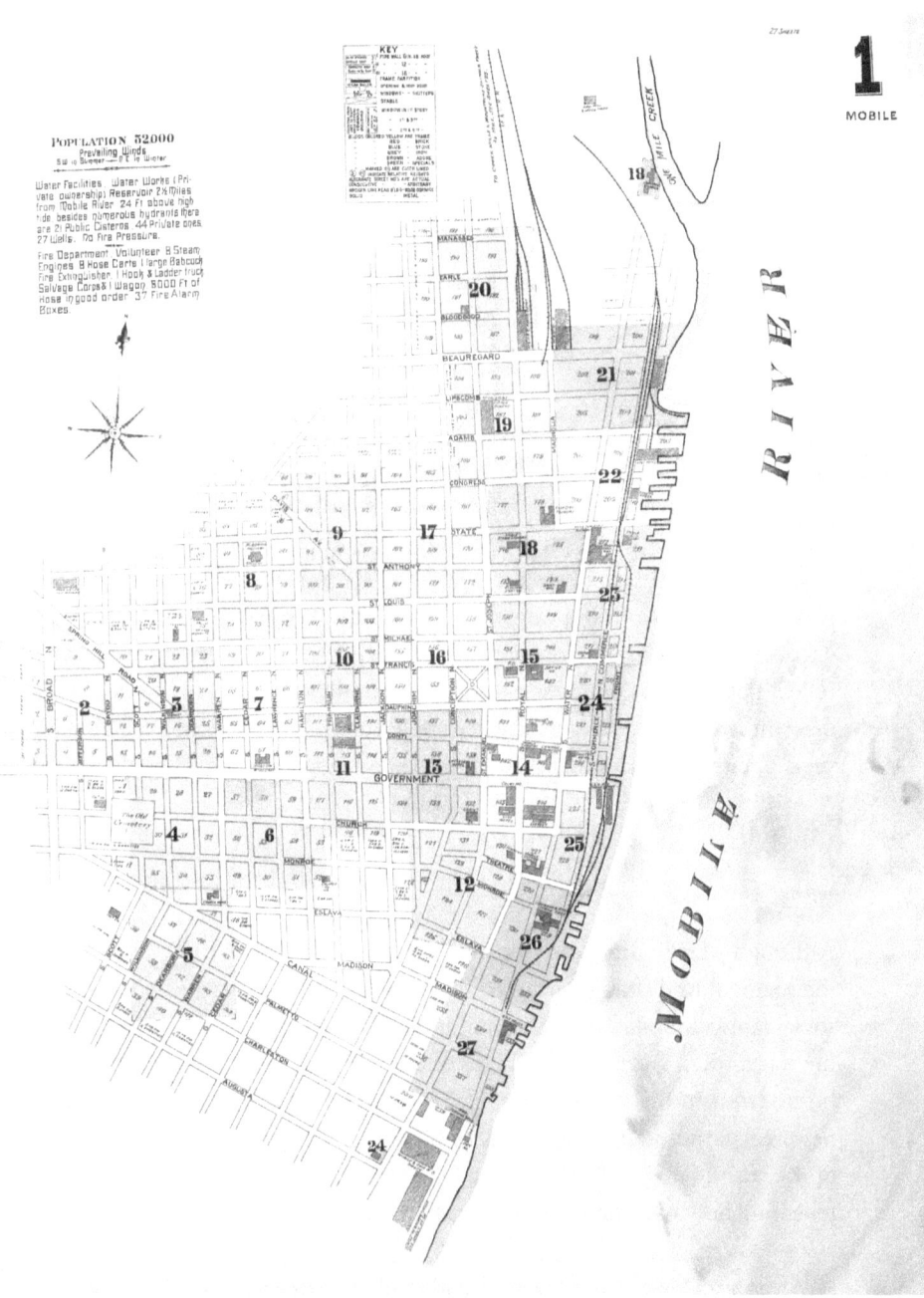

Sanborn Fire Insurance Map of Mobile County, Alabama (1891). Library of Congress, Geography and Map Division.

The history of downtown Mobile reflects the US urban boom during the Second World War, as well as its postwar decline. According to Alison Isenberg, in "a divided city (microcosm of a divided nation), the downtown has served as a potential place of interaction and negotiation of difference—a place of community gathering as well as all kinds of conflict."[2]

Downtown Mobile was and remains a contested space where people's experiences can be quite different according to the places their identities occupy in the city's sociocultural hierarchies. That explains the contradictions in how the people interviewed for the MGSCOH project remember and describe downtown Mobile in the second half of the twentieth century. Isenberg recognizes downtown's duality, as its "formulations of development" simultaneously represent inclusion and exclusion. As with the rest of the country, in Mobile, official plans and legislation helped determine "who should be downtown and why." Processes such as urban renewal, beautification, and modernization were often aligned with "policies designed to attract certain types of people downtown while explicitly rejecting others." Race, gender, class, and sexuality played important roles in how that played out.[3] People's segregated experiences of Mardi Gras did not happen by chance. They happened by design and reflect government policies and socioeconomic and racial hierarchies that determined the different experiences of groups of people who lived parallel yet separate existences that were nevertheless inexorably connected.

Mobile & WWII

Although Mardi Gras festivities were suspended during the WWII years, the sociocultural changes ushered in during the conflict permeated the city's social fabric. Mobile was such a quintessential US war boomtown that documentarian Ken Burns selected it as one of the four cities that represent the home front in his epic documentary series *The War* (2007).[4] The period newsreel narration used to introduce Mobile in the film paints a vivid picture of the rush of migrants who arrived in search of better opportunities, while revealing how newcomers were perceived as interlopers:

> An army of 150,000 men, women, and children invaded an American city—Whites, Negroes, Indians, Creoles, Cajuns. They came from every corner of the land, their roots in every curve of the globe: Moscow, Indiana; Warsaw,

These two photographs of groups of children posing in front of drug stores in segregated parts of town illustrate well the segregated existence of Black and white Mobilians from an early age.

Black children, members of Youth Training, posing for the camera in front of Eagle Drugstore in 1951. Erik Overbey Collection, the Doy Leale McCall Rare Book and Manuscript Library, University of South Alabama.

White children posing for the camera in front of Oakdale Drugstore in 1950. Erik Overbey Collection, the Doy Leale McCall Rare Book and Manuscript Library, University of South Alabama.

North Dakota; Hamburg, California; Milan, Missouri; Baghdad, Kentucky. Some came out of patriotism, some out of grim necessity, some for a richer life. All came to do a war job. This could be any one of a hundred great American war centers. It happens to be Mobile, Alabama.[5]

Allen Cronenberg claims that "no city in the American South was transformed by World War II more than Mobile." A former cotton city that had been in decline since the Civil War, it emerged from the Second World War as a "major industrial and commercial center linked to world markets."[6] Federal defense money helped rebuild the city in a process that began before the United States joined the conflict, when Democratic congressman Frank Boykin convinced the army to build the Brookley Army Air Field (commonly known as Brookley Field) in Mobile instead of in Tampa, Florida. The defense contract secured by Boykin transformed Mobile's municipal airport into a $26,500,000 Army Air Force supply depot and bomber modification center, creating thousands of jobs. It was the city's largest employer during the war.[7]

The flow of defense capital also meant a population boom. Between 1940 and 1944, Mobile County's population increased by 64 percent, leading to "housing shortages, rising rents and overcrowding on public transport."[8] The war industry affected the city's social configuration with the influx of women (especially white) in the workforce and an increase in its African American population.[9] While there are currently no studies of Mobile's LGBTQIA+ history, it is quite likely that, as in other documented cases throughout the country, this port city also received an influx of gay and lesbian newcomers.[10]

Although this presented an opportunity for African Americans to improve their socioeconomic status, attempts to integrate the workforce were met with white backlash. One of *The War*'s interviewees, African American veteran John Gray, recalls: "Mobile was a pretty fair-minded city. And before this time, whites and blacks got along pretty good as long as you had the status quo. Oh, but when the blacks began to get homes, to buy homes, and to ride in big cars it turned some people off."[11] On May 25, 1943, a group of white workers rioted for two days at the Alabama Dry Docks and Shipbuilding Company (ADDSCO) when the Fair Employment Practices Commission (FEPC), pressured by civil rights leader John LeFlore, convinced the company to promote twelve Black welders.[12] Supported by the League of White Supremacy, a group of white men and women attacked African American workers, leaving over one hundred of them injured. The plant had to close for four days.[13]

Another legacy of Mobile's legally segregated past, the "white" and "colored" bus signs.

Bus interior showing "colored" section sign. Undated. Erik Overbey Collection, the Doy Leale McCall Rare Book and Manuscript Library, University of South Alabama.

Bus interior showing "white" section sign. Undated. Erik Overbey Collection, the Doy Leale McCall Rare Book and Manuscript Library, University of South Alabama.

Wartime prosperity was not distributed equally. In August 1945 the City Planning Commission of Mobile released a "Housing Market Analysis" that provides relevant data on the racial disparities of family incomes in the city. The document lists the average income for Mobile families in the $40–$59/week range, "with 35 percent of the families having incomes of $60 and over and 31 percent having incomes of $39 and less." The average income for African American families, however, was between $20 and $29, even though they represented a larger percentage of multiworker families (46%) than whites (31%). Yet only 8 percent of Black families surveyed planned on moving away after the war, as compared to 19 percent of white families.[14] Analyzing race alone reveals only part of the picture. Although this US southern city functioned on the basis of systematic racism and white supremacy, Black elites had a more comfortable existence than regular Black folks and were therefore at times less invested in upsetting the status quo. Hence, when we hear complaints that Mobile changed after the war, we must keep in mind the racial and class-based nature of that discontent.

Although most of the people interviewed for the MGSCOH project were too young to remember Mobile during the war years, some of them expressed the prevailing sentiment that something changed in the city after the war, that the influx of newcomers somehow altered the character and identity of the city. Their recollections also show how the collective memory of a historic event can vary depending on the experiences of individuals and social groups.[15] Archivist Charles Torrey, born in Mobile in 1942 and descendant of some of the city's prominent white families, explains:

> New Orleans retains her identity. Mobile basically lost her identity between 1941 and '45. With the influx of so many people from elsewhere, upriver, out of state. They came for building the ships that were manning World War II. At the beginning of the war, there was a ship turned out every six weeks; at the end of the war they were turning out a ship once a week. And it took an immense amount of workers to do that. And Mobile just changed completely with that. Religion, ethnicity, race."[16]

George Moore, local historian at the Battle House Renaissance Mobile Hotel & Spa, was born in Mobile in 1933 and has worked in downtown Mobile since the 1950s. As an African American man who has navigated the city's white elite circles, he believes racial relations deteriorated after the war: "Yeah, it changed because a lot of people that came were not highly educated, 'cause they just needed people to build ships. So they came, taught them to weld, taught them to rivet, and that was it. And they stayed, yeah. Why go back to the farm?"[17]

Retired police officer Jack Bishop, born in Jones County, Mississippi, in 1938, moved to Mobile during the war with his mother, who came to work in Brookley Field. His recollections provide a glimpse into the experience of white rural families who moved to Mobile in search of new opportunities at that time:

> OK, when I came to Mobile it was during World War Two. And it was a lot of people coming into the city at the time to work at the shipyard and work at the air force base. My mother came here from working in the courthouse in Chatom, Alabama, which is the capital of Washington County. And she came down to work on the rationing board. And that's when gasoline, and sugar, and flour, everything was rationed. And her job was to dispense the rationings during that period. And being in that position, she was able to get us a brand-new-built house. It was two bedrooms, and a bath, a kitchen, and a dining room, and it was built by the government for government employees. And that's how we managed to end up with such nice housing to start out with.[18]

As an important staple in the city's annual calendar and a source of tourism revenue, the decision to suspend Mardi Gras during the two world wars was not taken lightly by city officials. Only three days after the attack on Pearl Harbor, Mobile's commissioner of public buildings Harry T. Hartwell wrote New Orleans mayor Robert S. Maestri to ask if New Orleans intended to celebrate Carnival that year, while assuring that they were "prepared to meet the Yellow Peril."[19] Three days later, the mayor replied that the festivities would indeed be canceled in the Crescent City.[20]

When the conflict finally came to an end, the acting mayor of Mobile, Robin C. Herndon, wrote a letter to the (white) king of Mardi Gras, Felix III, to welcome and hand him the city keys, while updating him on the developments since the monarch's previous visit, "after a lapse of five years":

> Much has happened here, and throughout the world, since your last visit to us and we believe you cannot help but rejoice with us that hostilities have ceased and that peace reigns throughout the known world. Also that you are proud of the part your subjects played in producing ships and materials, the necessities for the success of the allied nations in World War No. 2. Our population has largely increased as a result of war industry activities and living conditions have been rather inadequate, but thanks to the cooperation of your subjects, all new-comers have been privileged with living quarters.[21]

The tone here is notably different from the cheerful letters Herndon, and previous and subsequent mayors, wrote to the monarch.

Postwar Mobile

As Harvey H. Jackson III notes in his study of post–WWII Mobile, when the war ended, "some Mobilians thought it was time that workers who had come 'flocking from the backwoods' for jobs to head home."[22] That sentiment is still echoed today in statements by people who perceive the influx of newcomers during the conflict as ruining the city's genteel Creole Port City atmosphere. In a city characterized by a rigid social structure, an expanding middle class sought means of assimilation and social ascension. Jackson notes the important role of Mardi Gras in the city's social hierarchies:

Nowhere was this effort seen more clearly than in the yearly celebration of Mardi Gras, where local elites reinforced their status by entertaining the masses. What better way for nouveau Mobilians to announce their arrival than from a float looking down on their fellow citizens? And when older carnival associations refused to open their membership to newcomers, the newcomers organized associations of their own. . . . Though it remained a celebration of a closed society, it would never again be as closed as before.[23]

Although the festivities were somewhat subdued during the Korean War, 1950s Mardi Gras was characterized by the emergence of white women's parading groups, the creation of new mystic societies that accommodated those excluded from old elite organizations, and complete racial segregation. While "colored" Carnival was announced and respectfully described in the local white papers, it was always as a separate (marked) segment of the festivities. The news coverage praised Black elites' "civilized" celebrations and pageantry, which emulated those of the white elites.

According to the *Mobile Register*, revelers received a "special treat" in 1955 as the "Confederate Clad Band of the 31st Infantry 'Dixie' Division of the National Guard" joined several parades. Maj. Gen. Alexander G. Paxton was behind the idea of "costuming the band in Confederate uniforms," which he described as a "morale-booster." The article's author agreed, proclaiming: "You can bet every red-blooded Southerner in the band gets the boost out of the uniform that any red-blooded Southerner is supposed to get too. Even a Yankee or two playing with the band has a little feeling of pride."[24] It is likely that those who nurtured nostalgia for the Confederacy would need a "morale boost" less than a year after the *Brown v. Board of Education* Supreme Court decision. Yet this assertion seems to imply that only white people were "red-blooded Southerners," as it is unlikely that the sight of Confederate soldiers marching through downtown Mobile streets would have excited many African Americans.

The Experience of Segregation: Mobile's "Negro Main Street"

The 1901 Alabama constitution institutionalized segregation in the state. It established, among other things, the grandfather clause and other mechanisms for disenfranchising African Americans, as well as defining segregated

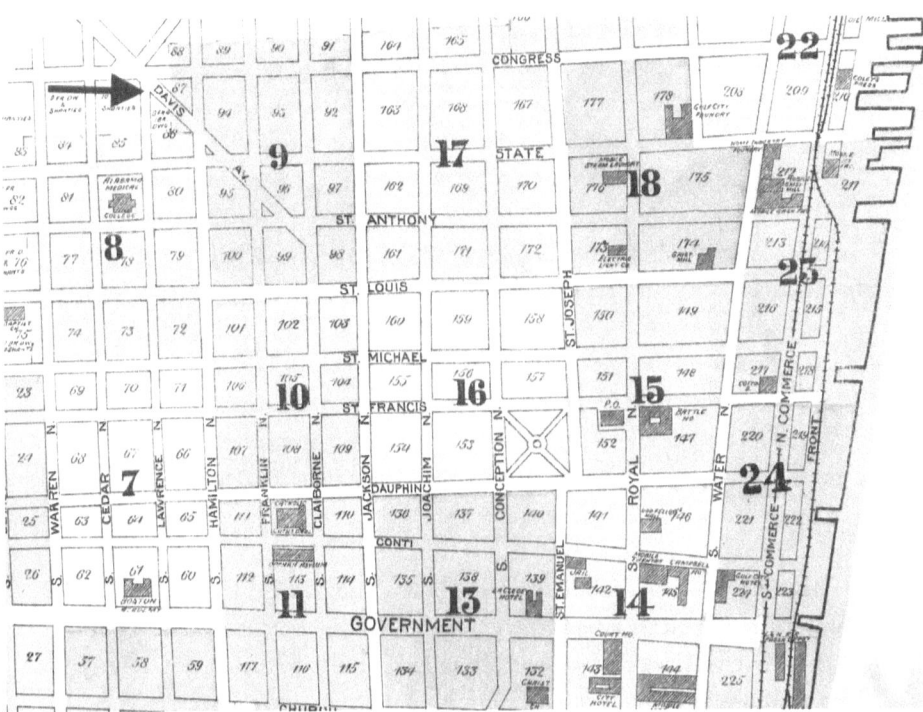

Detail of Sanborn Fire Insurance Map from Mobile, Mobile County, Alabama (1891) highlighting Davis Avenue. Library of Congress, Geography and Map Division.

public spaces. Business and shopping districts in African American neighborhoods derived from segregation, creating "new possibilities for [Black] consumers and entrepreneurs."[25] Davis Avenue, Mobile's Black commercial and social hub, was located close to downtown, but it was not exactly a part of it. As Wilmoth A. Carter defined it, it was Mobile's "Negro Main Street."[26]

Mobile's African American Mardi Gras was born, developed, and reinvented on Davis Avenue (now Dr. Martin Luther King Jr. Ave.). Until the downtown Mardi Gras parade route was desegregated in the 1990s, that is where all of Black Carnival's pageantry and celebration took place.[27] As downtown Mobile decayed, so did Davis Avenue, but it is still remembered fondly, and with nostalgia, by African American Mobilians old enough to have experienced it. As Mobile historian Paulette Davis Horton puts it:

> During Davis Avenue's hey days, neon lights were constantly blinking and glowing with the sounds of people walking on the crowded sidewalks. One of the

reasons that the Avenue was so popular to "out-of-towners" was because in some cases it was like home. Davis Avenue was like "being up North down South." ... Shopping was different than shopping downtown because you were somebody. You were home and you didn't have to worry about drinking out of the wrong fountain and going to the bathroom. On the "Avenue" you were out front.[28]

African American narrators interviewed for the MGSCOH project also shared their remembrance of that space:

Linda Dennison (born in Mobile in 1952): Let me tell you. For me, my family, my mother was a single parent. For us to venture even downtown to go to old Dauphin Street to Gayfer's, Hammel's, or something like that. It was something like a thrill. Because we did everything right there [on Davis Avenue]. We shopped, we played, we went to school, everything was right there.

Eric Finley (born in Mobile in 1952): Oh! It was just . . . it was the heart, it was the heart. I mean, any and everything that you needed done was done on Davis Avenue. There were three theaters you could go to the movies. There was a recreation center with a swimming pool. There were grocery stores, barbershops. I mean, the school that I went to, Heart of Mary, was on Davis Avenue. The church that we went to every Sunday was on Davis Avenue. There were clothing stores. There was one African American restaurant, The Best Grill. That was the Sunday place to go to eat. I mean, 'cause at the time we couldn't go to the white restaurants, in the fifties. It was everything that we knew and wanted. I really had no reason at the time to go to any of those other places 'cause everything was right there on Davis Avenue. I mean, our family was supported by the community because, you know, we had businesses in that area, so it was our life.

George Moore (born in Mobile in 1933): I lived only, like, three blocks from Davis Avenue. And that was our downtown area. And there were clothing stores, Black clothing stores, Black tailors, furniture stores, barbershops, cafés, barbecue cafés, movie theaters. There was the Pike. There was the Lincoln. There was the Ace Theater, and the Booker T. Theater. So, that was the area that Blacks went to shop, grocery stores. Some grocery stores were owned by Blacks and a lot of the businesses were owned by Blacks, so . . . There was Gomes Auditorium, which was a nice place to go and have parties, dance.[29]

Booker T. Theater, Davis Avenue 1959. Wilber F. Palmer Collection, the Doy Leale McCall Rare Book and Manuscript Library, University of South Alabama.

The memories of segregation from Mobilians of different backgrounds and identities provide an insight into the small ways in which racial violence was embedded in prosaic interactions in people's everyday lives. The narrators' memories show how racism, segregation, and racial hierarchies were taught, learned, internalized, and sometimes challenged in everyday actions. Racial violence was also delivered in symbolic gestures such as implying that a Black child's body was dirty or repulsive by forbidding them to try on clothes. Segregated facilities served the purpose of ingraining the belief that Black people were inferior and deserved less.

> **Eric Finley:** Well, you know, I can still see me wanting to go to the water fountain and your momma said: "No, you can't go." Going in and wanting to try some shoes or a hat, and they go: "No, you can't do that." Even though you could buy a suit. But you couldn't try on a hat. Unless you put some kind of cloth or handkerchief over your head. You know? It was just symbolic. You are African American, and if you put that hat on, nobody else would buy it. It was stupid stuff. Hum . . . not being able to go to the restaurant in Kress or . . . Oh yeah. It's, it's very vivid. . . . You know, like, we had theaters in our community,

but we didn't get the first slate of movies, so you would have to come downtown. And so, the Saenger Theater that's there now, it was beautiful, just like it is today, but we couldn't come to the front, we'd have to go around the side and walk upstairs to the balcony. Which, as a kid, you know, it didn't have that much of a negative impact on us then as it does now. Because at that time you were really just excited to go 'cause you were going to see some girl anyway. [laughs] But we were still boys, we'd thumb popcorn, you know, do silly stuff like that until a guy would come up and shine the flashlight. Yeah, so you remembered that, and you knew that it wasn't right, but in the fifties you kinda accepted it.

Palmer Richardson (born in Mobile in 1938): Downtown Mobile back when I was coming along and in high school, up until high school, downtown was a hustle and bustle, it was a lot going on, everybody going downtown to shop in the various stores and stuff and, especially on, like, a weekend you could hardly get down the streets because there was so many people. Dauphin Street was the street for shopping. [...] Everybody could go in any store, but I recall if you went into, say, Woolworth's, if I go in Woolworth's and I want something to eat ... all the way in the back was the lunch counter in the back. And whites' lunch counter was near the front side. I can see it today, alongside a wall. But, so, stuff like that was segregated. And the stores that maybe, if they did have a water fountain, you know, they were different. They had the Black water fountain and the white water fountain.

Bobby Dennison (born in Mobile in 1952): Well ... downtown was downtown. Downtown was open to everyone. When we were coming up, there were no places that we could not go. But once we got in those places, there were different areas for Black and white folks. Because we came up in the era where there was segregation, there was white water fountains and colored water fountains. So we both [referring to his wife, Linda Dennison, who was interviewed at the same time] remember that.

Linda Dennison: And we kinda knew ... when we were even growing up, and they would have, like, *The Popeye Show* down at the Saenger, and we would have to sit upstairs. We could not mingle with the kids, you know, the white children sat downstairs, we took the side entrance, and we had to go upstairs to the balcony to see that. And that was the late sixties, there, even still ... So we knew our place.[30]

White children, of course, had to be taught racial hierarchies.[31] White narrators who currently hold more egalitarian views look back on their "fond" childhood memories with some discomfort:

Kathie Hiers (born in Mobile in 1954): [sigh] . . . You know, I didn't think a whole lot about segregation when I was a child. Ironic, when I saw that movie *The Help* because we had a maid, [that] is what we called them back then, and, uh, she had been my grandmother's maid. So, she had helped my grandmother rear my mother and her brothers, then my mother had the same maid, Helen, when we were children. So she was like part of the family, and I didn't really understand the racial divide. Of course, clearly, I went to Leinkauf School that was all white.

Suzanne Cleveland (born in Mobile in 1938): Oh, absolutely, very segregated. I mean I can remember the water fountains that said colored and white. [. . .] One of the oddest things I remember about segregation was what is now the Little Sisters of the Poor was Hannon Park, and it was a white neighborhood, but there was one street that bordered on the, probably the south side of Hannon, where Blacks lived. And, so, we couldn't go there. We couldn't go in that side of the street. And, in my experience, I really, just accepted it. Although I didn't understand it. When I was in grammar school, I was at the cafeteria line and I said "yes, ma'am" to one of the cafeteria workers, and my teacher said, "Suzie, we don't say 'ma'am' to," and she used the n-word. I was just, I couldn't understand why, and I don't think I investigated it or anything, but I can just remember thinking, well, "that's not right." But it wasn't until much much later that I sort of put it all together. [. . .] I went [to downtown Mobile] with my grandmother some. And we had a housekeeper, and she would take us. Well, I need to say it, she was Black. And we called her then a maid, but she was like family. Her name was Clarabelle, and my sister and I, we would get on the bus with her, and she'd ride in the back and we'd ride in the front, and, at that time we didn't think anything of it. That was just what we did . . . don't know why we had these mores. Is that what they were when people just said you can't do this and you can't do that and no one ever questioned it?[32]

Mardi Gras played an important part in teaching racial hierarchies to Mobile's children, who grew up seeing racist imagery and Confederate memorials

Children in blackface posing on a float decorated as a steamboat, learning racial hierarchies and dynamics by participating in racist pageantry. Mardi Gras, Early Floral Parade near Ryan Park. Mobile, Alabama, 1936. Erik Overbey Collection, the Doy Leale McCall Rare Book and Manuscript Library, University of South Alabama.

being paraded and celebrated in the city's streets every year. Sometimes white children even got to participate in racist spectacles such as in this blackface performance at the 1936 floral parade.

Although Juanita Richardson did not grow up in Mobile and moved there only in the late 1960s, she perfectly describes how these traumatic memories leave indelible marks. She explains that to this day she cannot eat at a Krystal restaurant, because that would evoke the brutal mistreatment she met there by waitresses and police officers when, as a teenager, she participated in a sit-in in her hometown, Birmingham. She explains: "My daughter said I have to forgive, forget, and move on. I said I have forgiven, I have moved on, but I have not forgotten. That's the one I'm still working on."[33] Like her, most of the African American narrators interviewed for the MGSCOH project had a hard time letting go of their very palpable memories of segregation.

The Decline

Domingo Soto (born in 1946, in Aguadilla, Puerto Rico): The downtown was pretty much decimated. I mean, there was nothing here. The only reason that you would come to downtown would be, there were a couple of strip joints, like the Lucky Lady . . . The Stein & Still and then the gay bars . . . I think it was the place that was gonna have some cheap rent. It was the place that if you wanted to live an alternative lifestyle, you could, 'cause there was nobody down here to fuck with ya. The gay clubs were here, but the, the houses were in pretty horrible shape. It was a good place to get yourself killed. [laughs] It wasn't that much happening here. At least not in '69, '70, '71, '72 . . . Conception Street was featured in an American Friends Service Committee pamphlet back in the sixties . . . they looked like Walker Evans photos from West Virginia or something. This was Conception Street.[34]

The early 1960s brought significant changes to US downtowns as they became important sites in the Black civil rights struggle and stages of racial unrest and violence. As we will see in the following chapter, in Mobile, it would take a few more years for that to happen, as integration was (for the most part) less tumultuous there than in other Alabama cities. Yet in 1963 members of the White Citizens Council picketed in front of Mobile's Woolworth with signs that ironically proclaimed, "Help Integration. Trade at Woolworth," to protest desegregation.[35]

The decade also represents a critical turning point in Mobile's downtown history. A new Beltline Highway created to alleviate traffic contributed to suburbanization and westward expansion, along with the abandonment and decay of downtown. The city's first malls, Springdale Plaza (1959) and Bel Air Mall (1967), attracted retailers, marking the "beginning of the decline of the city's center."[36] Although jobs in other bases had already started dwindling in the early 1960s, the big blow to the city's labor market came in November 1964 when the Department of Defense announced its plans for closing Brookley Field.[37] The ensuing crisis should not have come as a surprise. In 1960 the Mobile Metropolitan Area Audit had warned about the city's dependence on defense funding, exposing the dangers of having its income and prosperity "tied closely together" to Brookley's fate. The report noted that its closing "would throw the area's economy into critical maladjustment," having the potential of "disaster," which could result in "severe depression" or "complete panic."[38]

As part of their revitalization efforts, government officials resorted to urban renewal projects. The Mobile Urban Renewal Agency was created in 1960, and by the end of the decade, the Mobile Housing Board had received $30 million in federal urban renewal funds. Arguably, the agency did not achieve its purported goals of using "rehabilitation, redevelopment and conservation . . . toward the total restoration of Mobile's blighted districts" and providing "a decent home in a suitable environment for every American family."[39] Most of the "blighted" areas listed for demolition and renewal were in African American sections of town, and Black people accounted for a disproportionate majority of the people displaced. Those in charge of the project were aware of the adverse reactions it would cause, and even their optimistic reports reveal how urban renewal affected the daily lives of the area's inhabitants while benefiting developers' interests.

In the summer of 1966, civil rights activists started attending informal meetings on Davis Avenue that would eventually give rise to the most radical voice of the Black liberation movement in Mobile: the Neighborhood Organized Workers (NOW). In June 1968 NOW launched Operation Ghost Town to boycott Mobile's downtown stores in protest of the lack of Black employees. According to Councilman Fredrick D. Richardson Jr. an original NOW member, the objective of the protest was "to boycott the merchants until such time as they agreed to hire blacks to responsible positions."[40] An ad published in the *Mobile Beacon* on May 31, 1969, announcing the third phase of the operation and summoning the city's Black residents to join the boycott explained:

DOWNTOWN MOBILE IS SURROUNDED BY BLACK PEOPLE AND BLACK PEOPLE HAVE NOTHING TO SHOW FOR SPENDING MOST OF THEIR MONEY WITH THE MAN.

WE, THE NEIGHBORHOOD ORGANIZED WORKERS, HAVE TRIED TO WORK ON THE CONSCIENCE OF THIS (WHITE) MAN. BUT WE HAVE COME TO THE CONCLUSION THAT HE DOES NOT HAVE A CONSCIENCE. WHY IN HELL! SHOULD BLACK PEOPLE CONTINUE TO SPEND THEIR MONEY WHERE THEY ARE NOT WANTED.[41]

Richardson would later recall that up until "1970, socially, in Mobile, Blacks still had to ride the back of the bus; drink out of a 'colored' water fountain;

GHOST TOWN
OGT-OGT-OGT-OGT
SUPPORT NOW

> DOWNTOWN MOBILE IS SURROUNDED BY BLACK PEOPLE AND
> BLACK PEOPLE HAVE NOTHING TO SHOW FOR SPENDING MOST OF
> THEIR MONEY WITH THE MAN.
> WE, THE NEIGHBORHOOD ORGANIZED WORKERS, HAVE TRIED TO
> WORK ON THE CONSCIENCE OF THIS (WHITE) MAN, BUT WE
> HAVE COME TO THE CONCLUSION THAT HE DOESN'T HAVE A
> CONSCIENCE. WHY IN THE HELL! SHOULD BLACK PEOPLE
> CONTINUE TO SPEND THEIR MONEY WHERE THEY ARE N
> WANTED. HERE ARE OUR RECOMMENDATIONS.

1. BUY FROM BLACK BUSINESSMEN IN THE BLACK COMMUNITY, OR ANY WHERE
ELSE EXCEPT DOWNTOWN.
2. DON'T SHOP ANYWHERE DOWNTOWN UNTIL BLACK PEOPLE ARE HIRED IN
PLACES IN MEANINGFUL POSITIONS SUCH AS:
   A. DEPARTMENT MANAGERS
   B. SALES CLERKS
   C. ACCOUNTANTS
   D. BUSINESS MANAGERS
   E. STORE MANAGERS
   F. CASHIERS & CHECKERS
   G. ADVERTISING SPECIALIST
WE DON'T WANT ANY MORE OF THIS ONE (1) TWO (2) THREE (3) JUNK.

SUPPORT N.O.W.

THE MAN (WHITE) DOESN'T UNDERSTAND REQUEST, SINGING, PRAYING, OR
MARCHING. BLACK PEOPLE HAVE BEEN MAKING REQUEST, SINGING, PRAYING,
AND MARCHING FOR YEARS AND THE WHITE DEVIL STILL WILL NOT HIRE BLACK
PEOPLE.
THE MAN ONLY UNDERSTANDS ONE THING- $MONEY - CUT HIS MONEY OFF JACK
AND HE'S HAD IT.

SUPPORT N.O.W.
PAID ADVERTISING BY THE

Paid Advertisement by the Neighborhood Organized Workers for the *Mobile Beacon*, May 31 1969. Courtesy of Local History and Genealogy. Mobile Public Library.

use the 'colored' rest room; live in 'colored' neighborhoods; work on underemployed jobs tailored for 'colored'; sleep in motels and hotels for 'colored only'; and eat in the 'colored section' of restaurants, if provided."[42]

Desegregation, along with the escalation of racial unrest, further contributed to the decline of downtown Mobile. Although integration meant undeniable advancements for African Americans, it also had its shortcomings. As Davis Horton recalls, in the 1960s it became clear that the Avenue "had seen its best days."[43] School desegregation meant the closing of Central High School, a social and cultural beacon for the city's African American community. While white flight, urban renewal, and the accompanying decline of the downtown area destroyed Black communities, it also represented an opportunity for people who defied gender and sexual normativity to find one another and start building a community of their own.

The Fruit Loop

An abandoned downtown was a place to be avoided unless you were looking for illicit pleasures. Although more work needs to be done to uncover Mobile's LGBTQIA+ history, evidence indicates that queer Mobilians took advantage of post–WWII urban decay, occupying undesired spaces and enjoying the relative anonymity that the area provided.

The Princess House on 254 Government Street was mentioned by some of the MGSCOH narrators as the first queer space they encountered in Mobile. It is unclear exactly how the Princess House Restaurant (later renamed Princess House Restaurant & Lounge) became a hangout for gay and lesbian Mobilians in the late 1960s and gained renown in the early 1970s for its fabulous drag shows. The space the Princess House would occupy for over three decades was listed as Mrs. Laura B. Ward's furnished rooms during the WWII years. In 1946 Theo Kouvarakis (Theologos Stamatios Kouvarakis), a Greek immigrant who "became a prominent figure in the restaurant business in south Alabama," is listed as the building's owner in the city's directory.[44] Geo N. Coumanis, who became the new owner in 1955, changed its name to Princess House Restaurant and Lounge and invested in an expansion and advertising in 1959. That year is also when the Golden Rod Social Club, owned by Geo E. and Mrs. Bessie E. Neal, another space that narrators remember being frequented by "queer folks," appears in the directory for the first time on 204 Government Street.[45] Furthermore, the YMCA, a place George Chauncey characterized as "one of the central institutions of gay male life" in the first decades of the twentieth century, was located less than a block away, on 168 Government Street.[46] A survey of the city's directories also reveals a progressive increase in vacant buildings in the area during the downtown decline period.

In 1970, after Geo's death, Nick G. Coumanis took over and rebranded the Princess House, putting out an ad in the directory with a new logo, which highlighted the word "Princess" in the foreground, superimposing a crown and a wand with a starred tip. The caption of the restaurant, which previously simply stated "Specialized in Steaks and Seafoods," was changed to "Specializing in Steaks and Seafoods, Party and Banquet Facilities, Open

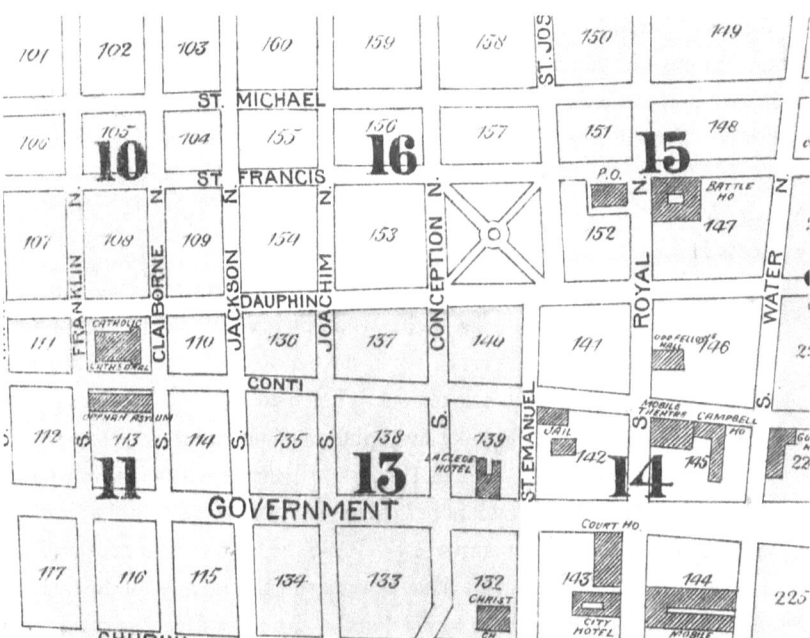

Detail of the Sanborn Fire Insurance Map from Mobile, Mobile County, Alabama (1891), highlighting the "Fruit Loop." Library of Congress, Geography and Map Division.

24 Hours." The ad also promoted the Tiara Dining Room. In 1972 a third venue mentioned by MGSCOH narrators as a space of gathering for gay and lesbian Mobilians appeared in the document: The Stein & Still Club, located on 215 Conti Street.

While it is, unfortunately, difficult to assess the extent and nature of the connection between Greek immigrant and queer communities in Mobile at that time, we do know that the different establishments that catered to different pleasure-seeking clienteles, such as the Lucky Lady strip joint and the 55 Club brothel, were in communication. As would be expected of a Port City, the transience of the space and constant movement of bodies generated interesting encounters. As Queen Richard IV (born in Mobile in 1957) recalled:

> There was a little Greek bar on Government Street, right there across from the Admiral. I remember one time the bartender at the [gay bar] French Quarter told me a ship is coming in. And I was really young 'cause he says: "You've got to come and go." And the thing was—it was the hookers that told him, because they always wanted some guys there when the Greek ship came in.

We were treated like royalty! I mean, it was the best night I ever had. The captain was—he couldn't speak a bit of English, but we all had a blast. You know, it was just like you see in the movies. Slamming the glass, throwing the ashtrays, dancing, the whole bit.[47]

Mardi Gras artist Homer McClure, born in Mobile in 1951, described the Princess House during its heyday:

Uh, let's see. Lots of vinyl. Like leather, you know, vinyl chairs. Kind of a 1940s look, linoleum. It was very dark in the bar area. But they did have a restaurant to the right-hand side that had a lunch counter with booths running down one wall, and I feel like it was pine paneling, and then there was a hallway that accessed both of them. So, if you were incognito, you would go to eat something at the restaurant part, then walk over to the . . . not have to walk outside and go in that entrance. [. . .] And the bar was next door right on North Jackson Street. But I feel like it was a straight bar most of the time, and like just certain nights were "gay." I don't know that for a fact, but that just seems to be stuck in the back of my mind. [. . .] They did have shows. It was one drag queen named Holy Dayworth who did lots of, uh, Lynn Anderson songs, I think. [. . .] And I feel like the guy that started Osiris, Neil Aldridge, was the choreographer for most of the shows at the Princess House, I can remember him there. And the waitress's name was Ann, I remember that. She had a hysterectomy that she had to tell everyone about [laughs].[48]

By the end of the 1970s, several openly gay bars had opened and closed in that area. As shown in chapter 5, these institutions would play a pivotal role in the development of Mobile's first openly gay Mardi Gras organization.

Some of the MGSCOH project narrators remembered "Gay Mobile" in that period:

Jack Bishop: Yeah, you had the Princess House, and then, on the side of the Princess House, was a little bar. And that was, that was for the gays, the gays went there. Nobody else bothered to go in there, that's where the gays went.

Kathie Hiers: Almost nobody went downtown anymore, and I can remember Gayfer's closing and Morrison's closing, and it became kind of rundown. And there really wasn't much down there for us, for me as a young adult but the gay bars. Of course, they were all near one another, but there wasn't a whole heck of a lot else down there. It was really rundown for quite a number of years. But for me, you know, when I started going down there in '78, there was nothing down there but the bars.

L. Craig Roberts: [sighs] It was totally abandoned, there was a gay bar or two, and a straight bar or two that were trashy, trashy, trashy. And everything was cut off at night on the weekend. It was like a dark place to be. And so, for gay people, I guess that was all right, because there was nobody around to see you if you were in the closet. You could go out and nobody would know the difference. 'Cause nobody was downtown. It was empty, and all the buildings were dark.

King Lawrence XV: You know where that big storage area is down on Government Street? You know where Broad Street is? Back from Broad, there's a big storage area there. Right there. And right across the street there's red-brick apartments. That was called Homo Heights. Everybody that lived there was gay, or crazy as hell, or drunks. [...] It was a fun place. [...] You know, I don't know what it is about it, but anything that has to do with gays, it starts downtown, and it stays downtown.[49]

Even when downtown Mobile's decline was at its nadir, Mardi Gras parades still took place in that area, which meant that at least once a year, Mobilians of all stripes gathered there to participate in the revelry. Although they often occupied segregated spaces, Mardi Gras served as a point of convergence or a place where people from separate worlds could at least see each other in a different context. Hopefully, future researchers will be able to uncover the origins and a more complete history of the Fruit Loop, but the area in and around the block formed by Joaquin, Conti, Conception, and Government Streets has been for decades a space where people who defy gender and sexual normativity congregate in the city. Including during Mardi Gras.

Remembering Downtown Mobile

Attempts to revive US downtowns since the last quarter of the twentieth century often rely on the power of nostalgia. Since people's memories are not a monolith, this use of the past to sell the present can be problematic. It is difficult to find a theme, or an image, that everyone can rally around when the memories of a space can be so subjective. It is also hard to create a sense of identity based on collective memory when a traumatic past affects a considerable segment of the population. As the *This Is Alabama* video suggests, promoting the image of an inclusive and diverse downtown Mobile that invites its citizens to celebrate a shared past can also mean forgetting or glossing over the baggage attached to it. Although the first part of that proposition is laudable, the second can be dangerous.[50] While the city's social structure was invented within a framework of segregation, classism, heteronormativity, and white supremacy, it can also be reinvented based on inclusion and diversity. But sanitizing the past is not the best means to achieve this goal. The actions and decisions taken by hegemonic groups (such as white flight and urban renewal) affected marked communities in different ways. Different marginalized groups used the urban spaces of Mobile to build community and assert their position in the city's society.

PART II
MARKED BODIES

CHAPTER 4

OFFICIAL "COLORED" MARDI GRAS AND MOBILE'S BLACK LIBERATION STRUGGLE

> You are looking at the history of Mardi Gras, and the social separation, that permeates Mobile society. And in a lot of ways there are people who I think self-subscribe to what I call the Mardi Gras mentality. There's a lot of fanfare and a facade of having a good time, as long as things stay separate. I wonder why that exists, I seriously wonder why if you work with folks, side by side, if you share a city, if you share a state, why you don't interact as much during this time of the year.
> —RICARDO WOODS[1]

In one of the most compelling scenes in Margaret Brown's 2008 documentary *The Order of Myths*, further discussed in chapter 7, Mobile's African American Mardi Gras queen realizes that her people came to that city in a slave ship owned by the white queen's people.[2] This is not only a piece of documentary filmmaking gold; it is also emblematic of how general audiences understand Mobile's Carnival. Whether denounced as a product of racism or defended as a proud tradition, Black participation in Mobile's Mardi Gras is often analyzed through the prism of segregation. The greatest (and often cited) evidence of that segregation is the fact that every year two separate official Mardi Gras Associations crown two pairs of monarchs, parade on separate routes, and have different sets of balls, creating different symbolic systems. What that analysis fails to account for is the fact that these organizations represent the experiences of only a limited segment of the city's population, even though their pageantry and events have been passed on as *the* history/experience of Mardi Gras.

Since the late nineteenth century, Carnival organizations composed mainly of members of the upper classes of the city's Black population have employed respectability politics as a means of combating racist stereotypes and achieving some level of social acceptance and ascension for affluent African Americans. In 1938 prominent members of the city's Black community formed the Mobile Colored Carnival Association (MCCA), allying with the Mobile Carnival Association (MCA), the white elite organization, in an attempt to "uplift the race."[3] That tactic eventually created a conflict between the MCCA's social pursuits and the more radical activism of the Neighborhood Organized Workers (NOW) in the late 1960s. While challenging Mobile's racial barriers and providing a means for African Americans to claim their space in their city's white supremacist society, organized Black Mardi Gras failed to confront systemic racism and often aligned with white elites reinforcing a classist exclusionary discourse.[4]

As Roger D. Abrahams notes, Black voluntary societies were created all over the Black Atlantic "in opposition to the socially exclusive color line, and in festivities these organizations often rehearse and express this opposition in resistance and derision performances."[5] Miguel Valerio explains how *pardo* brothers (mixed-race Afro Brazilians) asserted their place in the racist society of eighteenth-century Northeastern Brazil while making "potent statements about their subjectivities, or understanding of their personhood, sense of belonging, and beliefs, as well as their economic and artistic agency" through pageantry and public displays of devotion and affluence.[6] Elijah Gaddis sees African American processional culture as a means of claiming "streets and public places" in Wilmington, North Carolina, and as an "exercise in civic power."[7] In Mobile, however, official Black Carnival participation happened, for the most part, in Black neighborhoods and outside of the main parade routes. Furthermore, the expression of "opposition and derision" was curtailed there by the fact that organized Black Carnival celebration was developed in the molds of the city's accommodationist civil rights movement, that is, in collaboration with (and according to the norms imposed by) white elites. Nevertheless, it represented an important vehicle for African American Mobilians to combat racist stereotypes and discourses.

The Mobile Carnival Museum's timeline lists some of the important developments in the history of Black participation in the city's Mardi Gras. In 1894 the "Order of Doves, believed to be the first Black mystic society in Mobile, [was] formed." In 1938 Black Mobilians held their first Mardi Gras parade. A year later they created the first "colored" Carnival association, naming Mr. Samuel Besteda the First Mayor of "Colored Mobile." In 1940 the "Colored Carnival Association selected its first king and queen."[8] This timeline raises some important questions. Who created the Order of Doves, and how was it related to the emergence of African American mutual aid societies? Who was included in and excluded from respectable "Colored Carnival?" Furthermore, the timeline and museum exhibitions do not dwell on the reasons why people of color in Mobile needed to create a separate Mardi Gras celebration.

Although it is often told as a story of progress and achievement, this narrative also excludes and erases. In order for African Americans to enter the Carnival timeline in the late nineteenth century, and more importantly in the late 1930s, Mardi Gras needed to be articulated as a white spectacle and ritual. White chroniclers' accounts of Black participation in Mardi Gras reinforce the erasure and dismissal of popular participation while establishing a model for the "proper" performance of Blackness in Mardi Gras. Julian Rayford's "Colored Carnival" chapter, entitled "Fat Tuesday Invades Davis Avenue," is quite condescending, but also illuminating of white Mobilians' attitudes towards Black celebration. He notes: "For more than 200 years, the Negro enjoyed Mardi Gras by the sweat of his brow. Negroes carried the flaming torches that dripped fire along the parade route—and Negroes guided the mules that pulled the floats. Without colored people, there might never have been any Mardi Gras parades at all." There is no mention here that if that were true, for a long period of time, Mardi Gras parades likely existed thanks to the labor of enslaved people.[9]

Rayford also mentions a Black clown character who masqueraded on Mardi Gras day: "When you see him, suddenly, the whole drama of the carnival is concentrated upon him—a black domino hastening furtively through the rejoicing whites, a hobo, a vagabond, a masker stealing a quick moment of joy from this season." This spontaneous and unofficial "Negro humorist," he notes, presented "all the pathos, all the agony, all the poverty of his race."[10] While it denies this masker's agency and capacity for carnivalesque *jouissance*, this passage acknowledges the existence of spontaneous street masking, performed by Black revelers in white spaces.

Rayford also implies that the true (and acceptable) African American expression of Mardi Gras can be found only after the advent of the MCCA, when "the Negroes of Mobile present their own celebration of Mardi Gras with such dignity and pomp it is rumored the Negroes of New Orleans, in trying to escape the emphasis on burlesque in their own Mardi Gras, are planning to pattern their festival after that of the Negroes in Mobile."[11] This patronizing appeal to respectability is emblematic of the way in which white Mobile understood the city's racial dynamics. It is also yet another way that New Orleans served as the floating signifier in Mobile's identity formation, especially in the way white Mobilians *did not* want "their Blacks" to behave.[12]

Even a 1980 book produced by MAMGA and dedicated to chronicling Black participation in Mobile's Mardi Gras repeats the origin myths that center white elites in the history of the celebration while seemingly limiting "true" Black carnival participation to events led by the official organizations discussed below. They also describe Black participation in white events as a learning process that would teach them how to celebrate properly:

> When the time came, Blacks were very well prepared to stage their own show. They had worked with Mardi Gras since its inception, usually in less glamorous areas, as for instance, helping to build or lead horse drawn floats. In later years they supplied mules for the floats (as David Patton did for years) or rode the floats to manipulate animated figures—as Fred Williams did for the Infant Mystic's floats. These kinds of things were not only vital for the celebration but kept Blacks in contact through the years with this important festival.[13]

Edited by William J. Lovett Jr., *Mardi Gras in Mobile: A Chronicle of Black Participation* reinforces the markedness of the narratives around the city's Carnival celebration with two separate sections. "A History of Mardi Gras" traces the trajectory of Carnival revelry from its European origins with the "primitive people" of ancient Arcadia in Greece, to its being first celebrated in Mobile in 1703, to Joe Cain's revival. The section's concluding paragraph briefly introduces the first "black order," which is further discussed in a separate section entitled "Mardi Gras in Ebony Mobile."[14] While in many ways this book repeats the narratives created and perpetuated by white authors and commentators, it also claims these Black laborers' important place in the history of the festivities (not as subjects, but as historical actors), especially by listing their names.

"Colored" Mardi Gras at the Turn of the Twentieth Century

Accused of committing "sexual misconduct . . . against a white woman," two young Black men (seventeen-year-old Jim "Dick" Robinson and twenty-one-year-old Will Thompson) were taken to a Birmingham jail "for their safety until the trial" but were assaulted by a mob on the train trip back to Mobile in 1906.[15] Paulette Davis-Horton recounts: "Believe it or not, people wanted souvenirs, they took pictures, cut pieces of clothing from the victims and pieces of the tree from which they were hanging."[16] Davis-Horton alludes to the scars left upon African American Mobilians by the horrifying spectacle. Mrs. Rosie, whose house was located in front of the tree where the young men were hanged, "lived to be a very nervous woman and kept that window of her home boarded up so she would not relive that scene again." The author mitigates the narrative by concluding that only a "fraction" of Mobile's population participated in "these incidents" and complains that the "activity of a few made the whole city look bad."[17] Yet the kind of racialized violence that scarred Mrs. Rosie and her neighbors needs to be considered as part of the context in which Black Mobilians articulated their accommodationist and respectable social and political organizing. Mobile's white elites accepted, or at least tolerated, limited gains made by a selected group of what they deemed respectable African Americans, while disenfranchising and oppressing Black people in general. Hence, any discussion of Black and white experiences (including in and of Carnival) must take into consideration not only how the dehumanization of African Americans had concrete and deadly consequences but also how socioeconomic status shaped those experiences, despite systemic racism and white supremacy.

In 1845 people of color (enslaved or free) were prohibited from holding balls and public events in Mobile. By the last decade of that century, the main local newspaper respectfully announced "Colored Carnival" events.[18] Founded in 1890, the Order of Doves is referred to as the first African American mystic society in Mobile. They held their first ball on February 1894 in the Gilmer Rifles armory.[19] A couple of days later, the *Mobile Daily Register* noted the presence of "the elite colored" at the "affair" and its "grand success," declaring "Miss Florina Nicholas, attired in pink silk, with satin stripes . . . the acknowledged belle of the ball."[20] The 1892 city directory provides some clues about the men who chaired the event's committee of reception and their prominent positions within their community. Creole foreman

Francisco Gomez Jr. lived at the intersection of St. Madar and Davidson Streets. Physician Samuel S. H. Washington resided on 303 Michael Street. Frank Leavens was a barber who lived on 505 Church Street. Thomas R. W. Jackson owned a restaurant and oyster saloon on 564 Dauphin Street and lived next door. Willis Banks was the headwaiter at the Battle House hotel and resided on 455 South Dearborn Street.[21] Morgan Henderson worked as a US courts bailiff and as a messenger at the US district court, and his residence was located on Pecan Street, four doors west of Monday Street.[22]

The location of that first ball connects the mystic society to another respectable institution for Mobilians of color: Black militias. Although the US Congress had already opened state militias to Black men in 1870, in Alabama they came into existence over a decade later.[23] Black militias emerged when the end of Reconstruction led to a decline in Black political participation in Alabama, pushing African American leaders to resort to other, less direct, congregating activities. Assembled on August 25, 1883, Gilmer Rifles also had several Creoles of color as members.[24]

Gilmer Rifles leader Capt. Reuben Romulus Mims was a committed Freemason who served as head of the Grand Lodge of Alabama from 1886 until his death in 1901.[25] He was also vice president of the United States Letter Carriers' Mutual Benefit Association and the "highest-ranking black officer in the Alabama State Troops." Mims illustrates well the process by which, through collaboration with white elites, and by not defying the status quo, some Mobilians of color achieved a modicum of social status, while not directly challenging the city's discriminatory racial structure. In August 1892, when Gilmer Rifles' first encampment took place, the *Mobile Daily Register* praised the "well known, respectable colored men" who served as officers of the companies, and especially Captain Mims. When he died in March 1901, the same periodical eulogized him, noting he was "respected by whites and blacks alike."[26] Although the actual connections between Gilmer's Rifles and the city's "colored" Mardi Gras organizations need to be further investigated, the fact that the Order of Doves held its annual ball in the Black militia's headquarters shows the interconnectedness of Black organizations of the period.

In 1897 the *Mobile Daily Register* covered the fourth Order of Doves Ball, providing complimentary coverage, explaining that the society was composed of "some of our best colored young men."[27] The ball was again held at the Gilmer Rifles on the night before Mardi Gras. Before the formal affair, "the society marched from their quarters through Dauphin, Royal and St. Louis streets to the Gilmer Hall, making a very pretty show." The piece explained that the dancers followed a strict dress code (*costume de rigueur*) and that "admission was by invitation only." Some of the attendants wore "very handsome" costumes "made up of silk, satin and velvet, representing princes, knights and cavaliers," and the ballroom was "decorated with ever-greens" and "beautifully lighted with electric lights" that "showed off to great advantage the costumes of the maskers and those of their guests who wore evening dress." The note also comments on the "elegant supper" that "was served about 12 o'clock," telling the readers that the selected group of people sitting around the table "reflected great credit upon the society."[28] Although these notes were somewhat hidden in less prestigious sections of the paper, we can extrapolate that they offered white readers access to a flattering image of African American elites. More importantly, they reinforced the similarities between unmarked and marked sanctioned Carnival rituals. In addition, the section about the revelers' "march" indicates that at least part of the spectacle was public, which means it served a prescriptive function in performing proper Blackness to the "masses" in an African American neighborhood.

This reverence to members of the "colored elite" implies that any investigation of the experience of race in Mobile that does not consider its intersection with class would be incomplete. The 1880 census counted 18,955 whites and 12,449 "Colored" in Mobile, showing that this has for a long time been a city with a considerable population of people of color.[29] After the 1901 Alabama constitution established Jim Crow laws in the state, disenfranchising African Americans, the number of Black people eligible to vote dropped from 11,091 in 1896 to 4,572 in 1903. According to Nahfiza Ahmed, although the Jim Crow system created a separate "caste" for all people of African descent, in the nineteenth century a "class structure which emulated that of whites in the Old South was formed in black Mobile." Ahmed argues that this nineteenth-century structure, which privileged Black people who "descended from Creole and mulatto backgrounds," set the stage for the "bourgeois, accommodationist leadership" of the twentieth century. This pattern of Black leadership was present both in the city's civil rights activism and in its carnival organizing.[30]

The Colored Carnival Association

In the late 1930s, African Americans composed about 40 percent of Mobile's population and had accessed "a growing middle class."[31] Yet by 1939 only 224 Mobilians of color were qualified to vote.[32] At the end of that decade, three separate groups led efforts to organize Mardi Gras street revelry for African American people in the city. In a place that denied them the basic civil rights, Carnival afforded a symbolic system to affirm their humanity and dignity. While it would take over half a century for Mobilians to have Black people in actual positions of power in the city's government structure, the election and parading of Black mayors, monarchs, and courts sent a hopeful and empowering message.

Different sources claim that in 1938, the Knights of the May Zulu Club, led by renowned float builder Augustine S. May, performed the first mystic parade for/by Black people in Mobile. Unfortunately, none of them provide primary sources to support that information or elaborate on the particulars of what constitutes a "mystic parade."[33] While Mr. May was indeed a prominent figure in the city's Black community and organized parades and other Mardi Gras–related events, it is hard to affirm with certainty that this was the first Carnival parade organized and attended by African American Mobilians. It is even harder to imagine that before that specific event, Black people did not have some sort of street celebration or "ritual play."[34]

Born in 1902, May worked as a truck driver at Patterson Hardware and produced floats for some of the most prestigious white Mardi Gras mystic societies. Accounts of the Knights of May parades reveal similarities with the New Orleans Zulu Social Aid and Pleasure Club. According to independent Mobile historian Wayne Dean, their first parade "featured the rhythm of the members beating on buckets and tubs," and their float themes included "Flying Alligator of the Jungle" and "Monster of the Jungle."[35] They also crowned a Zulu king and a Zulu queen, and their 1946 parade, headed by African American war veterans, included the "King Haile Selassie in the Jungles of Africa" float.[36] As we will see, Mobile and New Orleans versions of Black Mardi Gras would eventually clash, as Mobile's "respectable" Carnival organizers repudiated what they perceived as their neighbor's "burlesque" pageantry. Perhaps that is why Mr. May's parade lasted only until 1952.

It should be noted, however, that the Mobile Zulus were quite popular while they lasted. On February 4, 1950, the *Gulf Informer* announced that the Zulus planned the "Best Parade in History," or "the most spectacular pageant ever presented on Davis Avenue." The Black periodical claimed that the spectacle, scheduled for that Mardi Gras Day (February 21) "would be composed of some of the most beautiful and graceful floats ever seen at a Mobile Mardi Gras parade." The article also announced that the Zulus' participation in

Mobile's Carnival was not restricted to the Fat Tuesday parade. They also held a coronation dance for the Zulu king and queen on February 10 at the Dragon Ball Room.[37] After so much success, it is unclear to this researcher why the group ceased its activities only two years later. It also seems odd that the organization has been relegated to small notes in Mobile Mardi Gras's official history. This chapter, unfortunately, perpetuates this erasure, as it is concerned with the creation of Mobile's Mardi Gras invented tradition and will therefore focus on the organization that has become the standard for Black Carnival in the city to the present day.

On Sunday, February 19, 1939, the *Mobile Press Register* announced that the "First Colored Mardi Gras Parade," sponsored by the recently established Colored Carnival Association "with the idea of creating interest among Mobile's colored residents in the annual Mardi Gras," had been scheduled for that following Tuesday afternoon. The note announced cash prizes for "best group displays," "best decorated bicycles," "best individual maskers," and "best decorated automobiles or floats," ranging from $1.50 to $20, which indicates that this was a community event open to the registered public rather than an organized pageantry exclusively performed by members of a closed group or organization. Those who did not register were "invited to watch" but "strictly forbidden to enter" the parade, which marched through the heart of the Black neighborhood, especially its "Negro Main Street." Starting at the Colored Community Center, it moved "east on St. Anthony to Hamilton Street; south to St. Francis, east to Warren; north to Davis Avenue, then west on Davis Avenue to Lafayette, countermarching east on the avenue to Lawrence and south to St. Anthony."[38] This prohibition of nonregistered revelers from joining the pageantry indicates that Black Mobilians didn't need such incentive to "create interest" in the celebration as suggested in the article. Instead, it reveals an attempt to organize and control a popular carnivalesque expression that already existed.

In a different column of the same page, the *Register* announced the coronation of the first "King of Colored Carnival," which would also take place the following Tuesday night at the St. Anthony Street Colored Community Center. Chosen by popular vote, Winston A. Allen, secretary-treasurer of Johnson-Allen Undertaking Company, received the title of King Tuttle.[39] Leslie Allen, Willie Turner, William Claiborne, and Webb Spencer were his knights. Dunbar High School student Ruby Morgan was his queen, and Wildora Wilkens, Elises Foster, Alice Glover, Ethel Corey, and Hilda

Richardson served as her assistants. Grand Marshal Emanuel Carter secured the parade's permit with Mayor Charles A. Baumhauer.[40] The court's evening parade took a similar yet slightly shorter route as the day parade.[41]

The fact that the "first" African American parade and Mardi Gras court were announced in the same newspaper, happened on the same date, and took very similar routes would appear to indicate that the same organization was behind both feats. Yet, on February 22, 1939, the *Mobile Press* clarified that different groups organized the two events: "The Mobile Colored Carnival Association, a group separate from that which conducted the evening parade, staged its procession at 3:30 pm." Among the African American organizations present at the parade were the Boy Scouts, Broad Street School, Dunbar High School, Williamson School, the "colored" YMCA and Alabama State Teachers' College. Bands from St. Peter Cleaver's School, Most Pure Heart of Mary School, the Bama State Band, the Excelsior Band, the Melody Masters, and "a clown band and a jazz orchestra from a traveling minstrel show" provided the musical accompaniment.[42] Although the newspaper article does not identify those responsible for the 1939 court, Davis-Horton, who interviewed people involved in the event, explains that the women of "The Smart and Thrifty Ladies Social Club selected Emanuel Carter to plan the first black carnival parade."[43]

All of these antecedents are fascinating and deserve to be further investigated, but since they did not last more than a year (in the case of King Tuttle's court), or a little more than a decade (the Knights of May Zulu Club's Parade), this chapter concentrates on the MCCA/MAMGA and its role in establishing Mobile's Black Mardi Gras "tradition." Among the organizations involved in the early years of the association were several Black mutual aid and social groups, such as the Utopia Social Club, the Krewe of Elks, the Dragons Social Club, the Gentlemen of Pleasure, and the Mobile Colored Insurance Company.[44] Dr. Wilborn L. Russell, a renowned local dentist, was its first president and led the organization until 1987. Other prominent race men collaborated with Russell in the endeavor: J. T. McKinnis (mortician), Sam Besteda (tailor), and Dr. James A. Franklin (physician), all of whom had successful businesses on Davis Avenue.[45] Besteda was elected by popular vote to become the first "mayor of Colored Mobile," chosen from a ballot that included R. R. Perry, William Howard, John Pope, and William Owens.[46] Tuskegee graduate Alex (Alexander) Herman was the first king crowned by the association, in 1940.[47] Herman would go on to serve as president of the

Photograph of Mobile Colored Carnival Association's first queen, Aline Jenkins, in 1940. Courtesy of Aline Jenkins Howard, the Doy Leale McCall Rare Book and Manuscript Library, University of South Alabama.

Unity Life Insurance Company for forty-two years and as a member of the Mobile branch of the NAACP. He was also the Exalted Ruler of the Gulf City Lodge 244. Alabama State College student Aline Necella Jenkins was the first queen. Jenkins earned BS, AA, and Educational Specialist degrees from Alabama State, as well as an MA from Columbia University's Teacher's College, and served as teacher, vice-principal, and principal in several different schools.[48] In other words, the two represented the best that respectable Black society had to offer. Black celebrities, such as baseball legend Hank Aaron, who served as "Mayor of Colored Mobile" in 1952, have also joined the organization's pageantry.

The monarchs did not participate in the pageantry that first year, watching it instead from a reviewing stand erected in front of the Black fraternal organization Elks Lodge located at the intersection of Warren and State Streets.[49] Many of the prominent early members of the MCCA were also members of the Utopia Social Club (est. 1914), whose debutantes served as the first ladies in the 1940 court. Former MAMGA president Eric Franklin Finley (grandson of founding member Dr. James A. Franklin) explains:

Dr. Russell represented in one of MAMGA's commemorative floats. Mardi Gras, 2017. Photo by the author.

The Utopia Club would host an annual ball and have debutantes that they would introduce to society, and those debutantes became the first ladies of the court. And the escorts for the debutantes became the knights. And the queen was one of the debutantes as well. And so that continued. It's just that as the organization became larger, then the knights and the ladies were selected at large, not just from the Utopia.[50]

The first MCCA parade, coronation, and associated events show the organization's role in congregating different elements of the racial uplift project. YWCA officials Lois Chandler, Deloris Dickerson, Vivian Pearson, and Juanita Rice hosted the royal Carnival Tea "assisted by nine girls from Mobile Branch Junior College," which gave "the city its first opportunity to meet the king, the queen, and the knights and ladies of the carnival court."[51] Among the distinguished guests in attendance were Alabama State Teacher's College president Dr. H. Council Trenholm and Tuskegee Institute president Dr. F. D. Patterson. Both schools provided bands for the parade, and the Tuskegee Institute's Swingsters animated the Tuesday night dance. Musician Edward Langster served as the chief marshal of the parade, which presented "leaders of the race in Alabama" in "decorated automobiles." Educator and Alabama Dry Dock and Shipbuilding supervisor Hershel Williams was the chairman of the publicity committee.[52]

Although the Colored Carnival Association/MAMGA was and still is a men's organization, Mrs. Frederica Glover-Evans, often referred to as the "mother of colored carnival," played a pivotal role in its inception, which shows that Black women were crucial to Black Mardi Gras's respectability politics project.[53] Although she is credited with the organization's inception, accounts of her participation often place her in traditionally feminine roles such as organizing the courts and teaching young monarchs and court members proper dress codes and etiquette as chairman of the coronation committee. She also came up with the name every monarch would take for the duration of the revelry. Eric Franklin Finley describes her role:

> The Utopia Social Club was initially started to provide cultural activities for young African Americans. 'Cause, again, we're in the Jim Crow era, and these gentlemen wanted to have some events that the kids could learn about etiquette, of different social events, and they had an auxiliary group of ladies, one of the most profound names is Mrs. Frederica Evans. She was kind of, what they refer to as the mother of Mardi Gras for the Mobile Area Mardi Gras Association. In fact, she tagged the name King Elexis the First. That was her creation. Because the first king was Alex Herman, and she changed that to Elexis the First, which still holds true today for the king each year.[54]

Mrs. Glover-Evans was more than an auxiliary lady. She was also an important educator appointed by US president Franklin D. Roosevelt to the National Youth Administration and was involved in the establishment of the Mobile branch of the Alabama State College.[55] Born in 1892, she earned a bachelor of science from the Alabama State College after also attending

Talladega College and Atlanta University as well as "workshops, institutes, and conferences held at Tuskegee Institute, Hampton Institute, Morgan State College, and many more colleges throughout the United States."[56] At the time of her death, on March 7, 1967, in a tragic house fire, she was "employed as an instructor at Mobile State Junior College, Chairman of Coronation of the Colored Carnival Association . . . a member of the Daughters Auxiliary of Knights of St. Peter Claver, an active worker for the March of Dimes and other organizations." Even after her death, she continued to empower young Black women through the Frederica Glover Evans Memorial Funds gathered in her name in lieu of flowers and awarded to "a worthy and needy young woman of the sophomores' class" at the Mobile State Jr. College.[57] Mrs. Glover-Evans's involvement in the establishment of the organization attests not only to the crucial role played by Black women in the racial uplift project but also to the importance of education as a means for them to ascend socially in a racist and patriarchic society. That is also evidenced by the roles of the Smart and Thrifty Ladies Social Club in the planning of the parade and by the YWCA officials in hosting the royal Carnival Tea.

The MCCA's official incorporation document, from January 15, 1946, provides a glimpse into the ways in which Cold War anticommunist paranoia affected Black people's attempts to organize, even if just for social purposes. It states that the organization was created:

> For patriotic purposes; to promote knowledge, arts and sciences; to create and cultivate interest in the celebration of Carnival activities at Mardi Gras; to unite the members in the bonds of friendship and fellowship that they may effectively promote the ideals of American freedom and democracy; to fit the members for the duties of citizenship and to encourage them to serve the nation ably as citizens; to maintain true allegiance to American institutions; to foster social and fraternal intercourse among the members and to urge and encourage active participation of all members in patriotic functions and in all things that have to do with civic, state or national betterment.

The document's eighth clause is even more explicit in its red-scare rhetoric, stipulating that the "Corporation shall be non-political, non-partisan, and non-sectarian and neither its name nor its influence shall be used inconnection [sic] with any political, sectarian or labor dispute."[58]

Official "Colored" Mardi Gras and Mobile's Black Liberation Struggle 89

MCCA's Carnival Court of 1950. King Leo Hagan and Queen Vivian Jones. *Gulf Informer*, February 18, 1950.

Mobile Colored Carnival Association Mardi Gras Court. King Hilliard Smith, Queen Edna Godwin, 1948. Archives Collection, the Doy Leale McCall Rare Book and Manuscript Library, University of South Alabama.

Mobile Colored Association Mardi Gras Queen Lya Battle (Lya Dowe) with children of the court, 1946. Courtesy of Marshall Wormley, the Doy Leale McCall Rare Book and Manuscript Library, University of South Alabama.

Mobile Colored Association Mardi Gras King Wayne Cheaere Lumpkins and Queen Gertrude Reese, 1964. Courtesy of Marshall Wormley, the Doy Leale McCall Rare Book and Manuscript Library, University of South Alabama.

Mobile Colored Association Mardi Gras Queen Carole Loretta Russell, 1958. Courtesy of Marshall Wormley, the Doy Leale McCall Rare Book and Manuscript Library, University of South Alabama.

Mobile Area Mardi Gras Association Coronation. Municipal Theater, 1972. King Dr. Tommy S. Thompson Jr. and Queen Felicie Bertille Hazeur. Mobile Press Register Collection, the Doy Leale McCall Rare Book and Manuscript Library, University of South Alabama.

The MCCA vs. New Orleans Zulus

Mardi Gras helped shape respectability politics and establish proper Blackness in Mobile as evidenced by the alleged 1947 feud between the founder of Mobile's Colored Carnival Association and New Orleans's Zulu king, which played out in the two cities' main white newspapers.[59] Although the Zulus remain one of the most important elements of New Orleans Mardi Gras celebration, the vision of African Americans in grass skirts and blackface at times also invited controversy.[60] When Louis Armstrong was crowned Zulu king in 1949, he faced outrage from other Black celebrities, and civil rights organizations called for a boycott on their parade in the 1960s.[61]

On February 15, 1947, the *Mobile Register* claimed Dr. W. L. Russell was "ashamed" of the antics in New Orleans, which he deemed "undignified." According to the paper, Johnie J. Smith, a theater manager who was crowned Zulu king that year responded, "We wouldn't go to Mobile and tell them how to have their Carnival." To which Dr. Russell allegedly replied, "We're not trying to tell them how to run their show in New Orleans . . . but I repeat that their burlesque is not the kind of celebration we care for in Mobile." He also noted that Black Mardi Gras events in Mobile were "carried out in a joyous, but intelligent, atmosphere," following "cultural and mystic principles."[62]

The *New Orleans Times-Picayune* version of the squabble quoted Smith as stating: "Nuts to those Mobile peoples . . . but not no coconuts—they's for our friends only." The article also claimed that Dr. Russell proscribed jitterbugging from his queen's coronation ball and lambasted "the Zulus for dressing in grass skirts and wearing rings in their ears, painting their faces black, and marking white rings around their eyes." According to the *Picayune*, the Zulu king retorted: "If those peoples don't want to see the Zulus they can stay right there in Mobile and mind their own business . . . As long as we like it, it's not their business."[63] The press in both cities was controlled by white elites, and by pitting these two Black Carnival organizations against each other, they were also presenting two competing images of public performances of Blackness. In Mobile it appears as if there was a concerted effort to curtail any form of pageantry and revelry that did not fit the molds of the MCCA's respectability politics. A note about the 1950 race for "Mayor of Colored Mobile" conveyed the organization's concerns "regarding reported obscene masking in previous seasons" and their plea for revelers to "refrain from such degrading masking."⁶⁴ It is likely that they are referring here to the street performers known as "Mollies," further discussed in chapter 6.

Dr. Russell summed up his organizations' goals: "People sort of looked for Mr. Colored Man to be a clown. But we have changed that attitude among our people. We seek dignity, and gradually, we are succeeding. We go in for the classical side. We follow Mardi Gras as it has been set by the fathers of Mardi Gras." These founding fathers, as previously established, were members of the white elites. He also acknowledges the support and influence of the Mobile Carnival Association in the creation of the Mobile Colored Carnival Association, noting that the two groups agreed that Black Mobilians "should have, as much as possible, a classical parade. We did not care for the burlesque." While expressing his hopes that Mardi Gras would play an important role in his community's uplift, Dr. Russell continued: "We choose our king and queen . . . exactly as the white king and queen are chosen. No amount of money can buy that honor. We select only the finest young people from the best families in the community."⁶⁵ This description provides a good example of how marked people appropriated dominant cultural norms as a means of social ascension and acceptance. Rayford's 1935 letter, discussed in chapter 1, confirms Dr. Russell's fears that white people conceived of Black people's public performances as ridiculous entertainment, so it is not surprising that his organization sought to counteract racist stereotypes with and through their pageantry.

MCA's influence can also be seen in MCCA's parade theme choices. Whereas the Knights of May Zulu Club were paying homage to Emperor Haile Selassie and Zulu royalty in 1946, the 1948 MCCA parade honored early American explorers, "gaily [portraying] important voyages and settlements in the Western Hemisphere":

Float 01 (Sponsored by the Utopia Social Club): "Leif Erikson and the Norsemen of Iceland"

Float 02 (Sponsored by the Krewe of Elks): "Columbus Discovers America"

Float 03: "Ponce de Leon Discovers the Fountain of Youth"

Float 04 (Sponsored by the Spartan Social Club): "Magellan Lands at South America"

Float 05 (Sponsored by the Night Hawks Social Club): "DeSoto Made Governor of Florida"

Float 06 (Sponsored by the Pirates Social Club): "Landing of the Pilgrims"

Float 07 (Sponsored by the Gentlemen of Pleasure Social Club): "Lemoyne and Bienville Founders of Mobile"[66]

While it is hard to confirm whether these themes were suggested (or imposed) on the MCCA by the MCA, it is truly confusing why an organization created to celebrate and uplift people of African descent would choose to pay homage to and identify with European settlers and *conquistadores* and therefore commemorate the violent colonization process that caused unspeakable harm to people of color. Another, more prosaic, interpretation would be that since Black organizations often rented floats from white organizations for their parades, they could have also incorporated some of their themes into the procession for practical reasons.

NPVL vs. NOW: Different Paradigms for Mobile's Black Liberation Struggle

This close relationship between the MCCA and the MCA occurred in the context of the larger movement for Black civil rights and racial uplift. In Mobile, moderate protests sanctioned by "good whites" have historically taken precedent over radical dissent in the way the city recounts its history of Black civil rights struggle and progress.

To understand how Mobilians came to perceive their city as a better place in terms of race relations than other major Alabama cities at that time, we need to look at the two protagonists in that narrative: civil rights leader John LeFlore and mayor Joe Langan. The city's only public monument to the civil rights struggle is a bronze statue of the two men side by side.[67] LeFlore was a postal clerk who became the executive secretary of Mobile's National Association for the Advancement of Colored People (NAACP) chapter in 1925, a position he held until 1955. When state attorney general John Patterson prohibited the NAACP from operating in the state in 1956, LeFlore dedicated himself to the leadership of the Non-Partisan Voters' League of Mobile (NPVL). According to his biographer, Kenneth A. Robinson, LeFlore embodied the "gentleman's approach" to civil rights, "forming alliances with liberal white leaders" and gaining "the respect of fair-minded whites." To the author, although racism existed in Mobile, it possessed a "genteel flavor"; hence, the "proper way" to confront it was to "engage intelligibly with white leaders and businessmen."[68] Under LeFlore's leadership, the NPVL sought the sociopolitical and economic inclusion of Mobile's African Americans through tactical alliances with "racially liberal" white politicians. Even the name of the organization sought to distance itself from radical political movements and organizations, creating an aura of impartiality similar to that expressed by the MCCA founding document. The NPVL also distanced itself from efforts by civil rights groups that proposed direct action and civil disobedience, such as the Southern Christian Leadership Conference (SCLC). LeFlore criticized the 1960s sit-ins as "a spurious and reactionary attempt on the part of feeble-minded individuals to incite the race into needless antagonization against whites."[69] This is not to say that Mobile was completely isolated from the national civil rights movement. In 1959 more than two thousand people came to hear Dr. Martin Luther King Jr. speak at the ILA 1410 Auditorium on Davis Avenue on Emancipation Day. A year later Rev. Ralph D. Abernathy and Rev. Fred Shuttlesworth led the Non-Violence and Social Change workshop at the Mt. Zion Baptist Church. Both events were organized by the Alabama Civic Affairs Association, which had LeFlore as its research secretary.[70]

As indicated by the celebratory statue, his most important partner was not another Black leader, but a white politician: Joseph N. Langan. As the story goes, Langan, a Catholic New Deal supporter of Irish descent, changed his opinion of African Americans by fighting alongside them during WWII. When he returned from the South Pacific, he supported their claims for civil rights.[71] He was elected to the Alabama House of Representatives in 1946 and was later elected to the three-man Mobile City Commission, thanks in large part to votes from predominantly Black districts acting under LeFlore's instructions.[72] In 1956 Langan created a biracial committee to promote "communication between the races during a period of rising confrontation elsewhere in Alabama." The committee did not produce significant results but contributed to the image of the city's racial progress. Critics denounced the committee, along with its successor, the Special Advisory Commission (1963), as a way for Langan to reward "those who had supported him in the polls and particularly his long-time friend, LeFlore."[73] Colored Carnival Association's Dr. W. L. Russell was one of the committee members.

In 1963 the *Wall Street Journal* praised Mobile's harmony and ability to build "racial peace as strife increases elsewhere."[74] The article lists the accomplishments of African Americans in positions such as police officers, bus drivers, and school crossing guards, as well as the integration of the city's golf course in 1961, while commending its "uneventful" lunch-counter integration. The piece also quotes an unnamed "Negro lawyer" who claimed Mobile was "a much better place for Negroes to live than any other city in Alabama" and concludes by emphasizing the role played by Black leadership in curtailing radical dissent.[75]

Although LeFlore's post–WWII strategy of allying with liberal white politicians resulted in limited gains for the city's Black population in terms of voting, housing, and employment rights, his accommodationist tactics were questioned in the late 1960s by the younger, more radical activists of the Neighborhood Organized Workers (NOW). The organization lasted only from 1966 to 1975, but in that brief period it challenged the model of Black political leadership that was dependent upon (and allied with) the white power structure.[76] In his memoirs, *The Genesis and Exodus of NOW*, Fredrick D. Richardson Jr. paints a vivid image of the city's racial relations, providing numerous accounts and personal anecdotes to support his argument that Black Mobilians were not afforded the same civil rights and opportunities as their white counterparts. According to Richardson, in the aftermath of the 1964 Civil Rights Act, the "word 'nigger' was tossed around freely."[77] He also acknowledges intraracial class dynamics:

> It was not the well-to-do blacks who faced the hate-filled whites at the initial stages of integration. It was the young, poor blacks. After things opened up, the well-to-dos took a front seat in eating establishments, frowning on anyone (black) who couldn't dress as well as they.... Throughout the fifties, every major city in the South organized a mass movement against segregated laws that kept blacks suffocating in the basement of society—except Mobile...We were told that we were 'better off' than other ignorant blacks.

Richardson criticizes LeFlore, as well as the work of the NPVL and the NAACP, that "remained in the courts, not in the streets," while taking only "token steps" that served as a means to "keep blacks under control."[78] In a 2001 oral history interview, activist Jerry Pogue also rebuked claims of Mobile's racial harmony:

Mobile was always known as a city that didn't hate, that was the word they used. The city that didn't hate, a city where white and black get along peacefully. Let me tell you what, lady, that's always been a lie in my lifetime! . . . It's a myth ma'am. And the black leaders were bought and paid for by the white folks that controlled this town.[79]

In his interview for that same project, Langan in turn accused NOW of being paid by his opponents to boycott the election that removed him from power:

. . . my opponent was attacking me entirely on a racial basis and was making race the prime campaign controversy to fight over, and yet the blacks who I supported through all these years and done all the things I had done for, taking the stands for them, and gotten them the right to vote, gotten a person appointed to the Board of Registrars to register them, and where we had gotten lots of them to go ahead and get registered to vote, and protect them, and opened job opportunities, and met with all the businesses and utilities and everybody else to open up job opportunities toward them, and all these things we'd worked for, and then to have blacks to boycott it was, the only reason that I can see was that they were paid to do it. Certainly there was no principle, no reason, or anything else for them to be opposing my candidacy against the person who was running on a racial basis.[80]

It is understandable that Langan would resent NOW's role in that important political defeat, but it is also revealing that he understood the advancements in African American civil rights in Mobile as something he *granted* to Black Mobilians rather than something they fought for.

The years 1968 and 1969 brought important developments that would affect the city's racial relations. While Langan lost his seat to more conservative Lambert Mims after NOW's concerted efforts to boycott LeFlore's strategy to grant him the Black vote, Dr. Martin Luther King Jr.'s assassination made it painfully clear that accommodationist tactics were not effective in the face of white supremacist horror.[81] When NOW organized a protest march through downtown three days after Dr. King's assassination, thousands joined them, even though city authorities denied their request for a permit. At the Municipal Auditorium memorial service, Dorothy Williams, one of NOW's original founders, took over the microphone "to chastise the ministers and political leaders in Mobile who did not show support for what NOW had been

Jerry H. Pogue carries the American flag, leading marchers in Mobile on April 7, 1968, mourning and protesting the assassination of Martin Luther King Jr. Palmer Studio Collection, the Doy Leale McCall Rare Book and Manuscript Library, University of South Alabama.

trying to do" but was removed from the stage by a white man after declaring that "the leadership in this town is rotten." She would later tell a reporter what she could not finish on the stage: that "a bunch of hand-picked Negro leaders and Uncle Tom preachers" impeded her from bringing Dr. King to Mobile because they were upset with his taking a stand on the Vietnam War. NOW was affiliated with the SCLC, who helped organize its high-profile direct-action protests such as the boycott of the American Junior Miss pageant at the Mobile Municipal Auditorium, which resulted in over three hundred arrests.[82]

In 1968, the year Noble Beasley became NOW's second president,[83] the organization brought Stokely Carmichael (later known as Kwame Ture) to speak in Mobile, clearly signaling their identification with more radical Black freedom fighters.[84] Audrey Bridges, who covered the event for the *Mobile Beacon*, described it as the "Speech of the Century" that galvanized over two thousand Mobilians who packed the Afro-American School in North Mobile and surrounding area. The space, which once housed the Warren Street Baptist Church, was "filled to capacity and beyond its limits," and the captive audience braved the Deep South July heat in a crowded space to eagerly hear the Black Power leader speak for three and a half hours. Carmichael/Ture spoke of Black Power and beauty, and of the importance of creating a united front. He also cautioned the public: "A speech is okay-we can clap and feel good. But we need to go *beyond* clapping and feeling good. We have to *do* something good."[85]

NOW vs. MCCA

The following year the organization managed to suspend Black participation in official Mardi Gras. On January 25, 1969, NOW published a piece in the city's premier Black periodical, the *Mobile Beacon*, entitled "NOW Outlines Position on Mardi Gras," which begins with the declaration:

> Just as almost everything in this community, Mardi Gras . . . was not founded nor meant to be founded with the Black man involved in any way except to take his hard earned money. Black folk in the community realized that they couldn't participate in white folks Mardi Gras so they endeavored to form their organization, namely the "Black" Carnival Asso. The forming of this asso. can be compared with Blacks of yester year conking their hair so it could be straight like the white man's. But the hair was not really straight so conked hair was a "trick bag" and Mobile's Black Carnival is a "trick bag" in its now existing form.

The piece compared the city's Black and white Carnival associations, calling the former "Parade Givers" and the latter "Mardi Gras Makers." It claimed that while Mardi Gras "making" produced year-round economic gains to the city's white folks, the "Parade Giver . . . buys the floats from the white man after he has used them, buys the costumes from the white man after the Mardi Gras maker has bought them, he buys candy from the white man to throw to little hungry black children." In the section outlining the reasons why the organization refused to "support Mardi Gras under its present structure," they argued that accepting a segregated Black organization "would be to admit inferiority."[86]

The same *Beacon* issue carried a note signed by Dr. Russell cancelling MCCA's activities for that year. It explained that "the Colored Carnival Association, because of conditions beyond its control . . . decided that it would be wise and expedient to forgo all of its usual presentations for Mardi Gras this season even though all plans were more than half completed."[87] An important detail in NOW's statement is the refusal to call the organization the Mobile Colored Carnival Association. Since the term "colored" was already being rejected by some activists, they used Black Carnival Association instead. Three years later the organization officially changed its name to Mobile Area Mardi Gras Association (MAMGA). This episode exemplifies the tough position held by the MCCA/MAMGA. It had to appease white elites while catering to a Black audience and community that was evolving with the times. It should be noted, however, that Noble Beasley served as MCCA's "Mayor of Colored Mobile" the previous year and, along with his wife, Marcella Beasley, hosted "several open house parties" to celebrate the occasion. He even thanked publicly "the courtesy bestowed upon him by his many friends."[88] The reason he went from throwing parties to throwing shade at the MCCA from one year to the next is unknown. Regardless, this is yet another episode that reveals the complex relationships and connections between different Black organizations in Mobile.

Richardson explains why the city repeatedly attempted to shut up (and shut down) NOW, and did not want them to appear in the national media: "The nation was to see only blacks selected by the system and proven to be OK (that is to say, the person selected must deny that Mobile had unsolved racial problems)."[89] They eventually succeeded by indicting two of the organizations' most prominent leaders, Noble Beasley and James Finley, on "trumped up charges of murder."[90]

Despite NOW's harsh assessment, Black Mobilians (as well as other marked people and groups) appropriated white/normative pageantry as a source of community pride and as a means of negotiating their space (sometimes literally) in their city. While being a part of an organized elite Carnival association represented an important step in the social ascension of those who had access to it, other folks also participated and derived pride and pleasure in their city's defining festival through their performance and labor or as spectators.

CHAPTER 5

QUEERING MOBILE'S MARDI GRAS

> The lights dimmed, the open bar was open, the buffet steamed, and the mystics appeared by space ship. You would have to have been here to have believed the spectacular presented to those present in white tie—long dress—and a number of representatives of the more straight community. The applause has not died. Apollo, watch out! There were many out of town guests from Birmingham, Atlanta and other parts of the southeast. Try to be here next year—if you can wrangle an invite. You know, Mardi Gras originated in Mobile and if you wish to journey south next year (the weekend before Ash Wednesday), "Joe Cain Sunday" is the day to catch.
> —RHETT'S BUTLER[1]

The enthusiastic invitation above was part of the coverage of the 1983 Order of Osiris (OOO) Ball. Founded in 1981, it is Mobile's oldest surviving gay Mardi Gras organization.[2] Around 2,000 people, many of them straight identified, attend the Osiris ball each year, which is held at one of the city's main convention centers. By creating an openly gay mystic society, Osiris members and their annual extravaganza have contributed to the visibility, organization, and (to a certain extent) acceptance of LGBTQIA+ people in Mobile.

In the wake of the Stonewall uprising, US southerners negotiated a climate of change and militancy with local traditions.[3] Daneel Buring acknowledged the role of "southern distinction" in the creation of gay and lesbian identities, noting that southern culture tends to discourage radical dissent. Buring sees this as the reason LGBTQIA+ political activism took longer to develop in southern cities than in other parts of the United States and shows that gay and lesbian Memphians, for instance, focused on "less obtrusive social pursuits" instead of direct political activism.[4] A similar process took place in Mobile. The city tends to be more open and accepting of LGBTQIA+ people when it comes to entertainment and social pursuits than when it comes to supporting their demands for equal rights. Yet the body is also political, and unapologetically expressing and celebrating one's identity and/or sexuality in public can often be as much of a political act as an organized protest or involvement in electoral politics.[5]

Gay Mardi Gras

The quote that opens this chapter, published in the well-known gay publication the *Alabama Forum*, shows how people who defied gender and/or sexual normativity in Mobile were also invested in the city's Carnival mythology and wanted to be a part of the festivities. Costuming and masking, whether in mystic societies' private events or in the streets, provided an outlet for Mobilians to express (or play with) their gender identity long before there was an organized gay movement in the city. It is possible (and confirmed by off-the-record gossip) that gender-nonconforming people used that as an opportunity to publicly express identities and practices that were usually kept private.

Rayford described how in gender-segregated floats and organizations, which followed old theater conventions (or the "Elizabethan custom," as he puts it), men and women played every role in the float, even if that meant cross-dressing.[6] As noted in the preface, it is not always possible to distinguish the instances in which cross-dressing served as a way of challenging heteronormativity from those in which the performances were actually reinforcing gender norms in the past.

Formed in 1884 by Dave Levi, a Jewish former vaudeville performer, the Comic Cowboys' satirical Mardi Gras performances supposedly attested that the city's elites did not take themselves too seriously by embracing this new "tradition." To Rayford they counteracted the "saccharine concept of Mardi Gras" by creating "a completely masculine parade, with men as the actors.

A good example of what Rayford called the "Elizabethan custom" of cross-dressing for a Mardi Gras tableau. The Spinsters (founded in 1911) was a group originally composed only of unmarried women. Spinsters Mardi Gras Ball/Tableau, "Only Hearts Are Trump" theme, 1941. S. Blake McNeely Collection, the Doy Leale McCall Rare Book and Manuscript Library, University of South Alabama.

Intellectually, it was tough and rowdy, nothing soft or feminine about it at all."⁷ Since 1917 Queen Eva, a burly man in grotesque drag, carrying an adorned plunger as a scepter, leads the Cowboys parade. Eva's intentionally unskillful portrayal of femininity clearly serves the purpose of reinforcing gender performance norms, making fun of male femininity rather than celebrating it.

But other instances are less clear. The press coverage for 1873's Mardi Gras claims that "as the day progressed, from all parts of the city maskers, rigged out in the most absurd and grotesque costumes, filed into Dauphin, Royal, Government, and other principal streets of the city." Among the menagerie of "every imaginable character attired in the most *outre* [sic] and superlatively ridiculous costumes," which included "Indian warriors, niggers, black as charcoal; a man monkey, led by a clown; jackassess, representatives of the infernal region, charcoal carts, filled with maskers, [and] zootic teams," there were also "'Chumpa' women, fairies, women representing men and men women."

Attendants of the 1899 Pink Domino Ball, held the night before New Year's Eve, experienced a combination of "merriment" and "consternation" as the unmasking ceremony revealed that "a mischievous young man had arrayed himself in skirts and a domino and had passed himself upon the unsuspecting boys as a winsome maid." He was later "pronounced the best two-stepper in the assembly and elected the 'Belle of the Ballroom.'"[8] When the *Mobile Daily Item* announced in 1902 that the "First Person Arrested under New Masking Ordinance Proved to Be a Man in Woman's Clothing," they did so in a humorous way. The note explained that when "the identity of the supposed woman was discovered there was considerable laughter from the crowd who followed the officer to the station. The make-up was a good one and the man could have fooled the best of them."[9] Under the headline of "Southern 'Belles' Display Charms," a 1947 newspaper clipping shows three individuals identified as men smilingly posing in drag for the camera.[10] The caption reads: "THREE LOVELY SPECIMENS of Mobile 'femininity' go in for a little 'cheesecake' during general masking day Tuesday in the Mardi Gras celebration here."[11] It is impossible to determine the gender identity and sexual orientation of the people mentioned in these notes or their intentions when they put on these outfits and beat their face up to go enjoy Mardi Gras. Maybe some of them felt humiliated by the ensuing events as they were "outed." Yet these news pieces do not indicate surprise by their writers, or by authorities and onlookers, that Mobilians would cross-dress during the festivities.

There were other gay Mardi Gras societies and balls before Osiris, such as the Mystic Krewe of Apollo, Apostles of Adonis, Daughters of Gaia, and Krewe of Pan, but they didn't last long enough to evolve into a "tradition."[12] The first Mobile (all-male) gay Carnival group identified by the MGSCOH narrators, Apollo, was a franchise from the New Orleans homonymous organization. Founded in 1969 in New Orleans, Apollo also had franchises in other US southern cities, such as Baton Rouge, Birmingham, Memphis, Lafayette, and Shreveport. According to Howard Philips Smith, the krewe's founder, Roland Dobson, "made sure his standards were met" by all of them.[13] King Lawrence XV recalls that the Mobile chapter had around twenty members and threw a single ball, which took place in a ballroom in Springhill located upstairs from a wholesale florist that had at one time served as a union hall.[14] Further research needs to be done to uncover with more accuracy the history of these pre-Osiris organizations. Since they did not last long enough to create significant records, their histories depend now on the

Mardi Gras Maskers, 1930s. Erik Overbey Collection, the Doy Leale McCall Rare Book and Manuscript Library, University of South Alabama.

memories of their few surviving members, which can be fallible. For instance, while King Lawrence recalls that the first and only king of Apollo was also the first Miss Gay Mobile pageant winner, the *Alabama Forum* lists someone else, renowned drag queen Miss Terrie Roberts, as the winner of the title and accompanying $400 prize, trophy, and roses.[15] Around the time that Osiris came about, the group Adonis was also formed but lasted only two years.

Some gay and lesbian Mobilians were able to enjoy mainstream Mardi Gras events, as long as they performed "appropriate" gender roles well enough. Homer McClure, who identifies as a gay man and whose family has a long tradition of occupying prominent positions in elite white Mardi Gras organizations, was able to participate both in the juvenile court and later as a knight in MCA's "big court." He explains:

> At that time, I was dating girls and everything. You know, 'cause that's what was expected. And I played my cards right, I was polite, I showed up on time, I didn't get drunk and leave 'em standing there. So, she asked me to be her

FIRST PERSON

ARRESTED UNDER NEW MASKING ORDINANCE PROVED A MAN IN WOMAN'S CLOTHING.

The first arrest under the new masking ordinance was made shortly before noon to-day when Police Officer Eastburn arrested a person in female attire. The party was taken to the station and turned out to be a man in woman's clothes. His name is said to be George Morris. When the identity of the supposed woman was discovered there was considerable laughter from the crowd who followed the officer to the station. The make-up was a good one and the man could have fooled the best of them.

Mobile Daily Item, February 11, 1902.

Southern Belles' Display Charms

THREE LOVELY SPECIMENS of Mobile "femininity" go in for a little "cheesecake" during general masking day Tuesday in the Mardi Gras celebration here. The trio is composed of Robert Brown (left), Travis Wheeler (center) and Roy Smith.

Maskers Take Over Mobile As 1947 Mardi Gras Closes

Young And Old, Bedecked In Outlandish Costumes, Crowd Downtown Streets Throughout Tuesday

Mobile Register, February 19, 1947.

knight. And everybody always says, you don't ask somebody to be your knight to fall in love. You make sure they gonna take care of you, you make sure they're not gonna get drunk and have more fun than the lady is having. That's what they always tell the girls to do. So, I minded my manners.[16]

Gay Mobile

As Queen Richard IV puts it, during the 1970s and 1980s, "if you were downtown in Mobile at night, you were either a prostitute or queer. Nobody was in downtown Mobile at that time. Other than Mardi Gras. Mardi Gras was totally different."[17] The "gay district" that emerged in abandoned downtown, the Fruit Loop, was also known as "the circuit," since the loop provided a cruising path for men to pick each other up for sexual encounters. Queen Richard IV explained how it worked:

> So, basically, what you did was whichever way you came in you would cruise, like, from the park, pass Miss Betty's [Society Lounge] down Joachim, pass the French Quarter, make a turn there, and go up to Government Street. And go back down to Conception again, and that way you are crossing again through the bar areas, and as you drive by you would kind of nod at somebody, or somebody would nod at you, and you'd come back around and sloooow down. Or you would follow somebody in front of you. It didn't always work out so well.

Although it would be imaginable that, as with most aspects of social life in Mobile, the city's "gay world" would be racially segregated, anecdotes and photographs show that African Americans frequented the Fruit Loop, and some of the MGSCOH narrators noted that interracial couples frequented gay bars looking for privacy.[18] In his recollections of his first visit to the Princess House Lounge, founding Osiris member and owner and president of the Miss Gay Mobile Pageant, Al Vaughan, provides an example of the ways in which queer Mobilians negotiated their sexuality in the complicated terrain of Alabama's racial dynamics:

> I walked through the front door and the place was packed with men having a great time. I flashed the bartender my fake ID and all was good. Then I felt these arms wrap around my waist and it was a Black man. I was not a prejudice person, but had never been hugged by a Black man. It was the 70s and I came from a redneck family. He asked: "Do you mind?" I replied: "It's my first time here and I wish you wouldn't." He let go. I got my beer and a then a good-looking man came up to me and asked: "Do you want to go someplace more quiet?" I said yes and off to Tee Jays we went.[19]

It is notable that even though Vaughn made sure he explained he was not a prejudiced person, the fact that he unwittingly contrasts a Black man and a good-looking man (whose race he doesn't feel the need to "mark") is indicative of how race was an important subtext in his lexicon of desire.

Although some interviewees described different lesbian and gay scenes, the gender line was somewhat more flexible in Mobile than in other larger cities. Unlike the early New Orleans gay Mardi Gras krewes, Osiris was a coed organization from the beginning. Some of the Fruit Loop bars, however, were described as more "female friendly": the Society Lounge, run by Miss

Betty (whom narrators identified as straight), and Grace's, whose eponymous owner, they claim, "was definitely a lesbian." According to the MGSCOH narrators, the Society Lounge had many nicknames, such as the "so shitty lounge" or "sweaty Betty's." Its bouncer, Chuck, would walk women to their cars after hours, and drag queen Miss Mazie Savage often performed there as Loretta Lynn. Queen Janette XII (born in San Antonio in 1948) describes Miss Betty as a "fixture in the community" who "smoked like a house on fire" and wore "bouffant hair-dos." She would place herself strategically in a corner where she could see everything that was going on, and knew everyone's names.[20] Writing about his first time at Tee Jays, Al Vaughn described his experience as a gay man in a lesbian bar:

> It was on the corner of St. Francis and Jackson Streets. It is also now a parking lot. It was a lesbian bar with a drag show. My first drag show! I was so impressed! Mazie Savage, Brenda Dee, Terrie Roberts and Bobbie Lord were the show girls. Even though it was a girls bar men were welcome. The gay bars in Mobile were always mixed with girls and guys. I remember going to New Orleans and the ladies were not allowed in the gay clubs, nor were drag queens.[21]

It is important to stress, however, that homosexuality was illegal in the state of Alabama until 2013. In and around Mobile, morality laws were used to arrest and shame gay men for public sexual activities.[22] Yet the people interviewed for the MGSCOH project did not recall bar raids or systematic instances of police brutality. They claimed downtown Mobile was so abandoned that it did not matter that "the queers" congregated there. Some narrators, however, recalled instances of homophobic violence: a friend who was shot at a gay club, a bar owner who got beaten, a dance instructor murdered by "rough trade." Police officer Jack Bishop's first homicide case when he was in patrol division was a man "beaten to death in the pavilion down at Bienville Square." He explains:

> The young guy that killed him was a senior in high school, and he was going down there, and his purpose was to roll him. It's what you call rolling queers. And he was gonna go down there and roll him. [...] I'm saying it would probably be 19 . . . 61 or 62. He beat the man to the ground, with his fists, and then he kicked him, until he was dead.[23]

But this project's narrators did not remember regular official persecution at the bars such as the one that inspired the Compton Cafeteria and Stonewall riots. Queen Vickie V (born in Mobile in 1951), another early Osiris member who worked in a few local gay bars at that time, noted:

> They might send in somebody undercover to see if we are selling to minors, but we never had any lewd or weird charges like that. Never raided. We were over there, and it was kind of dark, you know? There wasn't really a lot of businesses around there . . . it's not like being on Dauphin Street . . . and it is still a bit more secluded.[24]

Queen Richard IV, however, painted a more nuanced picture:

> I don't remember raids, no. But I definitely remember harassment. Police and public. I can remember police driving by if anybody was out in the street. [. . .] You could not be out in the street. I remember young boys riding by in trucks calling us faggots, sick, whatever. You're going to hell. I got a vodka bottle thrown at me one time. [. . .] There may not have been raids here because it was more isolated. [. . .] You think of these other cities, New York or whatever. Those bars were right in the city. And they had beat cops. [. . .] Downtown was dead. Nobody cared, what's the big deal, you're gonna raid it? Nobody cares. There was no reason to raid it. You're not gonna get any publicity out of it. You're not gonna get any political advancement out of it.[25]

Police officer Jack Bishop's recollections confirm that the general attitude of the police was to let people be in known gay establishments, yet they also indicate a level of frequent harassment:

> They had their places, and they had no trouble. If there was a problem in it, you went in and you serviced the call and you were the police, you were in charge, and you took care of it. And if somebody needed to be arrested, you arrested them and you left. [. . .] If somebody got drunk and got into a fight or something, you know, it might be it. But, for the most part, they just took care of themselves, and we didn't have to, to hound much of their business. And in the same way with the Black bars, they pretty much took care of themselves, and you would, you know, in dealing with alcohol and people, you gonna have to go in and service some of them. [. . .] No, we didn't raid. You know, if you

had a problem, in the early sixties, and it got to be too many calls, then about eight o'clock you would go in and you would stand everybody up against the walls, and then you would start shaking them down, no reason, you know, just shaking them down.[26]

Although most MGSCOH narrators denied that there were bar raids and systematic harassment in downtown Mobile, these testimonials reveal that the safe queer space provided by the Fruit Loop was not impermeable to intimidating incursions.[27] As Kathie Hiers recalls, that was true during Mardi Gras as well: "You'd go in and out of the bars, and I can remember the police would come at least one or two parades a year and just march like a military unit and line up in front of the door of the bar just to intimidate people. We'd just walk around them and go in. But it was a little bit scary."[28]

GAE: Lesbian and Gay Activism in Mobile

Though Mardi Gras helped to create a visible LGBTQIA+ community in Mobile, Mobilians who did not conform with gender and/or sexual normativity also organized in more directly political fashion. A good example would be the creation in 1978 of the Gulf Alliance for Equality (GAE). A result of the merger of three previous organizations, the GAE sought to:

> Stimulate interest and participation on the part of the general public in Alabama and elsewhere in protecting the individual rights of all human beings in the community, through education, social involvement, and social events, including specifically the individual rights of the gay (homosexual) men and women of the community, whenever discrimination and/or unjust deprivation of rights against a human being take place; provide assistance and conduct projects for the benefit of the community; interpret gays' needs and problems to other interest groups; promote good citizenship among the gays, including involving them in projects for the betterment and benefit of the community as a whole, thereby helping them and their heterosexual fellow citizens to be more tolerant and understanding of each other and also making other constructive contributions to society . . . endeavor to encourage among our membership, all persons regardless of race, creed, sex, or affectional orientation whose concern is human equality.[29]

GAE members organized to send a contingent to the 1979 National March on Washington for Lesbian and Gay Rights, published a newsletter with resources and articles for and by gay and lesbian people, and were responsible for the first Gay Pride week celebrations in Mobile. In a 1982 issue of their publication, they identified as "an organization of individuals, gay and straight," who sought to "educate people about homosexuality" by "confronting stereotypes that people have about us." Members of the organization often spoke in local colleges and universities for that purpose. Straight-identified people, especially "misfits" or folks who embraced the counterculture of the 1960s and '70s also frequented the Fruit Loop and participated in gay and lesbian organizations and events, which reveals how the boundaries of identity and community building can be porous at times.[30]

While they organized formal meetings and events, they also produced more carnivalesque performances staged in local gay bars that included drag and parody shows. GAE's "homegrown theater group, the Flaming Thesbians staged "high-teacup satire-thing" performances, and the Hats and Vests, a "four-woman band, along with their new conga, alternated with the one-man wonder pianist in providing the Society Lounge with a diverse range of entertainment."[31] Although a former GAE member described the organization and Osiris as two different/separate paths taken by Mobile's gay/lesbian community at the time, others, like Janette Curry, Diane Hampton, Kathie Hiers, and Joey Potter (who designed the GAE and Osiris logos), were involved in both. Curry, Hampton, and Hiers had also previously worked together in the feminist collective Women's Space.

Even though it wasn't a "gay" event, the 1974 Freakers Ball can be considered a predecessor of the Osiris Ball as a space for defying Mobile Mardi Gras's rigid social norms and for pioneering integration in the festivity (albeit the majority of the attendees were white). Domingo Soto described it as Mobile's "first alternative Mardi Gras event." Soto talks about the cultural ferment that generated the ball and the background of the folks who organized and attended it:

> You have to remember what a tight-assed community Mobile was in the late sixties and early seventies. A lot of how the progressive movement developed can be traced to the antiwar and civil rights work done, not just in the community but at USA [the University of South Alabama], which was in those

1974 Freakers Ball. Courtesy of Domingo Soto.

1974 Freakers Ball. Courtesy of Domingo Soto.

days the vanguard. We provided a bunch of the warm bodies needed for doing things like picketing the A&P, the Junior Miss Pageant, etc. We took over student government (Genesis) and then proceeded to bring in national speakers like Rosa Parks, Gloria Steinem, Florynce Kennedy, etc. Our Experimental Collage (sic, long story) had the first women's lib class here. Most of the folks involved, whether initially or later, got their sea legs from the events at USA.

We eventually set up a center for social change that was an umbrella for a bunch of groups, including environmental, peace, and gay groups.[32]

The Origins of the Order of Osiris

According to the Order of Osiris's official history pamphlet, "On the evening of March 16, 1981, an idea became a reality. Neil Aldridge convinced Budgie Atkinson and Larry Argo to meet at David's Lounge to hear his ideas and plans for a new gay Mardi Gras Organization."[33] In July of that year, the Birmingham-based *Alabama Forum* announced the creation of the "newest state organization," explaining that "both men and women [were] allowed to be members" but would have to pay a $100 yearly fee for a full membership, and, "in order to be considered," they would have to "be sponsored by a current member" and approved by the board. They also announced the next event to raise funds for the organization's first ball: "The Diamonds and Denim Revue" that would take place at David's on July 12.[34] Six months later their Mobile correspondent, Les Yeux, dispatching from the "mother of mystics, home of the hunks," advised readers to "save [their] pennies, and dust off [their] tuxedos and ball dresses," because "the walls" whispered "that the key words on the ball are 'hot' and 'flawless.'"[35]

The February 1982 issue of "Alabama's Lesbian/Gay Newsleader" educated its readers on Mardi Gras's history, explaining that "much to the surprise of many people, even some in Alabama, our Port City, Mobile, is the home of Mardi Gras in North America." The reason for this ignorance, the piece claims, is that "Mardi Gras in Mobile was for 150 years referred to as Boeuf Gras until about 1866," while "New Orleans has always referred to it as Mardi Gras." The author was clearly well versed in Mobile Carnival mythology, and the piece has all of the narrative's greatest hits: from the 1704 "*Societe de La Saint Louis* [sic], to Michael Krafft and the Mother of Mystics title, to Joe Cain reviving the celebration after the Civil War "along with six comic advisors on a coal wagon" (no mention of the name of the troupe). It is not the goal here to criticize the piece's lack of historical accuracy—the author clearly did their research with the materials available—but rather it is to show that, as with the book on Black Mobile Mardi Gras history mentioned in the previous chapter, this lesbian/gay publication was also invested in this particular invented tradition and mythology. Like the rest of the city's population, marked bodies

Joey Potter (top), Dr. Brue Head (center), Paul Von Bothmer-Davis (bottom). "The Diamonds and Denim Revue." David's Lounge, July 12, 1981. Mobile, Alabama. Courtesy of Joey Potter.

also derived pride, pleasure, and joy in proclaiming their city's protagonism in the celebration's history. The article above claims this pride, joy, and pleasure not only for the Port City but for the whole state of Alabama. The piece concludes with an invitation to out-of-towners to experience their state's historical Mardi Gras while partaking "of the wonderful hospitality of the Gay bars: Corral, Crew's Pub, David's, French Quarter, and Society," placing the city's queer communities and spaces at the center of the celebration.[36]

Gay bars like the ones mentioned above served as spaces for community building and identity formation in Mobile.[37] Several of the original members of the OOO worked in local bars, and that is where many of the activities leading to its creation took place. It is likely that the organization began with bar folks because they were the ones with less to lose from exposure, as they had already embraced an openly queer identity through their labor.

Wealthy gay men and lesbians, members of the aristocratic Old Mobile families (known as the A-gays or the lavender elite) were accepted, or at least tolerated, among the city's high society as long as they either did not flaunt their homosexuality or hid it behind an aura of European sophistication. At the same time, they also had access to traditional Mardi Gras events through family or social affiliations. According to architect L. Craig Roberts, who identifies as a gay man, "educated, and well-traveled" people would open their hearts to gays and lesbians "given the opportunity," even though in "a social setting they may prefer that you not be flamboyant and, as we might say, carry on the gay flag with you all the time, you know, they don't want you to do that."[38] Creative labor and connections also presented a point of access into the city's elite circles. Mardi Gras designer Ron Barrett (born in 1949, in Fairhope, Alabama) explained he never felt disrespected for being gay in his almost fifty-year career, despite not being born into an "Old Mobile" family. When asked why, he replied: "Probably a big fish in a little pond. See, people give me respect. People give me so much respect that . . . and I wouldn't get that in Los Angeles, or Washington, DC. Yeah, 'cause, see, I'm the only one doing this. I'm the go-to person for anything Mardi Gras. And that's because I live in our little city."[39] Yet he also admits that a close relationship with a member of Mobile's elite likely helped open some doors.

Middle-class gay men and lesbians appear to have been the ones with the most to risk. Many held public jobs and could be fired for "misconduct" if they were open about their sexuality.[40] Queen Julie III (born in 1958 in Montgomery, Alabama), for instance, lost her job and joined the Army Reserves when her boss found out, by learning about her relationship with the Order of Osiris, that she was lesbian.[41] King Lawrence XV noted his reservations in talking about his past:

> Well, I did too because I taught school. You could lose your job for teaching school and being gay. Whether you ever touched a soul or not. It was just the idea. So, you know, it's like, I know I'm kinda evasive on some of my answers. But, you know, I don't know what to say, because you were sort of . . . guarded, on a lot of occasions.[42]

Queen Janette XII explained the hesitations of some of the early Osiris members when attending the first balls:

> That was difficult for some people. And even though we were way over there, people were afraid. Our members were afraid of losing jobs and, you know, being outed in the community the way they didn't wanna be. So, they would

wear masks, when they got there. And they all wore masks for the performances [...] they didn't all work in LGBT businesses, you know? [...] They were afraid they'd lose their jobs. They were afraid their families might find out. There were a lot of people who had not come out to their families. They were afraid of losing their place in the out, the regular community, and friends, family.[43]

Osiris's founding father, Martin Neil Aldridge, born on March 23, 1952, in Robertsdale, Alabama, was a drum major, a dancer, and the bandleader at Robertsdale High School. According to his close friend Sherry Odom, he moved to Mobile in his late teens, to "find a place to be gay."[44] By several accounts Aldridge, who bartended in different gay clubs in Mobile, was the catalyst for a number of organizations and events that brought the city's LGBTQIA+ community together and out into the open. He bridged gender, race, and class gaps and combined unlikely groups of people in the Broadway-style performances he staged in local gay bars and on regional tours around the Gulf Coast.

He not only choreographed, directed, and performed in these shows but was also a talented costume designer. His amateur theater group employed bartenders, drag queens, public service workers, and even some straight folks, performing camp classics such as *The Rocky Horror Picture Show*, *Jesus Christ Superstar*, *The Wiz*, and *The Best Little Whorehouse in Texas*. The *Alabama Forum* describes Osiris's rendition of *The Wiz*, which took place on May 29 and 30 of 1982 at David's, as "widely publicized and more than well attended," noting that "since their first, stunning ball . . . Osiris' name has come to mean flawless entertainment."[45] These shows often served as fundraisers for future Osiris balls, as well as for other social causes that affected the city's queer community. Sherry Odom remembers performing as Janet Weiss in *Rocky Horror* to raise money for the support of people with HIV/AIDS. Joey Potter, who designed the first Osiris logo and performed in some of Neil's plays, credits these musical performances as the "grassroots organization that originated Osiris."[46] Neil also had the habit of walking the streets of Mobile during Mardi Gras (especially on Joe Cain Day) in extravagant costumes. According to Al Vaughan, people would throw things at him and yell homophobic slurs, but he used his training as a dancer to strut elegantly through it all.[47] Aldridge remained the driving force behind the OOO until his untimely death on August 13, 1990. He was one of the city's tragic losses to the AIDS epidemic.

Neil Aldridge as Dr. Frank-N-Furter; Sherry Odom as Janet Weiss, and Joey Potter as Brad Majors. Mobile, Alabama, 1980s. Images courtesy of Sherry Odom.

Al Vaughn, Queen Vickie V, Neil Aldridge, and Mark Fisher at the "Dreams"-themed fifth Order of Osiris Ball. Mobile, Alabama, 1986.

Queen Vickie V, who worked with him for many years, summarizes his personality and the strong impression he left on people:

> This guy from Robertsdale, Alabama, this Podunk place, he should have been a dancer in New York City. He should have been on Broadway. His expressions, his makeup, his dancing, just everything about him was . . . it was new to all of us, really. Nobody that talented had been around that I knew of. Neil didn't have a single enemy. No one disliked Neil. [. . .] He knew everybody, he didn't meet a stranger. And by the end of the night, if you came in a stranger, you certainly weren't one when you left.[48]

Neil's flamboyance and large personality did not please everyone. King Lawrence XV thought he was "an OK guy" but placed him in the category of "professional fags." Which he described as gay men who "never had a good, decent job [. . .] they never accumulated anything. To my knowledge none of them ever owned a home back then. [. . .] A lot of them were into pot and everything else. I just never was into that stuff."[49] Despite the offensive epithet, it can be argued that Neil chose a line of work in which he could live openly and unapologetically, which might have been uncomfortable for some. These different experiences in terms of race, gender presentation, and socioeconomic status reveal what Katie Horowitz articulates as "the trouble with queerness." While umbrella terms help people rally around common oppressions, they can also erase crucial differences in terms of lived experiences, evidenced by King Lawrence's middle-class disdain for gay men who did not accumulate wealth.[50]

Queering Mardi Gras

The Osiris Ball began as a separate safe space where gay and lesbian Mobilians could enjoy their city's most cherished tradition without having to hide their queer identities. Over the years, however, it became a sort of Trojan horse for LGBTQIA+ visibility and acceptance in the city. Joey Potter describes the inaugural dance, held on January 30, 1982, as "almost like an AA meeting," since they tried to downplay the fact that it was "gay men and women" to rent the Alabama National Guard's Fort Whiting Armory.[51] Queen Richard IV reflected on the decision to hold the event, and on why they would not have

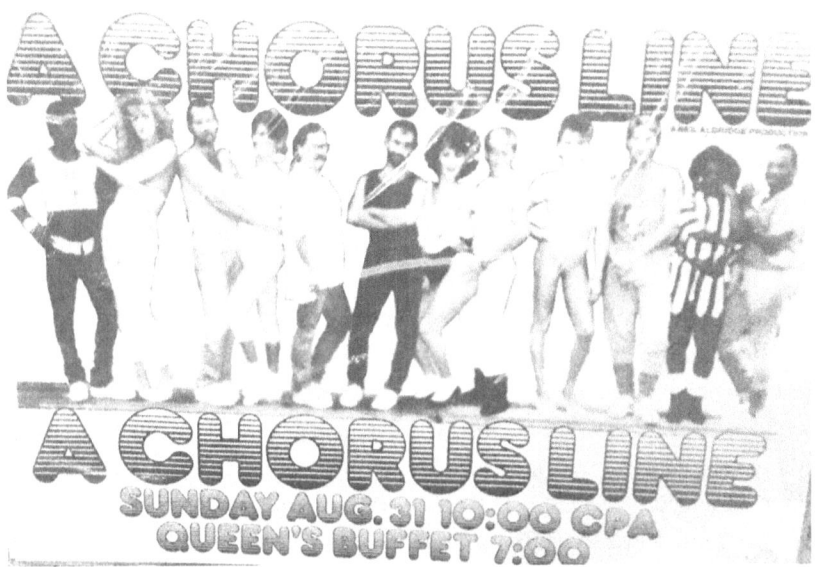

Poster for *A Chorus Line*: A Neil Aldridge Production. From left to right: Darren, Miss Cie, Felicity Lane, Queen Vickie V, Bunnie Hopson (who did the music for many of Neil's performances), Neil Aldridge, Erica Mills, Don Hall, Amy DeMilo, Patrick Stapleton, Monique Dubois, Dennis. Courtesy of Queen Danielle II.

Felicity Lane, Darren, Miss Cie, and Neil at the *Chorus Line* rehearsals. Courtesy of Miss Cie.

been able to openly parade in the streets: "Doing the gay ball was kind of like being in your face. It's like, 'Yeah, we are here. Yeah, we're gonna do this.' But it was all under certain restrictions, you know? Everybody said: 'Oh, you've got a fabulous costume, you should parade.' I said: 'We don't wanna get shot!' And that was the truth. We really thought we were gonna get shot."[52] Neil was the first ball captain, and King Jan I and Queen Budgie I (Miss Renee DeCarlo) were the first monarchs.[53] Budgie was a well-known drag performer who coached a women's softball team and worked as a med tech at the University of South Alabama. An anonymous reviewer penned a flamboyant dispatch for the *Azalea City News and Review*, noting that the OOO's "long tableau featured some of the most sumptuous costumes ever seen in Mobile."[54]

Previous gay Mardi Gras events were held in private spaces and were not widely publicized, so putting on a ball in a public space represented an important step toward LGBTQIA+ visibility in the city. Even simple details such as renting the location and formalwear required some level of exposure and identity affirmation. Danielle II, Osiris's first "female queen," had just arrived in Mobile from Bayou La Batre, heartbroken after ending a long relationship, when she saw the poster for the ball at one of the local gay bars. She purchased a ticket from the bartender and noted it required *costume de rigueur*.[55] This was exciting but also presented a challenge, since Danielle and some of her girlfriends wanted to wear tails instead of gowns. When she called the formalwear rental store Randal's and explained the situation, the salesperson asked them to come in after the store closed and all the other customers had left.[56] Other lesbian women expressed feeling out of place, or excluded from Mardi Gras tradition, because they were not comfortable wearing gowns. To them the possibility of participating in the festivities while wearing clothes that respected their gender expression was extremely liberating. Kathie Hiers's family belonged to the Order of Inca, and she relied on her "gay boyfriends" to help her fit in the organization's balls:

> I remember a friend of mine who was actually the very first HIV case in Mobile, and the very first client at Mobile AIDS Support Services, he and I were good friends, and I remember I would get him to go with me to some of those balls. And he'd dress up in his granddaddy's suit and we would go down there, and I'd have the floor-length gowns, and I felt a little like I was in drag, because that's not something that I would normally wear, and my mother just loved it. [. . .] So, yeah, I remember most of those years when that ball would

"Magnificent Monarchs"–themed first Osiris Ball: King Jan and Queen Budgie (right); Ball Captain Neil Aldridge as Zeus (center); Andrew D. as Osiris (left). January 30, 1982. Order of Osiris Archives. Montage by Daniel Wildberger.

Osiris

The beloved Lord & Pharaoh, as he embarks on a mysterious voyage invites you to experience the First Annual Ball of His Order

Saturday evening   January 30, 1982

Fort Whiting Auditorium
South Washington Avenue
Mobile, Alabama

Formal Attire
Floor Length Formals
Black or White Tie
BYOB
No Cameras

Tableau: 9:00 P.M.
Doors Open at 7:00 P.M.
Doors Close at 8:45 P.M.

Invitation for the first Osiris Ball. Courtesy of Joey Potter.

Ticket for the first Osiris Ball. Courtesy of Joey Potter.

Poster for the first Osiris Ball. Courtesy of Queen Danielle II.

be over, we would head down in all of our finery to the Club Park Avenue or the Fireside Lounge or some of the bars downtown and dance and have a more relaxed time.

Hiers believes that not being able to enjoy the party with their real partners was part of the motivation for creating a gay organization and ball. Another reason was the fact that more conservative, older societies "didn't really want gay people." Or, as she explains it, *some* gay people:

> I believe that people are born along a spectrum, and some are very gay and some are not as much gay. For the people who are born very, very gay, and it is very apparent that they are gay—those kinds of folks are not very welcome in these events. I hated putting on the damn gown. My mother would buy me a $400 gown, all the way to the floor, and, yeah, it was pretty, but it wasn't me. I wanted to wear tails.[57]

Women were involved and attended the ball since the beginning. Although she is not featured in the organization's first slate of officers and never served as a monarch or captain, Sherry Odom played an important role in the early years of the OOO. Queen Danielle II and Queen Julie III reigned over the second and third balls along with their fellow monarchs. Danielle was also the ball captain in its fifth year.[58] Yet men dominated the OOO at first. All of those listed in their first slate of officers were cisgender men. Queen Janette XII describes some of the male member's hostile attitudes toward women, and the experience of her partner, Diane Hampton, who has since passed away:

> There were some men who didn't really want to have women involved. 'Cause when Osiris started . . . they didn't wanna open up and have a whole lot of women. Although there were women who started it with the men, they didn't want it. There were men in there who actually voted against any woman who came up for membership, as they didn't want to be around women. [. . .] On a personal level, she [referring to Diane] could get along with them, but when it came to having more women join, I think they were afraid, the men were afraid that women would take over, and, you know, that never happened. Although some of the women who joined like [Queen Danielle II] was very vocal and determined and Sherry Odom was, you know, sort of a loud, in-your-face sort of person, and she didn't hesitate to say whatever she thought.[59]

Queen Julie III in the "Lost Lands"–themed third Order of Osiris Ball. (Neil Aldridge was the king that year). Mobile, Alabama, 1984. Courtesy of Julie Dunlap.

These anecdotes reveal a lot about the process of identity affirmation of a marginalized group of people through the adoption, appropriation, and adaptation of the culture that once excluded them. Mardi Gras is a defining feature of the city's identity. Yet, for LGBTQIA+ folks, it meant a time when they had to choose between different identities. To go to a straight ball meant embracing their Mobilian selves while concealing their sexual orientation and/or gender presentation. Even though some of the early members wore masks to hide their identity, they still expressed apprehension when the ball was moved to a less secluded location. Nevertheless, they wanted not only to participate in Mardi Gras festivities but to do so *as* LGBTQIA+ people. They appropriated the dress codes, rules, and format of traditional Mardi Gras societies. Only they made it their own. In doing so they also had to reach out to local businesses and authorities, initiating a process that connected the city's straight and queer communities.

A personal story from Queen Richard IV exemplifies this process well. As he puts it, he grew up in an *Old Mobile* family that had the right name, but not the money to go along with it. So he navigated the different circles of the Mobile gay world. He knew the *lavender elite* but worked in the service

Queen Richard IV in "The City That Care Forgot"–themed fourth Order of Osiris Ball. Mobile, Alabama, 1985. Courtesy of Richard Rain Perez.

industry and frequented the downtown bar scene. He says that his family was less concerned with him being gay than with him associating with *trash*. When it was his time to command the Osiris Ball as queen, he felt apprehensive when his family, especially his father, who was a prominent member in one of the city's oldest mystic societies, decided to attend.

> I was panic-stricken, I really was [. . .] I'm looking through the curtain, I can't see them, I don't know where they are, and I'm in full cocktail drag. I mean, I was queen, there was no two ways about it. I had red velvet, gold lamé, dripping glitter, the hair, the jewelry, the whole bit, face beat, you know? And I'm like: "Oh my God, what are my parents gonna think of this? Oh my God! Oh my God!" [. . .] I go down, down the line greeting everybody, and there's my mom, and she gives me a hug. I don't remember her saying anything. But then my dad [. . .] Now, this man has been doing Infant Mystics Mardi Gras, Old Mobile Mardi Gras, forever. He was gonna die on the float. I get up to him, he says: "Go for it, queen!" All he knew is I was leading a ball. He didn't give a shit what I was wearing. I was important. He knew that. [. . .] He couldn't have been prouder.[60]

As he acknowledges, despite the transgressive elements in his carnivalesque expression, he was able to connect with and be accepted by his conservative family by appropriating (even if by subverting) the signs and language of the hegemonic culture and occupying a place of prestige in the pageantry's hierarchy.

People who did not conform with gender and/or sexual normativity didn't just enjoy Mardi Gras in private balls; they also sought strength in numbers to enjoy the festivities in the streets of the Fruit Loop. But while the area created a queer space for LGBTQIA+ Mobilians to enjoy the parades, as Kathie Hiers recalls, the organizations were not always friendly with that crowd:

> Some of the older Mardi Gras societies, when they would pass the gay bars, they would throw hard stuff absolutely as hard as they could, trying to hurt people. It was a different era. I don't think Mobile has ever been as uptight as other cities because of its port city nature, but I do think that it's so much better now. [. . .] You know, they would know they were coming up on the Fruit Loop, and they would start just pelting us with stuff. So . . . you know, that's just another example of blatant bigotry and redneck-ism [laughs].[61]

So far there aren't accounts of a similar queer space in the African American neighborhoods. Although "gay Mobile" tended to be slightly more integrated than the city at large, the Fruit Loop experience was predominantly white. For LGBTQIA+ people, the process of community building and bonding during Carnival took place in private spaces (such as someone's home), in semiprivate spaces (such as a ball/party that required invitation), and in the very public space of the Fruit Loop.

CHAPTER 6

CARNIVALESQUE BODIES
Defying the White Gaze and Respectability Politics

Richard Schechner analyzes Trinidadian Carnival as both a top-down and a bottom-up cultural phenomenon, establishing that two different Carnivals exist "simultaneously and often intermixing with each other." The first, represented by official events, is "extremely hierarchical" and follows "a pre-arranged sequence and schedule." The other Carnival erupts "in the streets . . . permeating the many private parties and more hidden venues," dissolving the "boundaries between inside and outside, private and public." The top-down approach focuses on events controlled by authorities and official institutions, who exert control over spontaneous revelry. The bottom-up approach reveals "the Bakhtinian mode of rebellion, the mockery of authority, a freedom from constraints." In Trinidad, and throughout the Americas, these "tensions between top-down and bottom-up playing" are the essence of Carnival's experience.[1]

Publications about Mobile's Mardi Gras, however, tend to concentrate on its top-down aspects, looking at organized events and mystic societies. To a certain extent, that is what this book has done until now. While it has tried to decenter the narratives that created and perpetuated Mobile Mardi Gras's origins mythology and invented traditions, it has focused mainly on how marked bodies organized within a paradigm established by a heteronormative and white supremacist social structure. Although it is important to

Black men dancing and making music, likely during Mardi Gras, to a mostly white audience. Mobile, Alabama, 1930s. S. Blake McNeely Collection, the Doy Leale McCall Rare Book and Manuscript Library, University of South Alabama.

acknowledge that this was an important (if not vital) strategy implemented by historically marginalized groups to defend their right to participate in their city's invented tradition and therefore to claim their space in their city's society, it is only (a small) part of the story.

Mobile's version of Carnival may not be nearly as Dionysian as those in other parts of the Americas such as Salvador, Port-au-Prince, Port of Spain, or New Orleans. Yet the celebration's bottom-up expressions are just as important. Such expressions can be found in Black spectatorship in (Black and white) spectacles, the roles played by Black people in white parades, and disruptive performers in "respectable Colored Carnival."

As public spectacles, parades can serve as a means to prescribe behavior and social norms.[2] Social hierarchies were displayed through downtown Mobile as white elites on top of floats and horses threw trinkets at "common folks," while African American laborers performed servile roles in the pageantry. The public space of downtown Mobile was divided by intangible barriers as different groups of people watched Mardi Gras parades from different sections. Those separate spaces signaled not only racial divisions but also economic status. Watching the parades from the stands mounted in front of the Athelstan Club located on Bienville Square, for instance, was a status marker for elite white Mobilians, while finding the right spot and the right crowd to enjoy the spectacle assured the safety of marginalized people, as exemplified earlier in the case of the Fruit Loop.[3]

Mobile's parade routes were segregated until 1992, which meant that although white Mobilians were mostly oblivious to the celebration taking place in the Black section of town, African American Mobilians often moved between two physical and symbolic spaces: Black Mardi Gras, which took place on Davis Avenue on Fat Tuesday (and later also on Lundi Gras) and the white downtown parades.[4] Speaking about the present day, educator Pam R. Moore, born in Mobile in 1968, precisely describes the imbalance between people of color's understanding of the "white world" and white people's lack of interest in people of color's experiences:

> When you are the majority, you don't even have to think about how the minority experience might be. You just assume that the way it is for you. [. . .] Could there even be another way? [. . .] I mean, I just think about, in my life, the stress of having to code-switch constantly, and have to keep things in mind that are just so very different. [. . .] I think when I spoke to a colleague about having participated in Mardi Gras, did they really understand that there was a Black court and a white court? Because their only thought process was that the white court was the only Mardi Gras. Do you mean there were actually other people in town that did this? Because they didn't even think about it. Of course, when you think about the time that I was growing up, in the paper, if there was a front page, who do you think was on the front page? . . . But it's amazing to me when you talk to people and they truly have no concept that the other exists. And I guess because I always had to balance knowledge of both. [. . .] I mean, I couldn't exist without knowing that all these things exist.[5]

Black Mardi Gras Experiences outside of the MCCA/MAMGA

Peter G. Stillman and Adelaide H. Villmoare frame their analysis of Black New Orleanians' Mardi Gras parading traditions through the concept of "subaltern counter-publics."[6] They argue that through parades, groups of people "marginalized from formal political and economic power" negotiate their place in the city's social structure, creating an "informal political discourse."[7] Hence, while older, elite white Carnival organizations "represent and re-assert" hegemonic powers and hierarchies, Black popular traditions express "opposition and an alternative to those traditional powers," challenging official political discourses.[8] In Mobile it would appear as if that process failed to take place. Yet a closer look at Black Mobilians' bottom-up revelry reveals a different picture.

When Black people paraded exclusively for Black audiences, their performance was different. Although, as shown earlier, official Black Mardi Gras in Mobile rejected what were perceived as the more "burlesque" aspects of Carnival celebration, there were Bakhtinian elements in its earlier pageantry. The *Mobile Register* provides a glimpse into the Colored Carnival Association's first parade, describing the dancing majorettes as the "vogue" of the spectacle, and noting that "mummers and maskers, a number of them wearing grotesque animal heads, formed a notable contingent."[9]

The MCA-organized parades (or "white Mardi Gras") take place throughout a number of days leading up to and including Fat Tuesday/Mardi Gras Day and follow a rigid social hierarchy. Different organizations have their individual processions, and the closer to Mardi Gras Day they parade, the more prestigious they are. The official Black parade, however, happened only on Mardi Gras Day (and later also Monday/Lundi Gras). It is a conglomerate of different groups and social clubs forming one big spectacle under the general umbrella of the MCCA/MAMGA (also known as the Mammoth Parade). Until the last decade of the twentieth century, this performance took place exclusively in the Black part of town. With the exception of Mr. May's Zulu parades, Black organizations initially rented floats from white organizations after they were done with theirs. That is still the case for some groups, but, as described below, MAMGA has a contingent of original floats that celebrate the history, traditions, and accomplishments of Black Mobilians.

Some MGSCOH narrators shared their recollections of Black Mardi Gras:

Eric Finley: For the African American parade, it's always gone down Davis Avenue. It started in a couple different locations within three-tenths of a mile. But it's always gone down Davis Avenue, which is in the heart of the African American community 'cause that's where all the businesses were. So, strategically, back during that time I'm sure it was designed so that those businesses could reap some revenue.

> **Palmer Richardson:** Now, back in the day, we didn't have night parades of Blacks. We just had that Monday and that Tuesday over on The Avenue. On Davis Avenue. And that's when people would go by and camp with their foods and stuff.
>
> **Bobby Dennison:** People would set up their grills, they would barbecue, they would set up tents, they would have little parties on the side of Davis Avenue while the parade was going on because . . .
>
> **Linda Dennison:** We only had that one day. [. . .] Well, see, we only had a parade just that Tuesday. We didn't always have that Monday. That was the only parade we had, was that one parade on Tuesday when we would borrow the floats from the white . . .
>
> **Bobby Dennison:** . . . organizations. But now this parade route was totally different [. . .] our parade ran through the Black community.
>
> **Linda Dennison:** We had a fair, and they had their fair. Their fair, the white fair was downtown and, you know, along Government Street. [. . .] We didn't even do the fair with them.[10]

Black Bodies in White Spectacles: Watching White Mardi Gras

The fact that African American Mobilians had only one official parade day did not mean they would refrain from enjoying the rest of the city's defining festival. They occupied segregated spaces downtown to watch the white parades and see friends and relatives who participated in the pageantry:

> **Bobby Dennison:** We were relegated to being second fiddle, so to speak, even with the parades that were held downtown. We were not in a position to sometimes be on the very front of the streets, because the white people had those spots, those locations. So a lot of times we had to stand behind them, even catch candy that came off of the float. Some of the paraders were fine when they were on the floats, some didn't care who they threw candy or trinkets to. Some were still prejudiced, even in that manner. If they saw Black folks, they wouldn't throw us any candy.

"Mayor of Colored Mobile" saluting the public on Davis Avenue. Mobile, Alabama, 1946. Courtesy of Loretta Scott Galloway, Blue Light Studio, the Doy Leale McCall Rare Book and Manuscript Library, University of South Alabama.

Mobile Colored Carnival Association parade on Davis Avenue. Mobile, Alabama, 1946. Courtesy of Loretta Scott Galloway, Blue Light Studio, the Doy Leale McCall Rare Book and Manuscript Library, University of South Alabama.

Linda Dennison: If it was a crowd of us, yeah. They would wait and go, you know . . . where a crowd of whites, that's where they would throw. So we knew to just kinda get to the back so that if we wanted anything, or get around them so that we could get candy. Now Bob [Bobby Dennison] lived down this way, with me coming from where I was, we didn't venture too far downtown. We watched the parade on Springhill Avenue. We would walk down, my brothers and I.

Eric Finley: We would come downtown. It's interesting, during that time, though, we would only stand in front of Barton Academy. It was the safest place to stay in because you would not be harassed, 'cause usually there was a slate of African Americans that would stand in front of Barton Academy. Anywhere else you felt uncomfortable, because you never would know. [. . .] Racism was still kinda at its peak in Mobile. And people would do silly things, especially when they are in a crowd and they are feeding off of another person. But yeah, we would watch the parade and some of the high schools, some of the African American high schools would participate in the parades. And it was Mardi Gras, especially the last night on Tuesday, we always ended up downtown, 'cause that's the last parade of the year.

Palmer Richardson: When I was a child, say, seventh to eighth grade, when Mom and them started to let us go, we went to Barton Academy. That's where we stood. Barton Academy. Everybody would . . . looking for your friends? You got to stand by Barton Academy. Other people had other places, but Barton Academy was the place.[11]

When asked why he would go and watch the African American parades on Davis Avenue, and then catch the white parades on Barton Academy, Palmer Richardson replied, "Well, in the white parades, the bands were gonna be Black."

Black Bodies in White Spectacles: Labor and/as Performance

Thomas F. DeFrantz and Anita Gonzales argue that performance can be "resistant, affirmative, or several states in between."[12] Carnival, in its many worldwide manifestations, cannot be seen purely as a liberating ritual or as a mechanism of social control. Its power comes from its ability to be both things simultaneously.[13] Mila Cozart Riggio shows that "Carnival's primary source of energy . . . is located neither fully in inversion nor in affirmation but in the tension between subverting and affirming, or . . . in its dialectic between civilized respectability and vagabondage." Or, as Rebecca Dirksen puts it, "it's that very point of friction, the node of the crossroads, where the energy, excitement, and potential arise."[14]

In his pioneering ethnographic work on Mobile's African American Mardi Gras experience, folklorist Kern Jackson explains that Black Mardi Gras as we know it was born under Jim Crow segregation. But he refuses to analyze Black participation through a prism of victimhood.[15] Jackson recognizes the objectification of African Americans in Mobile's Mardi Gras but also their consciousness of that process, their understanding of the roles available, of how to play them, and of the importance of the interplay between performances of self and the white gaze.[16] While Black bodies were quite visible in white parades, occupying spaces that clearly displayed and taught social and racial hierarchies, the "othering" gaze could also be defied, enjoyed, or returned.[17]

Jobs carrying flambeaux and flares, as well as pulling mules, were popular with young Black men and teenagers, tying their labor to the white spectacle parading the streets of Mobile. Yet their accounts contrast with those of white commentators who saw only the "pathos" and labor exploitation in these performances. To be sure, the Mardi Gras labor system was (and is) exploitative, and the participation of Black people in white parades reaffirms racial hierarchies, but Black narrators also recall those performances as a financial transaction, as a source of personal and community pride, and as "fun," despite being perfectly aware of the power dynamics involved:[18]

> **Pam R. Moore:** You may not have been able to go to parties with folks, but who was doing all the work for your party? Who was catering your party? Who was making the costume for your party? Who was creating the mask? Who was building the floats? Who was taking the horse and wagon and pulling the floats? Or who was pulling it with their back and labor? People that looked like me.

> **Bobby Dennison:** Now, as far as Mardi Gras itself [. . .] when it first started there were no electric or portable, battery-powered lights. The lights were those that we call flares. The flares were what they used, because when Mardi Gras first started that was a tradition that they used to light the floats at night. Portable flares that were on sticks that people walked with. They would hire

people during Mardi Gras just for that. To carry the portable flares and the signs that identified each float during the parades.

Linda Dennison: And during our time it really would be African Americans that they hired to carry those flares.

George Moore: I used to as a kid, I guess twelve, would carry flares because they didn't have the lights like they do now on the floats. And they had these flares. Also, I would carry the signs. And then in high school I played in marching bands, so I participated in a lot of Mardi Gras [chuckles]. The flambeau was the big, the kerosene-type lanterns; they call those flambeaux. And they wouldn't let you carry those unless you were a full-grown man. But the flares, which were used for signaling on trains. [. . .] It's like a stick, but it burns; it's phosphorus, it's dangerous. And they let the kids carry those, because they paid the kids like two dollars, three dollars, and on the last night they would pay you five dollars and 50 cents. And the men would make five dollars carrying the flambeaux. [. . .] Both of those types of things were dangerous. The phosphorous would really burn you, and the gasoline, kerosene, could drip down on you and catch fire. So, it was dangerous, yeah. [. . .] All those were white organizations. [. . .] I enjoyed carrying the signs, I was gonna make some money. It was lots of fun.[19]

Brass bands were also a constant presence of people of color in white spaces during Mardi Gras.[20] Playing in white events provided a unique opportunity to access elite white spaces. The oldest and most famous of them, the Excelsior Band, was formed in 1883 to celebrate the birth of John Clement Pope, the son of one of its founders, J. Alexander Pope, president of the Creole Fire Company.[21] It is still an iconic feature in Mobile's Mardi Gras, as well as in tourism advertisements. While the original band began by playing at funeral processions in the "colored section" of the Magnolia Cemetery, it soon became a staple in a myriad of Mardi Gras events, as well as all sorts of year-round celebrations for the city's white elites.[22] To Jackson, brass bands such as the Excelsior "occupy a unique space," as they navigate "public, racialized settings" when they perform in white parades and other events. They know their performances have different meanings for "different cultural groups and audiences" and are keenly aware of expectations, performing (and code-switching) accordingly.[23]

Black man holding a mirror to white Mardi Gras masker from the Infant Mystics mystic society, 1937. S. Blake McNeely Collection, the Doy Leale McCall Rare Book and Manuscript Library, University of South Alabama.

Black men conducting the mules that carry a Mardi Gras float from a white organization, 1940s. Courtesy of Frank Daugherty, the Doy Leale McCall Rare Book and Manuscript Library, University of South Alabama.

Carnivalesque Bodies: Defying the White Gaze, Respectability Politics   137

Flambeaux. Black men carrying the torches that illuminate the Infant Mystics Mardi Gras Parade, 1939. S. Blake McNeely Collection, the Doy Leale McCall Rare Book and Manuscript Library, University of South Alabama.

When asked about how members of the band experienced segregation (now and in the past), Hosea London, current leader of the Excelsior Band (born in 1948 in Winter Haven, Florida), replied:

> I talked to them some. And I knew that it was very segregated. And they always, for some reason, they always treated the band like . . . you know, differently. Because even then they were going into mansions and being treated, you know, real nice. Even now, they treat you real nice. [. . .] A lot of times musicians kinda had that opportunity to go places that ordinary people probably would never see. [. . .] It's ok. But it gets kinda strange sometimes because you always wonder, you know, why are there no other ethnic people here.[24]

Interviewed by Kern Jackson in the 1990s for the Video Oral History Project of the City of Mobile's Tercentennial celebration, then–Excelsior Band director Robert Petty had a similar insight:[25]

> The [white] Queen might have a party at her house . . . [we would] go out there and play at her house. I've gotten drunk on many a night playing at par-

The Excelsior Band. Mobile, Alabama. Mardi Gras Day 2017. Photo by the author.

ties and places like when we play weddings and parties that they have. [. . .] When we play for the whites the music we play, like I say, we play "Stars Fell on Alabama" or a waltz, tunes like that. See, that is what white people like. We very rarely play for blacks, that is the whole thing about it. Most of our small group music we play, most of our gigs are played for white people.[26]

Black high school marching bands also played an integral part in the white parades. Several African American narrators name them as a reason to come downtown for white Mardi Gras. Central High School's band, also known as the Marching 130, gained the reputation as "the Untouchables." Davis-Horton describes them:

The "Marching 130" was a show stopper and was the pride of Davis Avenue. When they marched on Mobile streets during Mardi Gras people would automatically widen the streets so that this band could pass. It was a glowing example of teenage pride and school spirit. The band members were all living up to the reputation it earned through the years as being the biggest and the best.[27]

George Moore was a member of the Marching 130 and proudly jokes that some of the white high school bands were hesitant to play after them.[28] Bobby Dennison, who also performed in the band, explains what it was like playing for African American audiences:

Carnivalesque Bodies: Defying the White Gaze, Respectability Politics 139

Central High School Band: Edward Pratt Sr., director (in Melody Masters Band), Second from left: Joseph Malone on clarinet; first left front: Herbert Downs; third from right front: Helen Harris, 1950s. Courtesy of Marshall Wormley, William Lavendar photographer, the Doy Leale McCall Rare Book and Manuscript Library, University of South Alabama.

As a matter of fact, when we marched in all of the parades, people would make sure they came to see us perform during Mardi Gras because we had such a positive reputation, musical reputation, that everybody wanted to see Central's band march during the parades. [...] The barricades that you see now to protect the parade goers? Didn't have 'em then. There were no barricades on the Avenue, when the bands performed. We barely had enough room to walk, to march down the street because the people were so enthusiastic, they wanted to see us perform so bad. They were really in our way. We could not even parade for them. There wasn't really ever any problem, they were just excited. They were happy. That was a big time of the year for us. And we took full advantage of it, because this was the parade that really made us feel at home. [...] I would say 90 percent of the people who watched the parade then were African Americans. There were a few white folks that would venture over that way to watch the parades, but it was mostly Black folk. And it's as if we were in our own element. The bands even played louder, they even marched harder. Because we were performing for our people, so to speak. So we did our very best to please them.

Mobile County Training School majorettes, 1958. Burton Studio Collection, the Doy Leale McCall Rare Book and Manuscript Library, University of South Alabama.

And to white audiences:

We were not as comfortable, because I know personally, we had several incidents where we were actually picked on by some of the people in the downtown district that were watching the parades, for example. As you may be aware, most bands have majorettes. We didn't really have any flag girls at that time. We had majorettes. So, there were several incidents where someone may have put their hands on one of our majorettes. Well, of course we reacted. Because, as anyone else, you protect what's yours. So, we never really had any problem with the authorities, because [. . .] they realized that the people who did those sorts of things were wrong. But you put your hands on our majorettes? You paid for it. Our uniform consisted of a tall hat with a plume. The plume was made of ostrich feathers. One guy tried to light a match to one of the plumes on one of our members. Of course, he paid for it.

Isabel Machado: What happened?

Bobby Dennison: We beat his behind. We didn't bother anyone. But we were not afraid to protect ourselves either. This was in the late sixties.[29]

Bobby Dennison's recollections show how Black performers felt and behaved differently in different racialized spaces. African American musicians' ability to inhabit those segregated spaces, code-switching between performances for "the community" and for the white gaze, provides a rich source for understanding cross-racial interactions in Mobile's Mardi Gras. Furthermore, his depiction of Black women's bodies and womanhood as something that belonged to, and should be protected by, Black men, reveals the complex intersections of race and gender in these performances. Yet marked people's bottom-up experiences of and participation in Mardi Gras were not limited to their labor and spectatorship. They also defied sociocultural barriers in different public performances. Independent maskers who stayed in Black neighborhoods provide insight into intraracial, class-based interactions and intersections.

"Deviant" Black Bodies: The Mollies

The most emblematic of those street performers were the Mollies, to whom the current MAMGA Mammoth Parade dedicates a float in their yearly spectacle. Davis-Horton describes them as revelers "known for doing comedy acts such as dressing up unusually funny, or having a dog in a baby carriage with a bonnet on its head." One of the popular characters, Poolroom Joe, "would have on old ragged shoes, old hat, stuffed bra, extra padding on his buttocks and a dance routine of his own. People looked forward to seeing this unusual clown who was not officially part of the parade, but just popped in from the sidelines."[30] Yet the gender-bending and more subversive elements of the characters have been sanitized or erased in the MAMGA float. Instead, they look more like early twentieth-century caricatures with characters such as Big Mary, a mammy-like figure, or Hotfoot Sam, a bug-eyed slender Black man in striped pants and top hat holding a cane. While Jackson sees Big Mary's "exaggerated breasts, behind, and mouth" as a nod to the cross-dressing performers, it is not likely that spectators who do not have previous knowledge of the history of the performances alluded by the float get that referent.[31] Hence, even if the artist/s who designed and produced the float and/or the person who commissioned it had that in mind, it does not have the same symbolic meaning to the people consuming the pageantry if the narrative behind it does not fully embrace and celebrate the "deviant" performances they claim to be commemorating.

MAMGA Mollies float. Mobile, Alabama. Mardi Gras Day 2017. Photo by the author.

It is urgent that we pay more attention to the history of those practices, since, as Cathy Cohen notes, "It just might be that after devoting so much of our energy to the unfulfilled promise of access through respectability, a politics of deviance, with a focus on the transformative potential found in deviant practice, might be a more viable strategy for radically improving the lives and possibilities of those most vulnerable in Black communities."[32]

A 2012 AL.com article explains the Mollies in the float as "a symbol both of carnival fun and MAMGA tradition," describing them as "a group of people in the 1940s who dressed up like comic characters and joined the procession." According to the article, the name derives from Disney's depiction of B'rer Rabbit and was an allusion to the character's girlfriend, Molly Cottontail. That is why, they say, children followed the Mollies shouting: "Molly Molly Cottontail/ Take your tail. And go to jail."[33] In his ethnographic study, however, Kern Jackson has it as "Mollie, Mollie, catch your tail?"[34] Although it is likely that, as with any oral tradition, the chant varied according to who was reciting it and over time, this official account of the name's origins is unconvincing. While it is hard to point out precisely when the Mollie "tradition" began, it seems to have been already established by the mid-1940s, and the character made her debut in the Disney comic strip only in 1946.[35]

It is also hard to determine whether the term Molly/Mollie, which was widely used in England in the eighteenth and nineteenth centuries to refer to homosexual and/or gender-nonconformant men, was available and employed in Mobile, Alabama, at that time in the same capacity.[36] Also, while thus far it is impossible to make any direct connection between Mobile Mardi Gras's Mollies and Cape Town Minstrel Carnival's gender-bending performers, the "moffies," they seem to perform a similar function.[37]

We do know, however, that it was used nearby to refer to men who cross-dressed and/or otherwise defied gender and sexual normativity in the nineteenth and early twentieth centuries. In a chapter dedicated to entities that terrified "the colored folks of New Orleans," the authors of the 1945 compilation of Louisiana folk tales, *Gumbo Ya Ya*, mention the Hugging Molly, a character that "haunted the city of Baton Rouge for several years during the early [eighteen] nineties," as a "white-robed individual who would hide among the bushes along North Boulevard until some girl came along; then he would rush out and crush the terrified female in a passionate embrace. Disguised in a sheet, his intention was evidently to appear as a woman to the casual observer." While the authors explained that the haunting was nothing but a "relatively harmless creature" who "had committed no crimes other than his amorous squeezings," they also note that the "resemblance of his drapery to that worn by the" Ku Klux Klan terrified Black people.[38] Although they do not specify the Hugging Molly's racial identity and minimize the violation of these women's bodies, this association between the robed specter and the Klan evokes the horrors of the pervasive sexual violence that Black women suffered at the hands of white men.[39] In Pensacola, Florida, on the other hand, two men arrested in 1901 for "dressing in women's clothes" were referred to as Hugging Mollies by the press.[40] Finally, at least one of the MGSCOH narrators, Linda Dennison, remembered hearing grown-ups refer to queer men as Mollies when she was a child in Mobile, which seems to corroborate the association between the term and gender and sexual nonconformity:

> I basically heard my mom talk about it. I didn't know much about the Mollies [. . .] 'cause momma would call somebody a Mollie or what have you. [. . .] And I think it was, from what I gather, I kinda sort of remember 'cause, you know, you just heard the grown-ups, the adults, talking that they . . . gay men in drag, or men in drag is basically what I took away from it as a little girl. But we didn't really ask.[41]

Although the 2012 article glossed over the gender-nonconformant subtext of the Mollies, it provides hints of the socioeconomic status of these "natural entertainers," who would emerge from "the bottom," or the area located "near the old city dump, in the north part of town." According to Mobile History Museum's then–assistant director Sheila Flanagan, the "historical Mollies turned MAMGA's procession into 'a people's parade,'" dressing "up in discarded clothing" and spoofing "the royalty and majesty we portray in the court." That Flanagan contrasts the Mollies' (they/their) mischievous performance with organized pageantry (we/our) is telling of how official discourses see popular revelry as "other."[42]

To late Mobile historian Dora Finley, the Mollies served as a cautionary tale of what happens when you exist outside the boundaries of Black respectability politics. Her father took her to "the bottom" to see the reality of the people who embodied the trickster characters and told her: "I want you to see that, but for the grace of God, this could be you." Yet he also "taught her . . . that the dwellers of the hard-luck neighborhood had created their own social order, including a king and queen." On Mardi Gras Day, they would emerge from "the bottom" to become "celebrities" who "fascinated . . . delighted . . . but also scared" children. The Mollies float is a good example of tradition reinvention and the sanitization of more subversive elements of past revelry, as their debauchery clearly conflicted with Dr. Russell's appeals to a middle- and upper-class Black respectability.[43]

Most of the MGSCOH narrators who shared their memories of the Mollies downplayed the gender-bending aspect of their performance, echoing the official discourse:

> **Eric Finley:** Back in that time, the Mollies was a very unorganized group of people. They were just people that costumed. And they would put on these costumes, and then accentuate all parts of their body, and then they would just come out of these different communities around the parade route. One area is called the bottom, one is called the campground, fishers' alley, and someway somehow, they had no meetings, they had no planning of this, they would just assemble. And they would march always before the parade. And it was like the crowd would start looking for the Mollies. They were the group that they anticipated seeing. They would always precede the parade and march the whole route. So, it became kind of something you would look forward to. 'Cause it was impromptu, you didn't know what kind of costume

While not much information has been preserved about this image—not even the date on which it was taken (probably the 1930s)—it captures unbridled carnivalesque Black joy outside of the boundaries of organized Mardi Gras. It is also possible that it captured the Mollies in action. This appears to be Davis Avenue, and the person on the left has fashioned some rags over their outfit, while their dance partner seems to be in drag, wearing a cinched-waist dress (or a skirt and feminine shirt) on top of masculine clothes, and their head is covered by a bonnet or some type of headpiece. Their hand on their waist also indicates that their gestures and movements were evoking femininity. "Miscellaneous Parade Images from a Rickarby Family Album." Image courtesy of Ann Rickarby, the Doy Leale McCall Rare Book and Manuscript Library, University of South Alabama.

they would have on, and it was always kind of the highlight before the parade actually started.

George Moore: They were people, ordinary people, that just wanted to celebrate Mardi Gras, so they designed their own outfit, and you could wear mask at that time. And they would put a mask on and design their own outfit and then they would follow the parades. [. . .] They just danced and walked behind, they walked behind a particular band and maybe a float, but they just wanted to be a part of it.

Palmer Richardson: I heard you mentioned the other day about the Mollies. And people used to dress up and oh, just clown, and just be walkin' down the street. And they would just be putting on a show and stuff. You might have a couple doing different little acts and stuff. It was just "look at that Mollie." That's what they used to call 'em. "Look at that! Uh, look at that!" And those were fun days, but you just don't find that anymore.[44]

Kern Jackson wrote the only academic investigation of the Mollies, who, he argues, performed a "key role in ritualistic play" in Mobile's Black Mardi Gras. As he notes, while brass bands "perform in large part for the gaze of the elite white majority during Mardi Gras, the mollies exist and primarily function within the context of the traditional black neighborhoods."[45] Although Jackson also had trouble finding someone who openly identified as a Mollie to interview, his narrators provide a fascinating picture of unofficial African American Carnival revelry in Mobile. One of Jackson's informers, Edley Hubbard, remembered maskers from the Black neighborhood of Plateau/Magazine Point (or Africatown) who also played with gender identity and presentation:

> They call 'em now transvestite or something like that. Well, they didn't use that name during that. It was just somebody putting on feminine clothes. One of the men named Gina Dexter, and the other . . . I believe he was Simpson, but we called him Beady, but they looked nice, and you couldn't tell who they were if you didn't know who they were. That's just one of their doings.[46]

An important feature of the Mollies was their hidden identity. They concealed their faces, so spectators knew who was behind the mask only if the performer allowed it. Two participants in Jackson's project seem to confirm that women also took advantage of the carnivalesque time and space to express or play with their masculinity. Myrtle Martin Fisher described the Mollies as "people who would dress up in any kind of way that they wanted, the men would have on women looking clothes, the women might have on a men clothes or; you couldn't tell who they were, unless you really knew them." Annie Kersh recalls:

> Most of 'em were men. Not many of 'em were ladies. And they would have on these short skirts, beautiful dresses, and wild faces. And you really couldn't see who it was . . . But it was something about their faces; the costumes was

pretty but if you ever seen a screened-wire face and then there's another face underneath it. They had two sets of eyes and it was just . . . they looked like they were unreal.⁴⁷

Of course, as a common practice in carnivals and other festivities worldwide cross-dressing does not necessarily entail that those involved in the practice were gender-nonconforming people. Yet, as shown earlier, it presents an opportunity and a safe space for exploring forms of performing gender that would not be accepted under different circumstances. A good example would be the Puerto Rican Fiestas de Santiago Apóstol, where, as Lawrence La Fountain-Stokes explains, "the character of *la Loca* has traditionally been played by ostensibly masculine, heterosexual Afro–Puerto Rican men in blackface who cross-dress for the occasion and aggressively tease passersby." As time went by and the practice expanded, however, "effeminate gay men and trans women also [began to] enact the role."⁴⁸

To the people interviewed for the MGSCOH project in the 2010s, the Mollies were a much more distant memory, filtered through current representations. The people interviewed by Jackson in the 1990s had more personal recollections. It is also possible that the narrators felt more comfortable discussing the more subversive nature of the Mollies with Jackson, an African American man from Mobile, than with a foreign stranger. Both sets of accounts, however, show that despite the city's overall conservatism, people who defied gender and sexual normativity existed and unapologetically took advantage of the festivity to express themselves. Moreover, it shows how the boundaries of respectability were crossed, and that audiences interacted with and, in some instances, revered them. More efforts are needed in order to recover the history of this and other carnivalesque expressions of historically marginalized people in Mobile, which would undoubtedly inspire new transgressive public performances and help us reframe and decenter the narrative of Mobile Mardi Gras's history.

In a sense the Mollies embodied what Rebecca Dirksen calls *creative vagabondaj*, or "a roguish and unruly but also playful and resourceful way of inhabiting space that emphasizes, celebrates, and even flaunts the daily interventions that bring possibility to an otherwise uncertain existence." Dirksen poses a question that is quite pertinent to an analysis of the Mollies: "What if *creative vagabondaj* were one way to work toward political personhood and embodied power?"⁴⁹

Cathy Cohen shows that respectability can be a useful concept to analyze the "process of policing, sanitizing, and hiding nonconformist" or "deviant behavior of certain members of African American communities." Yet Cohen also contends that we cannot ignore that "for many African Americans it was not only a mechanism to leverage dominant power but also a means to demonstrate" their "basic humanity and equality" while counteracting the dominant racist discourses and constructions.[50] Cohen underscores that this process entails positioning oneself as the one who is respectable, acceptable, and deserving in comparison to, or in contrast with, the "others" who exist outside of the boundaries of Black respectability. Importantly, Cohen also shows how studies that use respectability politics as a theoretical framework risk ignoring "the agency and actions of those under surveillance, those being policed, those engaging in disrespectable behavior," arguing instead "for a renewed focus on those acts of perceived deviance in Black communities, not to explain their functional or dysfunctional characteristics" but for "their potential" to produce "counter normative behaviors and oppositional politics."[51] Heeding Cohen's advice, I argue that the Mollies and other "deviant" public performances in Mobile's Mardi Gras should take the center stage when we rewrite a more inclusive narrative to tell this history, as they offer a great counterpoint to the accommodationist approach represented by official Black Carnival organizations.

It is difficult to define precisely when and why the Mollies stopped doing their thing. Some narrators dated their demise to the 1960s and 1970s, while Jackson credits the 1992 change in the parade route for their complete disappearance. But "deviant" performances did not end with them. They would be reinvented in new sociohistorical contexts.

CHAPTER 7

PLUS ÇA CHANGE?

Downtown Mobile at the Twilight of the Twentieth Century

The last couple of decades of the twentieth century brought important developments for Mobile. It also represented another turning point in the city's Mardi Gras reinvention as once marginalized groups became increasingly a part of the mainstream. The 1980s began and ended with tragedy. While the 1981 lynching of Michael Donald escalated racial tensions and left an indelible stain on the city's racial-harmony image, the decade ended with the HIV/AIDS epidemic devastating the city's fragile LGBTQIA+ movement and taking many of its gay Mardi Gras pioneers. Yet the 1985 changes in Mobile's government structure, which came as a result of a long legal battle, led to more political power for African Americans. In 1992 the Mardi Gras parade route was partially desegregated as the MAMGA Mammoth parade made its way to downtown Mobile and the Black spectacle reached wider white audiences for the first time. Meanwhile, the Osiris ball became increasingly popular and mainstream, and new LGBTQIA+ groups, some of which were started by Osiris dissidents, were created. Despite these changes, when the 2008 documentary *The Order of Myths* exposed Mobile Mardi Gras's segregation and connected it to the city's turbulent history of racialized violence, outsiders were shocked, and insiders upset.

The 1995 Civic Index Review: Milestones in Community Development, Mobile, Alabama 1960–1994 assessed "the issues that have most concerned Mobilians over the years."[1] The document provides a good example of the competing impulses pulling the city's reinvention process in different directions and the complicated position of a city that tries to change with the times while remaining the same. Some of the "major trends" examined in the document include: the transition from war economy to peacetime economy and the accompanying shift from dependence on federal funding to a more diversified economy and international outreach in the 1990s. The index also looked into the process that led to downtown's "destruction" in the 1960s and the subsequent "Downtown Renaissance of the 1990s." The document admits, however, that the "issue that has dominated these decades has been race," noting that since "Mobile emerged from racial segregation in the 1960s, African Americans have moved into positions of power and influence. Traditional racial attitudes have steadily receded. For a large black underclass, however, conditions have not improved" and had actually worsened in the 1980s and 1990s.[2]

Echoing the city's split personality and identity, the document encourages changes and recognizes Mobile's "unlimited potential . . . to become an international city," while defending the need to preserve its "distinctive character and unique sense of community." It also explained that although "many whites" still tried to hold on to "Mobile's racial traditions," it was "not as aggressively pursued."[3] This seems odd, considering that the period witnessed two of the most vicious episodes of racialized violence in the city's recent history. If the 1980s brought important milestones in Mobile's long path toward racial equality and justice, it also revealed the appalling truth of white supremacy's most savage facets.

1980s: Bolden and Michael Donald

In October 1975 civil rights leader Wiley Bolden, along with other prominent Black Mobilians, filed a class action suit, *Bolden v. City of Mobile*, to challenge the constitutionality of the City Commission and Mobile's form of municipal government. In its seventy-four years of existence, not a single Black person had served in the commission.[4] They contended the system of at-large elections discriminated against the city's African American residents, since "their concentrated voting strength" was cancelled out by the city's demographic white majority.[5] The case went to trial in July 1976, but it would take ten years for it to be settled, making its way to the US Supreme Court and back to the local court.[6] Neither the *Bolden* case nor the new developments in Black Mardi Gras can be understood outside of the context of the turbulent racial tensions enveloping the city at the time.[7]

In March 1976 two young African American men, Glen Diamond and James A. Jones, were stopped by Mobile police officers because of allegedly fitting the description of a robbery suspect. While Jones stayed to answer questions, Diamond ran and was chased by the policemen. After dragging him from under a porch where he was hiding, they took a rope that was in officer Michael K. Patrick's patrol car and placed it on Diamond's neck and over a tree branch. As journalist Kevin Lee described it: "He was pulled upward, heels off the ground, the noose untightened but bearing his weight. He choked and nearly passed out before it stopped."[8] The lynching was stopped only because another officer passed by and told them "We can't hang any niggers tonight." As a result of what became euphemistically known as the "mock hanging," Patrick was dismissed, and the others involved were suspended for fifteen days without payment. Black Mobilians were outraged, especially after police commissioner Robert Doyle explained in a press conference that "the officers were 'just playing' with Diamond."[9] As Scotty Kirkland explains, the Diamond case resulted in "the largest internal investigation in the history of the city's police department" but also brought forth a "rash of cross burnings" as well as harassment and intimidation of civil rights leaders and activists.[10]

Six months after the city's first appeal of the *Bolden* case, authorities approved a request by "Imperial Wizard" Robert Shelton to hold a United Klans of America (UKA) rally in downtown Mobile, which turned into a violent confrontation near Bienville Square. According to Kirkland, the "publicity from the *Bolden* case, and the city's decision to appeal it, along with the Diamond lynching and the Klan rally shattered Mobile's respectable image irrevocably."[11] Things would only get worse before they got any better.

On March 21, 1981, in a random act of retaliation for the killing of a police officer by a Black man named Josephus Anderson and his subsequent mistrial, two members of the local UKA chapter kidnapped Michael Anthony Donald on Davis Avenue, lynched him in the woods near Baldwin County, and hanged his dead body downtown near a house owned by local Klan leader Bennie Jack Hays on Herndon Avenue.[12] Hays was the "Great Titan" of the southern Alabama UKA. According to Laurence Leamer, he was outraged by what he perceived as "the rise of black people," and abhorred the idea of "whites watching black Mardi Gras parades," so he commanded Klavern members to slash tires around the African American parading area.[13]

During the aftermath of the lynching and ensuing trial, tensions were high in the city. In his speech at a rally "protesting the inaction of the investigation," Rev. Jesse Jackson compared the Donald murder to the "'political lynching' perpetuated on all blacks in the area by Mobile's form of government" in a clear reference to *Bolden*.[14] The FBI was involved in the case, and Henry Hays (Bennie Jack Hays's son) and James "Tiger" Knowles were charged with the murder. Henry Hays was the second white man sentenced to death for killing a Black man in the history of the state of Alabama. The other big development in the case was that after the Southern Poverty Law Center cofounder Morris Dees got involved in the case, he decided to also charge the UKA. The process resulted in Donald's mother, Beulah Mae Donald, being awarded $7 million in damages in 1987, which bankrupted the UKA and Robert Shelton.[15]

The Mobile area Klansmen did not channel their bigotry and violent hatred solely toward African Americans. A few days before they lynched Michael Donald, the killers deceived a gay white man into accompanying them to a nightclub, but instead "they put a knife to his neck and drove him to the causeway into the wilderness." Luckily, he was able to escape while they "debated what to do with him."[16] Although many Mobilians (including some MGSCOH narrators) expressed their shock and disbelief that such horrifying and blatant acts of racialized violence could happen that late in the twentieth century in their city, as Leamer notes, "five years before the Michael Donald lynching, the Klan had been sufficiently accepted that the *Mobile Register* listed its rallies the way the paper did high school football games."[17]

It is important, however, that when we tell that story, we focus not only on white supremacists' blatant demonstrations of their perceived power but also on African Americans' resistance to such displays. As mentioned above, the September 24, 1977, UKA march was met with a counterprotest. A crowd of about a hundred UKA members and sympathizers, several of whom "had handguns tucked in their belts," were met along the way by interracial couples openly embracing, Black youth shouting obscenities, and "throngs of Black protestors, who rushed to meet the marchers" on Dauphin Street, confirming the declaration by Mobile NAACP's president Robert Gilliard that "Black people no longer fear the Klan."[18] Scotty

Plus Ça Change?

United Klans of America march in Mobile, Alabama. September 24, 1977. Photo by Claire Matturro. "Photographs of United Klans of America March in Mobile, Alabama" Collection. Alabama Department of Archives and History.

Protestors at a United Klans of America march in Mobile, Alabama. September 24, 1977. Photo by Claire Matturro. "Photographs of United Klans of America march in Mobile, Alabama" Collection. Alabama Department of Archives and History.

Kirkland paints an evocative picture as he counterposes the chorus of Black protestors clapping and singing "Amen-Freedom" and the UKA marchers' racist slurs and in his description of the ensuing violence.[19] But we also have a powerful visual record of the episode, thanks to Claire Matturro's photographs.[20] In the collection, we clearly see the contrast between the "overwhelmingly male and middle aged" white marchers and the Black protesters and onlookers.[21] In Matturro's shots, most of which were likely taken before the confrontation, we see a Black woman with an Afro wearing bell-bottoms leading the protest and a Black woman in hair rollers carrying a Black baby on the sidelines observing the commotion. We see a Black man carrying a radio and Black children smiling at the camera. These are Black Mobilians claiming their space and making it clear that they are not turning the other cheek to this afront. This is a protest that would soon turn violent. But this is also a celebration. There is music, singing, clapping. There is revolt and defiance, and there is also immense joy and pride in these images.[22]

Two months after Donald's murder, testimony in the Bolden case resumed. In 1985 after a referendum, Mobile voters chose to have a mayor-council plan, dividing the city into seven districts, three of which are predominantly African American, while the mayor would still be elected at large. Furthermore, the Alabama legislature enacted the supermajority law requiring five out of seven votes in the council's decisions, to avoid the Black vote being once again suppressed by a white majority.[23] In July 1985, for the first time, Mobilians elected African American officials: pharmacist Irmatean Watson; Charles Tunstall (pastor of Stone Street Baptist Church, who defeated Joseph Langan for the position), and Rev. Clinton Johnson. Arthur Outlaw, the former finance commissioner (and former white Mardi Gras king), was elected as the city's first mayor under the new system.

The HIV/AIDS Epidemic: The Demise (and Reinvention) of the Fruit Loop

The 1980s and 1990s brought renewed attempts to revitalize downtown, which meant that "undesirable" or "deviant" behavior could not be as visible as it had once been. The "Downtown Renaissance" meant the demise (and subsequent reinvention) of the Fruit Loop. When asked if he remembered when the Fruit Loop began to "disappear," Homer McClure replied:

Mobile AIDS Support Services (MASS) pamphlet. Early 1990s. Gordon Tanner Collection. Invisible Histories Project.

On Conception Street, where the Flipside is now, used to be a very chichi French restaurant called Quatorze run by Yannick Marchand. And Yannick, I mean, that was such a nice place that everybody from Springhill [affluent neighborhood] would come down and go there. Well, you know, you're not gonna go down there and cruise ... so it would have been about then. And then, now I'm trying to remember, that would have been in the nineties, I'd say. So, I guess the nineties. I stopped about that time. But I would say the nineties was when kinda, downtown picked up again. They were trying to promote Dauphin Street like a Bourbon Street, you know, for young people. And then, when they started concentrating on Dauphin Street, I'd say that probably took care of the Fruit Loop.[24]

But even before that, the fabulous atmosphere of the Fruit Loop's disco days had been interrupted. In 1981 the health department reported the first death from AIDS (Acquired Immune Deficiency Syndrome) in Mobile County.[25] By the end of the decade, it had taken many of gay Mobile's most exuberant characters. Others, afraid of the still indecipherable disease, retreated to a more domestic existence. As drag performer Miss Cie explained on AL.com in 2019, "'One day we had love, disco music, freedom and gay liberation, then suddenly someone turned the music off, turned on the lights, and I looked behind me and everyone was just gone.'"[26] The pain and the trauma of losing so many loved ones is quite vivid in some of the MGSCOH narrators' memories. Queen Richard IV's recollections reveal the complexity of the experiences of those who survived the plague:

> God! I remember one night, we had somebody on [each side] of Dauphin Street—funeral homes—across the street from each other. That's something . . . I mean, that was the whole attitude. We had to laugh and joke you know to get past the anger and the frustration to begin with, and then this situation. [. . .] I remember the first person that died was a guy, a young guy that was a couple years behind me at McGill Toolen [Catholic high school]. And he was totally open. And then I remember people that got sick early on that lived for quite some time. [. . .] I was right there with them. I might have done the same drugs, or . . . with the same . . . but I was right there. And, uh, to this day I'm negative. You know, why? I don't know. I mean, I literally dodged a bullet. How? I don't know. And then I remember Neil [Aldridge] being sick and then dying. That was, that was really hard . . . plus, the stigma.[27]

Although the story of the HIV/AIDS epidemic often centers on (mostly white) gay men's experience, as in other parts of the country and the world, in Mobile lesbian women played an important part in the crisis response.[28] L. Craig Roberts, who was chairman of AIDS Alabama in the early 2000s, credits Mobile lesbians' "motherly instincts" as the driving force behind the creation of organizations such as the Mobile AIDS Support Services (MASS).[29] MASS provided educational programming, counseling, and services that attended to the basic needs of those affected as well as their caregivers. While different narrators provided different years for the creation of MASS, varying from 1986 to 1988, the organization first appeared in the *Alabama Forum* directory in the July/August 1989 issue.[30] Before that the organization listed was the Mobile AIDS Buddy Program. Queen Janette XII explains how her late partner Diane got involved:

> It was very upsetting to her that the government had no interest, and the general medical field had no interest, in helping or doing anything about

it. [. . .] We had counseling for caregivers. She did a lot of research on how the disease spread, 'cause right at first they didn't know, people were just ostracized 'cause they didn't wanna be in the same room. There was so little known about it. She found all the facts, they did, we did. We just made sure to put out information sheets in the bars. [. . .] She just thought about it from all angles of what a human being would need to do the best they could with this awful disease, and she was there for anybody who needed anything.[31]

Kathie Hiers, current CEO of AIDS Alabama, talks about the early experiences that ended up defining her career path:

Well, you know, it was growing up here in Mobile, the men and women were not as separate here as they are in Birmingham. You know, half my friends were always the gay guys, and they were so funny and fun, and I had my best friend was a gay guy. And then the plague of my generation hit. I mean, I just started losing people right and left, and, you know, back in those days there was nothing to do. We started after a friend of mine who was actually the first case at Mobile AIDS Support Services passed away. We started a little non-profit in his name called the Lee Simmons Fund for people living with AIDS. [. . .] Back in those days people used to separate them in the hospital, so we would go see them in the hospitals and bring them flowers, and all that stuff, and it was kind of a Make a Wish Foundation for gay people. [. . .] I'll never forget that day in 1985, when my ex and I were sitting in a Denny's up near the Interstate and six of my gay male friends walked in, and they had just all tested over in Pensacola anonymously. Back then you had to give your name here, but you [didn't have to] there. And they had tested as Daisy Duck and Minnie Mouse and so on, and all six of them were positive. And today five of those six men are dead. I would say of all my gay male friends from those days at least 90 percent are dead, if not more. [. . .] I think back to those days too and how the lesbian community really rose up to help. And we took care of so many of those guys. And I guess that's where I got my passion for the HIV work.[32]

Despite losing many of its prominent members, the OOO and its annual ball continued to grow, eventually becoming a crossover hit with straight audiences.

Marked Mardi Gras Goes Mainstream: The OOO's Crossover Success

It is hard to point out precisely how or when the Osiris ball ticket became such a hot commodity. The organization's official history pamphlet explains that the OOO was "widely accepted and recognized in the Mobile Carnival celebration" by the time it moved to a larger venue, the Municipal Expo Hall, in 1987.[33] Some members, however, remember a bomb threat in one of its early years.[34]

The ball's newspaper coverage illustrates the changes in the organization's visibility. While gay publications like the *Alabama Forum* covered Osiris events, except for a colorful review of the inaugural ball in the *Azalea City News and Review*, not much was written about them in mainstream periodicals during the 1980s.[35] Nowhere in the *Azalea City* piece is Osiris directly referred to as a gay or lesbian organization, but the anonymous reviewer provides some hints: "This latest star in the crown of the Mobile Carnival Association had a distinctly cosmopolitan flavor. Warm breezes from Rio de Janeiro were blowing that night, and festive rhythms from Christopher, Castro and Bourbon Street were hovering in the air."[36] But by the late 1990s, the Osiris ball was covered along with the other "traditional" dances. In 1998 the *Mobile Register*'s society editor Susie Spear Cloos revived the international motif, describing the ball as a "Rio-meets-Vegas-meets Mobile scene with men and women in elaborate and clever museum quality costumes."[37] Rather than focusing on the organization's distinctiveness, the columnist stressed its inclusiveness: "Membership is diverse—the group is the first in Mobile to include both men and women, white and black, as well as straight (about 40 percent by most estimates) and gay members."[38] The writer of *Susie's Parlor* returned to the ball four years later and confirmed Osiris's crossover success: "The always-creative ball, hosted by members of Mobile's gay and lesbian contingent, drew hundreds of mainstream Mobilians who so enjoy this annual party."[39] In 2001 the Masked Observer, a columnist known for his humorous portrayal of Mardi Gras festivities, also acknowledged the ball's popularity but stressed its difference from traditional organizations: "The Observer has heard for years that this particular event is among Mobile's hottest tickets. This year, he is fortunate enough to look at the group's 20th anniversary, which boasted two kings and no queen (it's a long story, ask us later)." In a passage describing the costumes of a particular member's escorts, who at some point in the tableau removed their bath towels to reveal G-strings, the Observer exclaimed: "Try doing that at the Order of Myths!"[40]

It seems clear from these articles, most of which appeared in the city's primary newspaper, that by the early 2000s the OOO had already been integrated and accepted into the official Mobile Mardi Gras tradition. Yet, while the Carnival Museum's website lists the creation of Osiris in its historical timeline, it had none of the OOO monarchs' trains, crowns, photographs, or scepters in its permanent exhibition when this author last visited it in 2015. A 2013 special issue of the independent weekly newspaper *Lagniappe* entitled "Insider's Look at Mardi Gras: Alternative Lifestyle Organizations" portrayed the city's LGBTQIA+ Carnival societies: Osiris, the Order of Pan, and the Krewe of Phoenix.[41] It is a positive representation and, once again, praises the organizations' tableaux, "the distinctive factor of all these balls." But the fact that homosexuality was still considered an "alternative lifestyle" in 2013 implies that there was a norm with which they failed to comply.[42]

This emphasis on the spectacle is important because it shows the process through which a marginalized group of people can be embraced by the mainstream after they appropriate the language, structure, and symbols of a dominant culture. The Osiris ball gets bigger each year, attracting more straight revelers. Yet, as the OOO gains more acceptance and respect from the city's straight community, it inevitably loses some of its original identity. As audiences became bigger, the participants in the spectacle began to not only express but also *represent* themselves and what they believe their community should look like to heteronormative audiences.[43]

Marked Mardi Gras Goes Mainstream: Black Mardi Gras Arrives Downtown

The decision to relocate the MAMGA Mammoth parade route in 1992 from "The Avenue" to downtown was controversial and made some people in the city's Black communities feel excluded and abandoned.[44] That is why they now start on MLK Avenue (formerly Davis Avenue) and parade all the way to join the downtown route. But the long trajectory brought its own set of problems. One of the main issues is that it put a strain on the performers who accompany the parade. Another parade organized by the MLK Business and Civic Organization, MLK Monday Mystics, and Northside Merchants remains exclusively on The Avenue on Monday (Lundi Gras).

Kern Jackson believes this represented an important turning point. Jackson argues that the moving of the parade from Black neighborhoods to the white parade route affected opportunities to mask, as the performers were now subject to the white gaze. It also marked the transition in Black performance from "mollie-like behavior" to the "mask of objectification," which he defines as "a mask that works among white people in commercially codified situations, utilizing the mixed gazes that one uses the rest of the year."[45] Linda Dennison recalled that the parade route change "sent just a shockwave through the community." And, although he "didn't really necessarily agree with it" at first, Bobby Dennison later understood the reasons behind the change and gave MAMGA credit for trying to level the Mardi Gras playing field: "I think that was one way they tried to put us in the forefront, to put things on an even keel by changing that route. Even though some people were opposed."[46]

The current MAMGA floats reveal a lot about the organization's vision for their role in the city's racial uplift project, reflecting the stories they want to tell about their organization and their community. They present a narrative that starts in Africa, honors race men, memorializes The Avenue in its prime, and subdues subversive Mardi Gras traditions. To commemorate their diamond anniversary in 2013, artist James Finklea designed two new floats. The Home of Diamonds float depicts ethnic groups from different parts of Africa such as the Xhosa, Masai, Fanti, and Dogon, connecting the organization to African ancestry and diaspora. The Seventy-Five Years Diamonds float depicts old Davis Avenue buildings and businesses, educating the audience on the heyday of Mobile's "Negro Main Street."[47] The other two main floats pay homage to the organization's past leaders and to the Mollies. While the Presidents Float memorializes the prominent men who led the organization, the aforementioned Mollies float presents a more sedate image of the street maskers.

Together, these floats tell a story. Although it is a sanitized version of the history and trajectory of African Americans in Mobile, it enshrines their place in that city's society. As the parade winds its way from The Avenue to downtown Mobile, passing through narrow residential streets, its symbolic meaning changes. Although they only have one day in the festive calendar to tell that story, it is emblematic of Black Mobilians' "two-ness." Just like the parades, they often have to navigate two worlds, while white people have the privilege of acknowledging only their spaces and experiences.[48]

MAMGA "Home of Diamonds" float. Mobile, Alabama, Mardi Gras Day, 2017. Photo by the author.

MAMGA "Seventy-Five Years Diamonds" float representing old Davis Avenue buildings and businesses. Mobile, Alabama, Mardi Gras Day 2017. Photo by the author.

MAMGA Mollies float. Mobile, Alabama, Mardi Gras Day 2016. Photo by the author.

MAMGA Presidents float. Mobile, Alabama, Mardi Gras Day 2017. Photo by the author.

The Order of Myths

In *The Order of Myths* (2008), filmmaker Margaret Brown follows the two Mobile Mardi Gras queens from the moment they receive the honor, through their preparations, to the coronation of the two separate courts. The plot gets much deeper as Brown shows that the white queen, Helen Meaher, is the direct descendent of Timothy Meaher, the slave trafficker who smuggled the last "black cargo" to the United States in the *Clotilda* ship after the abolishment of the transatlantic slave trade to the US. Stephanie Lucas, the MAMGA queen, descends from the marooned enslaved people who took refuge and built a community in the area known as Africatown, located just outside of downtown Mobile.[49] The film's director is the daughter of a former (white) Mardi Gras queen, and as we see throughout the film, her family has been involved in the higher echelons of white elite Mobile Mardi Gras for generations, which grants her uncensored access to the inner machinations of a very closed society. In return they seem to have expected a more flattering portrayal. Some Mobilians I spoke with expressed discomfort with the film. They were particularly upset by the fact that the filmmaker included an image of Michael Donald's lynched body, complaining they didn't see the connection between segregated Mardi Gras and that particular extreme act of violence. Others, however, appreciated how the film exposed the hypocrisy of Mobile's high society. Attorney Domingo Soto explains:

> Well, I like Mardi Gras. But I don't . . . I don't like a lot about it . . . like that film we were talking about the other day. It's like, you know, what I liked about the film was that it talked about the reality of it. It's like, maybe there are gonna be some folks that only wanna be in Black Mardi Gras. Maybe that's true [laughs]. But we won't know until we make 'em go together, you know? The excuse is that that's the way people want it, it's bullshit. It's complete horseshit. It's like, no way. It's a highly segregated, class-based deal and Black class too.[50]

Although it would seem as if white Mobilians would be more bothered by the documentary's depiction of the city's racial inequality, some people involved in Black Mardi Gras organizations also had their reservations. Pam R. Moore relayed the negative critique she heard from African Americans who watched the film:

> I heard different things about it. I mean, when I saw it, I took it for what it was, a documentary, one person's viewpoint. But I did hear some blowback. That it felt like the Black royals were striving to be a part of the white group a bit more than the white group was striving to include them, and that I thought was unfortunate, that people felt that way.[51]

In her laudable efforts to denounce the racist and white supremacist origins and practices in Mobile's Mardi Gras, the filmmaker did not account for the intraracial class divisions that permeate Black Mardi Gras. And, by focusing on African Americans as the victims of segregationist practices and racist violence, she unintentionally removes some of their agency. Nevertheless, the film also showed attempts to integrate the city's Carnival experience and raised awareness of how certain "traditions" look from the outside, leading to more efforts from the MCA and MAMGA to present a united front. For instance, the monarchs of each organization visit and pay homage to their counterparts in their respective coronations.

In 2004 a new Mardi Gras association, the Conde Explorers, "was founded . . . to bring together men and women of all races to celebrate Mardi Gras together." Their website proudly advertises that they were featured in "the 2008 award-winning documentary on Mobile's Mardi Gras" and declares: "It's a new millennium, but Mobile's signature event—Mardi Gras—is still largely segregated by race. In the home of the original Mardi Gras, young children raising their arms for beads at the downtown parades see that every single float rider is white—with the exception of one society."[52] Yet the membership of the association is still mostly composed of African Americans. In 2005 Mobilians elected their first African American mayor, Samuel Leon Jones, who was reelected in 2009 without opposition. A year after he took office, the Mobile City Commission unanimously approved a bill to rename Herndon Avenue in honor of Michael Donald. The year Sam Jones was reelected, Black people "constituted a slight majority of Mobile's population" for the first time.[53]

It is unclear what these sociocultural and political changes will mean for the future of Mobile's race relations and to their annual celebration. Former MAMGA president Eric Finley concluded his interview reaffirming his belief in the organization's longevity and its continuous role as a pillar of Mobile's Black community:

> The Mobile Area Mardi Gras Association, African American group, it's about tradition. It was started back during the Jim Crow days, which I'm sure when someone listens to this they will not have a clue of what the Jim Crow days were all about. But we lived in separate areas, we attended separate schools, we had separate social events, and a lot of that changed in the sixties. But, however, the Mobile Carnival was always about tradition from a Mobile Area Mardi Gras Association perspective. Meaning that it was about families, it was about the connectivity from grandmother to grandchild. The king was pretty much a legacy that was passed on from one family to another. [. . .] So, when

we talk about the longevity of the Mobile Area Mardi Gras Association and the potential merger with Mobile Carnival Association or the dissolvement or dissolution of both, I don't see it happening. I can't even visualize that taking place. I see it as almost like a perpetual kind of organization because the families keep the legacy going. That's the string that binds this organization.[54]

To support his point, he then provided the example of the five generations of people involved in Mardi Gras in his family, from his grandfather Dr. James Franklin, one of the founding members of the MCCA in 1938, to his grandchildren who currently participate. Finley concluded:

I mean, we've been organized now for eighty years. And the interesting thing is that it's African American men, and we have survived several wars and outlasted a lot of institutions in the city. There are not many churches and other organizations that have been active for that period of time. [. . .] And it just seems to continue to get stronger, the foundation seems to be as solid as one would expect, and it would just be a jewel if I could come back in one hundred years and see how it's evolved. But I think it will still be here and be strong, and that common thread of all of these families will continue to stretch out.[55]

Whether or not MAMGA persists, as in the past, it will not represent the totality of Mobile's Black Mardi Gras experiences. With a music video shot entirely in Black Carnival spaces, and including the floats and other symbols of the respectable top-down celebration, the 2 Major Twinz's "Mardi Gras Song" provides an alternative and vivid image of Black Mobilians' Mardi Gras experiences. Theirs is a Black Mardi Gras outside the confines of respectability politics, populated by "thick baby mamas" and smelling of "dro." Where folks dress up "like it's a fashion show" but still fear they might get "pitaroll'd" by the police if they are perceived to have stepped out of line. Yet it is also one where folks from MLK Avenue, the Bottoms, and the Campground are proud to declare they are from the birthplace of Mardi Gras. Hence, what started as an origin myth that supported a white supremacist Lost Cause discourse has provided a sense of belonging and identity affirmation to marked Mobilians.[56]

CONCLUSION

NOW YOU DO WATCHA WANNA

> Cultural identities come from somewhere, have histories. But, like everything which is historical, they undergo constant transformation. Far from being eternally fixed in some essentialised past, they are subject to the continuous "play" of history, culture and power. Far from being grounded in a mere "recovery" of the past, which is waiting to be found, and which, when found, will secure our sense of ourselves into eternity, identities are the names we give to the different ways we are positioned by, and position ourselves within, the narratives of the past.
> —STUART HALL[1]

On April 22, 2015, the Oxygen Channel debuted *The Prancing Elites Project*, a reality show about an "African American, gay and gender non-conforming dance team."[2] Adrian, Kentrell, Kareem, Jerel, and Tim are all fascinating to watch, but another character stood out in in the first couple of episodes: the city of Mobile. The Prancing Elites, and Mobile, had risen to sudden internet stardom when Shaquille O'Neal retweeted a video of their performance at the Christmas parade in the small town of Semmes, a few miles west of the city. In trailers, interviews, and the show, the members of the group introduce themselves by stressing their Blackness, their nonconformant gender and sexuality, and their place of origin. Rephrasing Lady LaBeija's iconic *Paris Is*

The Prancing Elites parade with the Order of Venus during Mardi Gras. Mobile, Alabama. February 1, 2016. Photo by Sharon Steinmann. ©2016. AL.com. All rights reserved. Reprinted with permission.

Burning opening lines in one of the program's teasers, team leader Kentrell explains: "We have three strikes. We're gay. We're Black. And we're in Mobile, Alabama."[3] In the opening episode, producers attempted to re-create the images that made them famous. The group, dressed in sequined leotards, tries to crash another small-town Mardi Gras parade and is antagonized by redneck authorities and spectators. The artificiality of scripted reality television does not detract from the lived experiences expressed through their performances to both parade audiences and the camera. Scripted or unscripted, in high definition, or through shaky handheld cellphone cameras, the image of their queer Black bodies occupying "respectable" white spaces and being gazed at by curious, supporting, or hostile white eyes said more than any witty commentary the screenwriters and the Prancing Elites could concoct.

The morning after the premiere, *Mobile Mask*'s Steve Joynt posted a photo of the group on Facebook with the following comment: "Speaking only for myself—a white, middle-aged male from the South who is a dedicated and practicing heterosexual—I think these guys are a hoot, and they are what Mardi Gras is all about. They're different, they're entertaining, and they aren't afraid to be themselves."[4] Yet that is not what Mardi Gras has always been "all about." The fact that the Prancing Elites are celebrated by a publication dedicated to support and promote Mardi Gras "tradition" seems to confirm that "tradition" is not a fixed concept. It is subject to reinvention.

The group embodies what madison moore brilliantly articulated as a "politics of fabulousness." moore explains that fabulousness "isn't just about sequins; it's what happens the second we stop trying to fit in and start daring to inhabit space in our own terms," and "fashion, glitter, and sequins ... are not only shiny, conspicuous, and look great on Instagram, but they underscore the pleasure and power of creativity for queer and marginalized people and other outcasts."[5] So by choosing to occupy public spaces in their own terms, unapologetically embracing and celebrating their queer Blackness, the Prancing Elites have rewritten Mobile Mardi Gras's tradition in more diverse and inclusive terms.

While they still make special appearances in Mobile Mardi Gras parades, to the delight of their faithful fan base, *The Prancing Elites Project* has since been cancelled. But other groups have also challenged Mobile Mardi Gras's rigid boundaries, structures, and conventions. Although they do not necessarily identify themselves as a Mardi Gras organization and hold their ball after the pre-Lenten season, the Mystic Womyn of Color is a social group that includes queer women of color and organizes a series of events throughout the year. Their main annual event is modeled on traditional Mardi Gras balls.[6]

The Joe Cain Day celebration still provides a space for experimentation. In 1974 a new tradition was born with the creation of the Cain's Merry Widows mystic society. On Joe Cain Day, their members "dress in black mourning clothes with veils, lay a wreath at Cain's burial site at Church Street Graveyard, wail over their 'departed husband's' grave, then travel to Joe Cain's former house on Augusta Street to offer a toast and eulogy to their 'Beloved Joe.'"[7] In 2003 they were joined in their performative grief by the Mistresses of Joe Cain. Dressed in red, they join the procession, taunting the Widows, proclaiming that Joe loved them best.[8] Both groups conceal their whole bodies and faces, and their identities are supposed to be a well-guarded secret. Although they are identified as women's organizations, there are rumors that men have occasionally taken advantage of the anonymity and joined the procession dressed either as a Widow or as a Mistress. The Joe Cain Secret Misters "tradition" started in 2012 with a group of mostly straight-identified young misfits who work in and/or frequent the downtown bohemian scene and parade on Joe Cain Day in revealing gender-bending outfits, carrying rainbow flags and provocative signs. The group's straight organizers are aware of the problematic ethics involved in representing "gay culture," yet as time passes their membership becomes more diverse. One of the Misters' founding members, Nick Shantazio (born in Mobile in 1983), who is the son of an Iranian immigrant, explains:

> So, our group is a bunch of, for the most part, straight white males who dress and act as flamboyantly as possible. The first year it was six straight white men. Over time it's become [...] we've got African American members, we've got homosexual members, we've got female members who dress as men. So, our group is different. It is different than any other society in Mobile 'cause we jump every line intentionally. [...] I always worry about that. I think we definitely straddle a real close line on, hopefully, on the side of, we're not, I don't ever think of this like we're making fun of gay people.[9]

The Misters also provide an example of the importance of an intersectional approach when judging who belongs to and has the right to represent a particular "culture," and the importance of downtown as a locus of identity formation for some Mobilians. The group's straight members are not complete foreigners in Mobile's gay world. Through their position as misfits, and through their labor (many of them work in the downtown service industry), they share a particular experience of that space with the people who work in and frequent the Fruit Loop. Stephen Gaudet, born in Tampa, Florida, in 1981, explains:

> Gabriel's is one of the gay bars, it's been our close-out bar for years and years. Those of us who are the kind of people who're used to stay awake all night, and drink all night, are intimately connected to that scene. Our final night hookups are happening alongside those dudes, like, we're having conversations with them every night, we're talking to them regularly. You know, I mean, we're getting invited to parties and stuff. It's not like we're unconnected to the thing. But Mobile has always had a particularly nasty small-town mentality about certain things, and gay culture happens to be one of those things.[10]

The Misters also embody the Bakhtinian Carnival spirit by openly challenging and ridiculing normative organizations' classist efforts to look "nice" and respectable:

Joe Cain Secret Misters founder Nick Shantazio. Mobile, Alabama, Joe Cain Day 2020. Photo by the author.

Joe Cain Secret Misters. Mobile, Alabama, Joe Cain Day 2017. Photo by the author.

Stephen Gaudet: Typically, Mardi Gras was started by people with money. And their entire purpose was to appear un-ridiculous. Their entire thing is they don't wanna be ridiculous. So, everything that they do is designed to echo their power over these peasant masses that they're gracing with their presence and throwing things to, and that doesn't fit into us. We're not, that's not us, that's not what we're doing. And that doesn't fit into their thing.[11]

In their first five years, the group grew from six to thirty-eight members and moved from a spontaneous second line on Dauphin Street to marching in the official Joe Cain procession. Yet they seem committed to remaining outsiders. They see themselves as allies to the city's LGBTQIA+ community, who want to defy Mobile Carnival's classist and normative structures. So far, they have refused all the offers to be part of official events and commercials. As Shantazio notes: "I've had the Joe Cain parading procession board ask if the Secret Misters will show up for city events. Trying to market tourism, and I've denied, I said: 'That's not what we're for.' We're not here to market the city. We're the antithesis . . ." Gaudet adds: "We're the definition of what you don't want." Shantazio further explains that his goal "with the group is to be the stick in the wheel, kinda, to cause that disruption."

Being such eye-catching figures, they immediately attract the camera lenses of photographers and journalists. They are often on the cover of the local news and in national and international outlets. Outsiders and younger folks, unencumbered by Mardi Gras norms and traditions, see those images in the media and think that *this* is what Mobile's Mardi Gras is all about. Although they identify as a group of "fuck-up drunks," they are conscious of and take pride in their role in reinventing their city's Mardi Gras tradition.

In 2015 Luis Diemert's descendants created the Order of Many Faces to honor what they call "Mobile's Second Original Tradition" and rectify their ancestor's "status among Carnival luminaries." They seek to be "as accessible as possible to as many people as possible" and include people of "all races, genders, and sexual orientations."[12] In 2018 members of the Rainbow Mobile coalition participated in the parade organized by the Order of Doves, a new incarnation of the first known African American mystic society, waving rainbow flags. And the current MLK Business and Civic Organization, MLK Monday Mystics, Northside Merchants parade, which takes place on The Avenue on Lundi Gras, had a Zulu float. These examples show how Mobilians are looking to the past for a more inclusive invented tradition.

Zulu float. MLK Business and Civic Organization, Monday Mystics, Northside Merchants parade. Mobile, Alabama, February 24 (Lundi Gras), 2020. Photo by the author.

Yet, when the *Mobile Bay Magazine* introduced the 2021 "Kings and Queens of Mardi Gras!" on Instagram, they were referring to the pairs of monarchs from the MCA's regular and junior courts, not to MAMGA royalty, which they specifically identify as that particular organization's kings and queens in a different post. To them, "unmarked" Mardi Gras is still the one created for and by the white elites.

On the eve of Mardi Gras 2021, the city of Mobile was at yet another crossroads as it faced a global pandemic and a crucial municipal election. Fredrick D. Richardson Jr. (former NOW member) challenged incumbent Sandy Stimpson in the mayoral election. Stimpson, who is white, had been the city's mayor since he defeated Sam Jones in 2013 (and again in 2017). In the year of his reelection, he was involved in some Mardi Gras scandal when his connection as a paying member of the Comic Cowboys raised protests after the group included some particularly racist posters in their parade. He has since terminated his membership in the group. On February 9, 2021, Kim McKeand officially announced on social media her candidacy for Mobile's City Council using the hashtags #OutforMcKeand, #mobilepride, #seatatthetable, and #lgbtqcandidate. Marriage equality is a reality for Mobile's

Conclusion

Fruit Loop drag shows. B-Bob's, Mobile, Alabama, Mardi Gras Day 2017. Champagne Munroe (left), Venus Shante DaVis (center), Lauren Mitchell (right). Author's photos. Montage by Daniel Wildberger.

gay and lesbian couples, thanks in no small part to McKeand and Cari Searcy's legal battle so that Searcy could legally adopt their son, Khaya.[13] While neither McKeand nor Richardson secured enough votes to occupy the positions, their candidacies represent new possibilities for LGBTQIA+ and African American activists in Mobile politics. Even the Fruit Loop has gone mainstream as late capitalism's commodification of drag brings throngs of queer and straight-identified fans to B-Bob's and other clubs to enjoy shows from *RuPaul's Drag Race* contestants and local performers.[14] According to B-Bob's owner Jerry Ehlen, who has been in charge of different Mobile gay bars since the early 1990s, about half of the audiences in his club's drag shows are straight.[15] It is common to see folks in ball gowns and tails enjoying late-night drinks, karaoke, dance floors, and shows at the area's gay bars after Mardi Gras balls. It is unclear what that will do to the district's status as a safe queer space.[16]

The 2020 census shows that, while the trend of Mobile establishing itself as a Black-majority city remains relevant, the city is also becoming more racially and ethnically diverse.[17] The survey registered that 51.3 percent of the population identified as Black, and only 40.8 percent as white. While the city's overall population decreased by 4.1 percent since the 2010 census, that decline was more pronounced in its white population (-13.1 percent) than in the number of Black residents (-2.7 percent). Even though the percentage of people identified as American Indian and Asian also declined by 1.1 percent each, the number of folks who identified outside of the Black and white binary increased significantly: Pacific Islanders (+48.1%); "Other" (+44.3%);

The Original Dragons Ball. Mobile, Alabama, February 26, 2017. Photo by the author.

Joe Cain Secret Misters. Mobile, Alabama, Joe Cain Day 2017. Photo by the author.

"Two or More" (+187.3%). Furthermore, the percentage for those who identified ethnically as Hispanic or Latino also increased by 31.2 percent. Hence, future works that explore the city's society and celebrations will need to go beyond the Black and white divide.[18]

While the COVID-19 pandemic cancelled official Carnival celebrations worldwide in 2021, revelers have found alternative ways to either work within, circumvent, or defy official prohibitions. From the "socially distanced drive-through" parades in Saraland, to Mobile's "Yardi Gras," to Saraland's boat parades, South Alabamians still found ways to observe the festive season.

One song echoes in my head as I try to wrap up this long journey of investigating Mobile's Mardi Gras: Rebirth Brass Band's "Now You Do Watcha Wanna." It is the song played in Black Mardi Gras balls cuing the guests to join the second line, waving their elaborately adorned umbrellas. Its words written in the seminaked white body of one of Joe Cain's Secret Misters. It reminds me that traditions don't just happen. They are invented and serve a purpose. As Mobilians reinvent themselves and their Carnival, they once again have a chance to define what and who they *wanna* be.

APPENDIX
Narrators Index

All interviews conducted for this project are part of the "Mardi Gras and Social Change Oral Histories" (MGSCOH) collection available at the University of South Alabama's McCall Library archives. Those that deal specifically with LGBTQIA+ experiences were also shared with the Invisible Histories Project. Carnival Mystic Societies or krewes are secret organizations. In respect of that tradition, narrators that are currently members or have been monarchs in the past are identified in the text by their titles rather than by their legal names. Those who gave permission are also identified in this list by the name they provided in the consent form they signed. I updated these descriptions when I had access to new developments in the narrators' lives. Otherwise, the information provided here reflects their occupations at the time of our interviews.

Bobby Dennison: Interview recorded in Mobile, Alabama, on February 12, 2016. Born in 1952 in Mobile, Alabama, Bobby Dennison has worked, among other things, as an at-risk manager with the Mobile school system and played in the famous Central High School band.

Domingo Soto: Interview recorded in Mobile, Alabama, on February 1, 2016. Born in 1946 in Aguadilla, Puerto Rico, Domingo Soto is an attorney who for many years was involved in Mobile's social justice and counterculture movements.

Eric Franklin Finley: Interview recorded in Mobile, Alabama, in March 2017. Born in 1952 in Mobile, Alabama, Eric Finley is a past president and current executive board member of the Mobile Area Mardi Gras Association and the tour coordinator and member of the board of directors of the Dora Franklin Finley African American Heritage Trail.

George Moore: Interview recorded in Mobile, Alabama, on February 10, 2016. Born in 1933 in Mobile, Alabama, George Moore is the local historian at the Battle House Renaissance Mobile Hotel & Spa. He has worked in downtown Mobile for over half a century and has been a member of several African American organizations in the city.

Homer McClure: Interview recorded in Mobile, Alabama, on January 26, 2016. Born in 1951 in Mobile, Alabama, Homer McClure is a Mardi Gras designer and artist. For generations members of his family have held prominent positions in Mobile's traditional white elite Mardi Gras organization and events. He also used to frequent the Fruit Loop.

Hosea London: Interview recorded in Mobile, Alabama, on January 26, 2016. Born in 1948 in Winter Haven, Florida, Hosea London is the current leader of the Excelsior Band and has lived in Mobile for over four decades.

Jack Bishop: Interview recorded in Mobile, Alabama, on January 21, 2016. Born in 1938 in Jones County, Mississippi, Jack Bishop is a retired police officer.

Joey Potter: Telephone conversation (not recorded) conducted on October 14, 2014. Born in 1954 in Fairhope, Alabama, Joey Potter is a photographer and graphic designer and currently lives in Atlanta, Georgia. He worked at the Mobile Public Library and designed Osiris and GAE's logos and participated in many of the organizations' public performances.

John Alton Vaughan/Al Vaughan: One of the founding members of the Order of Osiris, and owner and president of the Miss Gay Mobile Pageant. He is currently the owner of Clippendales Pet Grooming in Fairhope, Alabama. Written account, sent on October 5, 2015.

Juanita Richardson: Interview recorded in Mobile, Alabama, on January 27, 2016. Born in 1943 in Birmingham, Alabama, Juanita Richardson is a retired educator and a civil rights activist. I interviewed her and her husband, Palmer Richardson, together.

Julie Dunlap/Queen Julie III: Born in 1958 in Montgomery, Alabama. Third Osiris Queen. While I never had a chance to officially interview Queen Julie, she provided information and shared photographs via Facebook Messenger.

Kathie Hiers: Interviewed twice: First interview recorded in Mobile, Alabama, October 12, 2014. Second interview recorded in Mobile, Alabama, January 27, 2016. Both interviews were conducted in collaboration with Cari Searcy. Born in 1954 in Mobile, Alabama, Kathie Hiers was involved with LGBTQIA+ social and activist organizations and is currently the CEO at AIDS Alabama.

King Charles XXIV/Charles Torrey: Interview recorded in Mobile, Alabama, on August 12, 2014. Born in Mobile, Alabama, on February 1, 1942, Charles Torrey is a former monarch and emblem in different gay Mardi Gras organizations and is currently the research historian at the History Museum of Mobile.

King Lawrence XV: Interview recorded in Mobile, Alabama, on January 28, 2016. Born in 1943 in Mobile County. At the time of the interview, King Lawrence XV was a retired schoolteacher and had been a member of several of Mobile's gay Mardi Gras organizations as well as "traditional" organizations. Sadly, he passed away on September 9, 2020.

L. Craig Roberts: Interview conducted in Mobile, Alabama, on February 11, 2016, in collaboration with Cari Searcy. Born on April 13, 1952, in Guntersville, Alabama, L. Craig Roberts is an architect, Mardi Gras specialist, and author of *Mardi Gras in Mobile* (2015). He also frequented the Fruit Loop.

Linda Dennison: Interview recorded in Mobile, Alabama, on February 12, 2016. Born in 1952 in Mobile, Alabama. Linda Dennison is currently the Accountant and Business Operations Support at AIDS Alabama South.

She used to live close to Davis Avenue. I interviewed her and her husband, Bobby Dennison, together.

Nick Shantazio: Interview recorded in Mobile, Alabama, on March 5, 2017. Born in 1983 in Mobile, Alabama, Nick Shantazio is an unofficial ambassador of Mobile's downtown bohemians and works in some of the downtown bars. He is also one of the founders of the Joe Cain Secret Misters parading group. I interviewed him and Stephen Gaudet at the same time.

Palmer Richardson: Interview recorded in Mobile, Alabama, on January 27, 2016. Born in 1938 in Mobile, Alabama, Palmer Richardson is a retired educator who served as school principal in different Mobile schools. I interviewed him and his wife, Juanita Richardson, together.

Pam Richardson Moore: Interviewed in Montgomery, Alabama, on February 2, 2016. Born in 1968 in Mobile, Alabama, Dr. Pamela Richardson Moore is Assistant Professor at the Department of Counseling and Instructional Sciences at the University of South Alabama. She is also a former member of the MAMGA court, and the daughter of Juanita and Palmer Richardson.

Queen Danielle II: Interview recorded in Mobile, Alabama, on October 15, 2014. Born on December 10, 1956, Queen Danielle II was the second female Osiris queen, served as ball captain twice and was still an active member of the organization when she left us on December 30, 2020.

Queen Janette XII/Janette Curry: Interview recorded in Mobile, Alabama, on February 13, 2016 in collaboration with Cari Searcy. Born in 1948 in San Antonio, Texas, Janette Curry is a librarian and has been involved in several social justice movements and LGBTQIA+ organizations in Mobile.

Queen Richard IV/Richard Rain Perez: Interview recorded in New Orleans, Louisiana, on October 14, 2014. Born in 1957 in Mobile, Alabama, Queen/Empress/Prince Richard Rain Perez is a costume designer and artist, and a former member of the Order of Osiris. He is currently a member of the New Orleans chapter of the Radical Faeries, where he has been crowned Empress and Prince of Perversion in different balls.

Queen Vickie V/John G. Uptagrafft: Interview recorded in Mobile, Alabama, on October 15, 2014. Born in 1951 in Mobile, Alabama, John Uptagrafft worked in some of Mobile's gay bars in the 1970s and was involved in the Order of Osiris since its inception. He is currently retired.

Ron Barret: Interview recorded in Mobile, Alabama, on July 27, 2015. Born in 1949 in Fairhope, Alabama, Ron Barret is a renowned Mardi Gras designer.

Sherry Odom: Telephone conversation (not recorded) conducted November 10, 2014, and several other communications via email and Facebook Messenger. Sherry Odom owned and operated famous gay nightclubs and restaurants in the US Gulf Coast while fundraising for AIDS research and education. She is a founding member of the Order of Osiris and is the founder of Pensacola's oldest gay Mardi Gras association, the Order of Zeus.

Stephen Gaudet: Interview recorded in Mobile, Alabama, on March 5, 2017. Born in 1981 in Tampa, Florida, Stephen Gaudet describes himself as a "lifelong lover of Mobile." He works security for bars and is one of the founding members of the Joe Cain Secret Misters.

Suzanne Cleveland: Interview recorded in Mobile, Alabama, on January 16, 2016. Born in 1938 in Mobile, Alabama, Suzanne Cleveland retired in 2020 from the downtown law firm where she worked for thirty-seven years. She is a founding member of Mobile's PFLAG and a member of Conde Explorers, the first integrated Mobile Mardi Gras mystic society. She is also a former Azalea Trail Maid queen and was voted "Quintessential Mobilian" in the 2018 Nappie Awards.

NOTES

Front matter epigraphs

1. James Baldwin, *The Fire Next Time* (New York: Vintage International, 1993), 81.
2. Pierre Nora, "Between Memory and History: Les Lieux de Mémoire," special issue "Memory and Counter-Memory," *Representations* no. 26, (Spring 1989): 9.

Preface

1. Isabel Machado, "Never Too Big, Never Too Much: How the Order of Osiris Helped Build a Visible LGBTQ Community in Mobile, Alabama," *Oral History* 46, no. 1 (March 2018), 80.
2. Mikhail Bakhtin, *Rabelais and His World* (Bloomington: Indiana University Press, 1984), 7.
3. A *foliã* (fem.) or *folião* (masc.) is a reveler or someone who avidly participates in and enjoys the festivities.
4. For more information about the narrators interviewed for the Mardi Gras and Social Change Oral Histories (MGSCOH) project, see Appendix I—"Narrators Index."
5. Carl N. Degler, *Neither Black nor White: Slavery and Race Relations in Brazil and the United States* (New York: Macmillan, 1971).
6. In Brazil, for instance, a *criolo* (masc.) or *criola* (fem.) was a person of African descent (enslaved or freed) who was born in the South American country. See João José Reis, *Ganhadores: A greve negra de 1857 na Bahia* (São Paulo: Companhia das Letras, 2019). For discussions of Creole identity in Louisiana, see Virginia R. Domínguez, *White by Definition: Social Classification in Creole Louisiana* (New Brunswick, NJ: Rutgers University Press, 1986); Arnold R. Hirsch and Joseph Logsdon, *Creole New Orleans: Race and Americanization* (Baton Rouge" Louisiana State University Press, 1992); Carl A. Brasseaux, Keith P. Fontenot, and Claude F. Oubre, *Creoles of Color in the Bayou Country* (Jackson: University Press of Mississippi, 1994); Sybil Kein, *Creole: The History and Legacy of Louisiana's Free People*

of Color (Baton Rouge: Louisiana State University Press, 2000); Michele Grigsby Coffey, "The State of Louisiana v. Charles Guerand: Interracial Sexual Mores, Rape Rhetoric, and Respectability in 1930s New Orleans," *Louisiana History: The Journal of the Louisiana Historical Association* 54, no. 1 (Winter 2013): 47–93; and Daniel Brook, *The Accident of Color: A Story of Race in Reconstruction* (New York: W. W. Norton, 2020).

7. "The Charter and the Code of Ordinances of the City of Mobile." Mobile Commercial Printing Co., 1897. Compiled by City Attorney Joseph Hamilton, "Introduction: Definitions and General provisions" #4, 53–54.

8. See Paulette Davis-Horton, *Avenue . . . the Place, the People, the Memories, 1799–1986* (Mobile: Horton, 1991); Harriet E. Amos, *Cotton City: Urban Development in Antebellum Mobile* (Tuscaloosa: University of Alabama Press, 1985); Beth Taylor Muskat, "Mobile's Black Militia: Major R. R. Mims and Gilmer's Rifles," *Alabama Review* 57 (July 2004): 183–205; and Margaret M. Marshall, "The Creole of Mon Louis Island, Alabama, and the Louisiana Connection," *Journal of Pidgin and Creole Languages* 6, no. 1 (1991): 73–87.

9. Musicologist Emily Ruth Allen unpacks definitions of the term and the experiences of Creole people in Mobile (especially in relation to Mardi Gras) in "Brass B(r)ands in Mobile, Alabama's Mardi Gras (PhD diss., Florida State University, 2019).

10. matthew heinz, *Entering Transmasculinity: The Inevitability of Discourse* (Bristol, UK: Intellect Books, 2016), 5, 225.

11. See Jerry T. Watkins III, *Queering the Redneck Riviera: Sexuality and the Rise of Florida Tourism* (Gainesville: University Press of Florida, 2018), 5.

12. Mimi Marinucci, *Feminism Is Queer: The Intimate Connection between Queer and Feminist Theory* (London: Zed Books, 2010). For other recent works that engage critically with the term, see also Katie Horowitz, *Drag, Interperformance, and the Trouble with Queerness* (London: Routledge, 2019); Rahul Rao, *Out of Time: The Queer Politics of Postcoloniality* (Oxford: Oxford University Press, 2020); Lawrence La Fountain-Stokes, *Translocas: The Politics of Puerto Rican Drag and Trans Performance* (Ann Arbor: University of Michigan Press, 2021); and Amelia Jones, *In Between Subjects: A Critical Genealogy of Queer Performance* (New York: Routledge, 2021).

13. See Nicole Maurantonio, *Confederate Exceptionalism: Civil War Myth and Memory in the Twenty-First Century* (Lawrence: University Press of Kansas, 2019); and John Eligon, "A Debate over Identity and Race Asks, Are African-Americans 'Black' or 'black'?," *New York Times*, June 26, 2020, https://www.nytimes.com/2020/06/26/us/black-african-american-style-debate.html.

14. Sociologist Amy L. Stone, however, documented the experiences of queer African American Mobilians in contemporary Mardi Gras, looking specifically at the Mystic Women of Color, an organization created for and by LBQ women of color. See Amy L. Stone, "Making an Inclusive Collective Party or Building LGBTQ+ Community? Tensions in LGBTQ Festival Events in American Mardi Gras," *Journal of Policy Research in Tourism, Leisure and Events*, published online March 4, 2022, doi: 10.1080/19407963.2022.2046012; Amy L. Stone. *Queer Carnival: Festivals and Mardi Gras in the South* (New York: New York University Press, 2022).

15. "New Group Forms in Mobile," *Alabama Forum*, June 1992, 5.

16. In 1982 the *Alabama Forum* published a two-part series on the experiences of Black gay men in Tuskegee, Alabama. While it is likely that the experiences of Black gay men in the Port City were different from those in a smaller rural town, it is illuminating of intersectional experiences of race and sexuality in the state. Lee David Hoshall, "The Gay Side

of Tuskegee: Separate but Equal in Black America" (parts 1 and 2), *Alabama Forum*, July/August and September issues.

Introduction

1. In accordance with the segregationist 1901 Alabama constitution, the 1907 Code of Ordinances mandated the separation of races in streetcars. Those in charge of these passenger vehicles had to "separate the white people from the negroes, by seating the white people in the front seats, and the negroes in the rear seats." Exceptions could be made for Black nurses in charge of white children or sick white people. The document also conferred on conductors and other employees "authority of police officer to enforce provision of seating section . . . invested with the police power of a police officer of the city of Mobile to carry out the provisions." *The Charter and the Code of Ordinances of the City of Mobile with Appendix*, prepared by Saffold Bernew, Attorney-At-Law (Mobile: Commercial Printing, 1907), 330 and 331.

2. Interview with Suzanne Cleveland, recorded by Isabel Machado in Mobile, Alabama, January 16, 2016; interview with Eric Finley, recorded by Isabel Machado in Mobile, Alabama, March 3, 2017; interview with Jack Bishop, recorded by Isabel Machado, Mobile, Alabama, January 21, 2016, MGSCOH project.

3. Since the creation of the Order of Osiris in 1981, the members of Mobile's LGBTQIA+ mystic societies identify their organizations as inclusive groups that accept all people regardless of race, gender, or sexual orientation. Nevertheless, only a few African Americans or straight-identified people have joined these groups over the years.

4. Folklorist Kern Jackson's work provides a notable exception. See Kern Michael Jackson, "Listening to the Wise Ones: Personal Narrative as a Window into Traditional Black Neighborhoods in Mobile, AL" (PhD diss., Indiana University, 2004); Kern Jackson, "Going to the Boomalatta: Narrating Black Mardi Gras in Mobile, Alabama," *Tributaries*, no. 7 (2004): 38–74.

5. A 2004 study, commissioned by the Mobile Bay Convention and Visitors Bureau, estimated the "direct spending during the 2004 Carnival season in Mobile at $227 million," while forecasting "$20.8 million in total tax revenues." The study, however, did not mention the public cost of the festivity. John Sharp, "Can Mobile Unmask the True Worth of Mardi Gras?" AL.com, August 5, 2019, https://www.al.com/news/2019/08/can-mobile-unmask-the-true-worth-of-mardi-gras.html.

6. See Anne Janine Pond, "The Ritualized Construction of Status: The Men Who Made Mardi Gras, 1830–1900" (PhD diss., University of Southern Mississippi, 2006); James Gill, *Lords of Misrule: Mardi Gras and the Politics of Race in New Orleans* (Jackson: University Press of Mississippi, 1997); Amos, *Cotton City*; and Scott P. Marler, *The Merchants' Capital: New Orleans and the Political Economy of the Nineteenth-Century South* (Cambridge: Cambridge University Press, 2013).

7. Fruit Loop (discussed in subsequent chapters) is the name given to a section of downtown Mobile where most of the gay bars and clubs are located. In the past it was also a cruising spot and zone of prostitution. The official Mardi Gras parade route includes part of the Fruit Loop. For further theoretical exploration of the concepts of publics and counterpublics, see Michael Warner, *Publics and Counterpublics* (New York: Zone Books, 2014); and Nancy Fraser, "Rethinking the Public Sphere: A Contribution to the Critique of Actually Existing Democracy," *Social Text*, no. 25/26 (1990).

8. See Thomas J. Sugrue, *The Origins of the Urban Crisis: Race and Inequality in Postwar Detroit* (Princeton: Princeton University Press, 2005); Kevin Michael Kruse, *White Flight: Atlanta and the Making of Modern Conservatism* (Princeton: Princeton University Press, 2005); Robert O. Self, *American Babylon: Race and the Struggle for Postwar Oakland* (Princeton: Princeton University Press, 2003); and Matthew D. Lassiter, *The Silent Majority: Suburban Politics in the Sunbelt South* (Princeton: Princeton University Press, 2006).

9. See, for instance, Gill, *Lords of Misrule*; Errol Laborde, *Krewe: The Early New Orleans Carnival, Comus to Zulu* (New Orleans: Carnival Press, 2007); Arthur Hardy, *Mardi Gras in New Orleans: An Illustrated History*, 4th ed. (New Orleans: Arthur Hardy Enterprises, 2009); Reid Mitchell, *All on a Mardi Gras Day: Episodes in the History of New Orleans Carnival* (Cambridge: Harvard University Press, 1995); Henri Schindler, *Mardi Gras: New Orleans* (Paris: Flammarion, 1997); J. Mark Souther, *New Orleans on Parade: Tourism and the Transformation of the Crescent City* (Baton Rouge: Louisiana State University Press, 2006); Anthony J. Stanonis, *Creating the Big Easy: New Orleans and the Emergence of Modern Tourism, 1918–1945* (Athens: University of Georgia Press, 2006); Richard Brent Turner, *Jazz Religion, the Second Line, and Black New Orleans* (Bloomington: Indiana University Press, 2009); Kim Marie Vaz, *The "Baby Dolls": Breaking the Race and Gender Barriers of the New Orleans Mardi Gras Tradition* (Baton Rouge: Louisiana State University Press, 2013); Smith, *Unveiling the Muse*; Leslie A. Wade, *Downtown Mardi Gras: New Carnival Practices in Post-Katrina New Orleans* (Jackson: University Press of Mississippi, 2020); Shane Lief and John McCusker, *Jockomo: The Native Roots of Mardi Gras Indians* (Jackson: University Press of Mississippi, 2019); Jennifer Atkins, *New Orleans Carnival Balls: The Secret Side of Mardi Gras, 1870–1920* (Baton Rouge: Louisiana State University Press, 2017). In comparison, there are only a few books dealing specifically with Mobile's Mardi Gras, most of which were self-published and/or not written by professional scholars. The exception is Samuel Kinser, *Carnival, American Style: Mardi Gras at New Orleans and Mobile* (Chicago: University of Chicago Press, 1990), which investigates both cities' celebrations. See Julian Lee Rayford, *Chasin' the Devil Round a Stump* (Mobile: American Print, 1962); Wayne Dean, *Mardi Gras: Mobile's Illogical Whoop-De-Doo* (Mobile: Adams Press, 1971); Emily Staples Hearin, *Let the Good Times Roll: Mobile, Mother of Mystics* (n.p.: self-published, 1991); William J. Lovett, Charles W. Porter, and Jean Tolbert, *Mardi Gras in Mobile: A Chronicle of Black Participation* (Mobile: Mobile Area Mardi Gras Association, 1980); L. Craig Roberts, *Mardi Gras in Mobile* (Charleston, SC: History Press, 2015); Ann J. Pond, *Cain: The Man, The Myth, and America's First Mardi Gras* (n.p.: self-published, 2015); Ann J. Pond, *Cowbellion: The Antebellum Gulf Coast and the Birth of America's Mardi Gras* (n.p.: self-published, Lulu.com, 2015); Bennett Wayne Dean Sr., *Have a Good Time but Don't Get Bad!* (Mobile: Joe Cain Marching Society, 2019).

10. A new body of work has challenged that assumption. For instance, by looking at the role of performance in the identity negotiation and disturbance of gender, sexuality, and racial norms, Zandria F. Robinson and E. Patrick Johnson have shown that southern identity is not exclusively white and/or heterosexual. Zandria F. Robinson, *This Ain't Chicago: Race, Class, and Regional Identity in the Post-Soul South* (Chapel Hill: University of North Carolina Press, 2014); and E. Patrick Johnson, *Sweet Tea*, and *Black. Queer. Southern. Women: An Oral History* (Chapel Hill: University of North Carolina Press, 2018). Also on southern queer experiences: James T. Sears, *Lonely Hunters: An Oral History of Lesbian and Gay Southern Life, 1948–1968* (Boulder: Westview Press, 1997), Daneel Buring, *Lesbian and Gay Memphis: Building Community behind the Magnolia Curtain* (New York: Garland, 1997); John Howard, ed., *Carrying On in the Lesbian and Gay South* (New York: New

York University Press, 1997); James T. Sears, *Rebels, Rubyfruit and Rhinestones: Queering Space in the Stonewall South* (New Brunswick, NJ: Rutgers University Press, 2001); John Howard, *Men like That: A Southern Queer History* (Chicago: University of Chicago Press, 1999); Brock Thomson, *The Un-Natural State: Arkansas and the Queer South* (Fayetteville: University of Arkansas Press, 2010); Carlos L. Dews and Carolyn Leste Law, eds., *Out in the South* (Philadelphia: Temple University Press, 2001); Watkins, *Queering the Redneck Riviera*; Howard Philips Smith and Henri Schindler, *Unveiling the Muse: The Lost History of Gay Carnival in New Orleans* (Jackson: University Press of Mississippi, 2017); Julio Capó, *Welcome to Fairyland: Queer Miami before 1940* (Chapel Hill: University of North Carolina Press, 2017); Jaime Harker, *The Lesbian South: Southern Feminists, the Women in Print Movement, and the Queer Literary Canon* (Chapel Hill: University of North Carolina Press, 2018); Gregory Samantha Rosenthal, *Living Queer History: Remembrance and Belonging in a Southern City* (Chapel Hill: University of North Carolina Press, 2021).

11. Early works that established the base for carnival studies include: Roger Caillois, *L'homme et le sacré* (Paris: Presses universitaires de France, 1939); Natalie Zemon Davis, *Society and culture in early modern France* (Stanford: Stanford University Press, 1965); Emmanuel Le Roy Ladurie, *Carnival in Romans* (New York: Braziliar, 1979); Peter Burke, *Popular Culture in Early Modern Europe* (New York: Harper & Row, 1978); Mikhail Bakhtin, *Rabelais and His World* (Bloomington: Indiana University Press, 1984). See also Thomas Sebeok, ed., *Carnival! Approaches to Semiotics* (Berlin: Mouton, 1984); Kinser, *Carnival, American Style*; David K. Danow, *The Spirit of Carnival: Magical Realism and the Grotesque* (Lexington: University Press of Kentucky, 1995); and Aurelie Godet, "Behind the Masks," *Journal of Festive Studies* 2 (2020): 13.

12. See Thomas F. DeFrantz and Anita Gonzalez, eds., *Black Performance Theory* (Durham, NC: Duke University Press, 2014); E. Patrick Johnson, *Appropriating Blackness: Performance and the Politics of Authenticity* (Durham, NC: Duke University Press, 2003); Harvey Young, *Embodying Black Experience: Stillness, Critical Memory, and the Black Body* (Ann Arbor: University of Michigan Press, 2010); Nicole R. Fleetwood, *Troubling Vision: Performance, Visuality, and Blackness* (Chicago: University of Chicago Press, 2011); Michelle Ann Stephens, *Skin Acts: Race, Psychoanalysis, and the Black Male Performer* (Durham, NC: Duke University Press, 2014); Aimee Meredith Cox, *Shapeshifters: Black Girls and the Choreography of Citizenship* (Durham, NC: Duke University Press, 2015); Uri McMillan, *Embodied Avatars: Genealogies of Black Feminist Art and Performance* (New York: New York University Press, 2015).

13. Joseph Roach, *Cities of the Dead: Circum-Atlantic Performance* (New York: Columbia University Press, 1996), 3.

14. See Rayford, *Chasin' the Devil*; Dean, *Mardi Gras*; Hearin, *Let the Good Times Roll*; Emily Staples Hearin and Kathryn Taylor DeCelle, *Queens of Mobile Mardi Gras, 1893–1986* (Mobile: Museum of the City of Mobile, 1986); Jay Higginbotham, *Old Mobile: Fort Louis De La Louisiane, 1702–1711* (Mobile: Museum of the City of Mobile, 1977), 108, fn60; Jay Higginbotham, *Mobile: City by the Bay* (Mobile: Mobile Junior Chamber of Commerce, 1999), 184..

15. Mobile Museum of Art, "The Art and Design of Mardi Gras." http://www.mobilemuseumofart.com/exhibitions/art-design-mardi-gras.

16. Visit Mobile, "Born to Celebrate," YouTube video, 1:31 minutes, November 18, 2015, https://www.youtube.com/watch?v=IohsMHfMZqw; Ken Robinson, "Selling Mobile, 'Born to Celebrate,'" *Lagniappe Weekly*, May 18, 2016, https://lagniappemobile.com/selling-mobile-born-celebrate/.

17. Fred Góes, "Reinventando o Carnaval nas Américas," in *Teorias y formas de analisis de las relaciones entre globalidad y localidad en America Latina (1982-2005)*, ed. Ellen Spielmann (Berlim: Wissenschaftlicher Verlag Berlin, 2007). See also Fred Góes, "Apresentação: Pensando o Carnaval na Academia," *Terceira margem*, Rio de Janeiro, no. 14 (January–June 2006). For more on the diversity of the Pan-American Carnival, see Paulo Miguez, "Muitos (Outros) Carnavais," *Revista Observatório Itaú Cultural*, no. 14 (May 2013).

18. Linda Waugh, "Marked and Unmarked: A Choice between Unequals in Semiotic Structure," *Semiotica* 38 (1982): 299; Deborah Tannen, "Marked Women, Unmarked Men," *New York Times Magazine*, June 20, 1993. The concept was originally articulated in the 1930s by Roman Jakobson and Nikolaj Trubetzkoy, but has been applied to different areas of linguistics, most notably semiotics, and is often divided into two main currents: Noam Chomsky's generative grammar and Roman Jakobson's structural linguistics. See Noam Chomsky and Morris Halle, *The Sound Pattern of English* (New York: Harper & Row, 1968); and Roman Jakobson, "The Structure of the Russian Verb" (1932), in *Russian and Slavic Grammar: Studies 1931–1981*, ed. Linda R. Waugh, Morris Malle, and Roman Jakobson (Berlin: Mouton, 1984). See also Jacques Derrida, *On Grammatology* (Baltimore: Johns Hopkins University Press, 1976). A diverse range of fields such as music, arts, anthropology, and sociology has also appropriated it. Sociologist Claude Lévi-Stauss, for instance, used it in his famous analysis of cultural systems. Claude Lévi-Strauss, *Le cru et le cuit* (Paris: Pilon, 1964).

19. Martin Haspelmath argues that the use of the term/concept has lost its usefulness in linguistics since it has been used in too many different contexts to signify different ideas. Martin Haspelmath, "Against markedness (and what to replace it with)," *Journal of Linguistics* 42, no. 1 (2006): 25–70.

20. Linda Waugh applied the concept to hierarchic binary structures such as male/female, white/Black, heterosexual/homosexual, abled/disabled, etc. Waugh also points out that this process is subject to sociocultural developments, as the opposition to certain issues may change over time. Edwin L. Battistella demonstrated how markedness aids in the creation of symbolic systems. Waugh, "Marked and Unmarked," and Edwin L. Battistella, *The Logic of Markedness* (New York: Oxford University Press, 1996). French feminist Hélène Cixous noted the gendered and hierarchical character of binary oppositions and, as Deborah Tannen notes, suffixes "like ess and ette mark words as 'female.' Unfortunately, they also tend to mark them for frivolousness." See Hélène Cixous, "Sorties," trans. Ann Liddle, in *Modern Criticism and Theory: A Reader*, ed. David Lodge (London: Longman, 1988): 287–93.

21. Interview with Grada Kilomba in Djamila Ribeiro, *Quem tem medo do feminismo negro?* (São Paulo: Companhia das Letras, 2018), 111. Author translation.

22. As Chris Shilling notes, "the oppositions and differences inscribed in classificatory systems can *materially shape* our bodies in ways which contribute toward social inequalities." Hence, the body is not only the space in which we negotiate our identities, it is also where difference is constructed and experienced. Chris Shilling, "The Body and Difference," in *Identity and Difference*, ed. Kathryn Woodward (London: Sage, 1997), 65.

23. See Henrietta Moore, "Divided We Stand": Sex, Gender, and Sexual Difference," *Feminist Review* 47 (1994): 78–95.

24. Reference to Joan W. Scott, "Gender: A Useful Category of Historical Analysis," *American Historical Review* 91, no. 5 (1986): 1053–75.

25. Aside from the aforementioned books on Mobile's Mardi Gras, see Hearin and DeCelle, *Queens of Mobile Mardi Gras*.

26. Karen L. Cox investigates the role of southern women (more specifically, the United Daughters of the Confederacy) in preserving Confederate culture and promoting Lost

Cause ideology. Cox uses the term "Confederate culture" "to describe those ideas and symbols that Lost Cause devotees associated with the former Confederacy" and argues that those "ideas and symbols are based on a hierarchy of race and class and often reflect the patrician outlook of Lost Cause leaders." See Karen L. Cox, *Dixie's Daughters: The United Daughters of the Confederacy and the Preservation of Confederate Culture* (Gainesville: University Press of Florida, 2004), 1.

27. Katerina Sergidou, "'Living like Queens," *Journal of Festive Studies* 2 (2020): 153–78. White women's Mardi Gras organizations are often referred to just as "women's groups," exemplifying what feminists of color have criticized as the universalization of white women's experiences. As Kimberlé Crenshaw asked, "How can the claims that 'women are,' 'women believe' and 'women need' be made when such claims are inapplicable or unresponsive to the needs, interests and experiences of Black women?" Kimberlé Crenshaw, "Demarginalizing the Intersection of Race and Sex: A Black Feminist Critique of Antidiscrimination Doctrine, Feminist Theory and Antiracist Politics," *University of Chicago Legal Forum* 1989, no. 1 (1989): 139–67.

28. Here I am borrowing from Henry Louis Gates, *The Signifying Monkey: A Theory of Afro-American Literary Criticism* (New York: Oxford University Press, 1988). The idea of repetition and difference comes from Henry Louis Gates, "The "Blackness of Blackness": A Critique of the Sign and the Signifying Monkey," *Critical Inquiry* 9, no. 4 (June 1983): 696.

29. Korbena Mercer, *Welcome to the Jungle: New Positions in Black Cultural Studies* (New York: Routledge, 1994), 63.

30. Eric Hobsbawm, "Introduction: Inventing Traditions," in *The Invention of Tradition*, ed. Eric Hobsbawm and Terence Ranger (Cambridge: Cambridge University Press, 1983), 1.

31. See David Cannadine, "The Context, Performance and Meaning of Ritual: The British Monarchy and the 'Invention of Tradition,' c. 1820–1977," in *The Invention of Tradition*, ed. Hobsbawm and Ranger.

32. See Emily Ruth Allen and Isabel Machado, "Mobile, Alabama's Joe Cain Procession: A Confederate Memorial or The People's Parade?" *Journal of Festive Studies* 3 (2021): 92–120.

33. Maria Isaura Pereira de Queiroz, *Carnaval brasileiro: O vivido e o mito* (São Paulo: Brasiliense, 1992).

34. It should be noted that there was an important shift in the scholarship in the 1970s, as scholars like Emmanuel Le Roy Ladurie began to be concerned less with the origins and essence of carnival than with socioeconomic configuration of its participants. See Ladurie, *Carnival in Romans* (New York: G. Braziller, 1979).

35. The sociohistorical approach, which emerged in the late 1970s and has one of its seminal works in Jacques Heers's *Fêtes des fous et carnavals* (1983), reveals the ways in which society and Carnival are intertwined. Jacques Heers, *Fêtes des fous et carnavals* (Paris: Hachette Littératures, 2007).

36. For more on Brazilian Carnival, see Queiroz, *Carnaval brasileiro*; Felipe Ferreira, "O triunfal passeio do 'Congreso das Sumidades Carnavalescas' e a Fundação do Carnaval Moderno no Brasil," *Terceira margem* (Rio de Janeiro), no. 14 (January–June 2006); Maria Clementina Pereira Cunha, *Ecos da folia: Uma história social do carnaval carioca entre 1880 e 1920* (São Paulo: Companhia das Letras, 2001); Fred Góes, "Reinventando o carnaval nas Américas," in *Teorias y formas de analisis de las relaciones entre globalidad y localidad en America Latina (1982–2005)*, ed. Ellen Spielmann (Berlin: Wissenschaftlicher Verlag Berlin, 2007); Fred Góes, "Apresentação: Pensando o carnaval na academia," *Terceira margem* (Rio de Janeiro), no. 14 (January–June 2006); Gilberto Freyre and Mário Souto Maior, "Carnaval: De onde veio? Como era? Como evoluiu?" *História* no. 9 (February 1974): 81–91; Roberto DaMatta, *Carnivals, Rogues and Heroes:*

An Interpretation of the Brazilian Dilemma (Notre Dame: University of Notre Dame Press, 1991); Fabiano Gontijo, *O Rei Momo e o Arco-Íris: Homossexualidade e Carnaval no Rio de Janeiro* (Rio de Janeiro: Garamond Universitária, 2009); Eneida de Morais, *História do carnaval carioca* (Rio de Janeiro: Editora Civilização Brasileira, 1958).

37. These two narrators repeated the same expression in different interviews, without knowing of the other's comments. Interview with Juanita Richardson and Palmer Richardson, recorded by Isabel Machado in Mobile, Alabama, January 27, 2016. Interview with Bobby Dennison and Linda Dennison, recorded by Isabel Machado, Mobile, Alabama, February 12, 2016. MGSCOH collection.

38. An 1845 ordinance prohibited people of color (enslaved or freed) from holding balls and public events. Alderman document 1845: City of Mobile Aldermen's books. CMMA, Book # 1843–47. Ten years after the *Lawrence vs. Texas* decision, people could still be arrested for consensual same-sex relations in the state. In *Williams vs. Alabama* (2013), the Alabama Court of Criminal Appeals finally recognized the unconstitutionality of the "state's ban on consensual oral and anal sex, aimed at criminalizing homosexual conduct." Brian Lawson, "Gay Sex Ban Struck Down by Alabama Appeals Court," AL.com, June 13, 2014, http://www.al.com/news/index.ssf/2014/06/gay_sex_ban_struck_down_by_ala.html.

39. Alessandra Lorini investigates how African American New Yorkers appropriated and reinvented public rituals, which the author connects with respectability politics, noting the "concern for public behavior reflects the need among educated African Americans to defeat the racist stereotype of the notoriously unruly behavior of black people, in which the guilt of one single individual of their race was indiscriminately extended to all blacks." Lorini looks at the relation between mutual aid groups and other social organizations, such as Masonic Lodges, which were approved by whites as a means to curtail more radical dissent. This process can be compared to the relationship between white elites and early "Colored" Mardi Gras. Alessandra Lorini, "Public Rituals and the Culture Making of the New York African American Community," in *Feasts and Celebrations in North American Ethnic Communities*, ed. Gutiérrez and Fabre. See also Remco van Capelleveen, "West Indian Carnival in Brooklyn," in the same anthology. Historian Daneel Buring notes a similar process with gay and lesbian Memphians. Buring, *Lesbian and Gay Memphis*.

40. In *Lords of Misrule*, James Gill talks about the white supremacist roots of New Orleans Mardi Gras krewes and how social clubs served as a means to circumvent desegregation laws. Gill opens and closes *Lords of Misrule* in the present (1990s) with a participatory observation of the efforts to desegregate Mardi Gras krewes (along with luncheon and other social clubs) based on the notion that membership in them "conferred business opportunities that were being unfairly denied to blacks." The freedom of association defense is used by New Orleaneans to oppose Mardi Gras desegregation. That same argument has also been used in Mobile to keep people in "their place." Gill, *Lords of Misrule*, 20.

41. See Jack Santino, "From Carnivalesque to Ritualesque: Public Ritual and the Theater of the Street," in *Public Performances: Studies in the Carnivalesque and Ritualesque*, ed. Jack Santino (Logan: Utah State University Press, 2017), 3–15.

Chapter 1: Official Narratives, Origin Myths, and Tradition Invention

1. *Sweet Home Alabama* Facebook Page, "Mobile's Mardi Gras in Times Square," Facebook post, uploaded June 15, 2017, https://www.facebook.com/AlabamaTravel/videos/vb.85442653844/10154833390873845/?type=2&theater.

2. John Sharp, "Alabama Trolls New Orleans with Billboards: 'You Are 114 miles from America's Original Mardi Gras,'" AL.com, February 5, 2018, https://www.al.com/news/mobile/index.ssf/2018/01/alabama_trolls_new_orleans_wit.html.

3. Michelle Matthews, "Mobile's New Mardi Gras Flag Symbolizes the Birthplace of Carnival," AL.com, January 15, 2018, https://www.al.com/living/index.ssf/2018/01/mobiles_new_mardi_gras_flag_sy.html.

4. Mobtown Merch, accessed November 29, 2021, https://mobtownmerch.com/products/official-mobile-mardi-gras-flag-3×5. They also sell "We Started It" Mardi Gras cups.

5. https://omg1703.com/.

6. See Emily Ruth Allen and Isabel Machado, "Mobile, Alabama's Joe Cain Procession: A Confederate Memorial or The People's Parade?," *Journal of Festive Studies* 3, no. 1 (2021): 92–120.

7. See, for instance, Louis de Vendel Chaudron, *Mobile Mystics and the Story of Mardi Gras Societies* (Mobile: Bienville Historical Society, 1910); Erwin Craighead, *Mobile: Fact and Tradition, Noteworthy People and Events* (Mobile: Powers Printing, 1930); and François Ludgére Diard, *The Tree: Being the Strange Case of Charles R. S. Boyington* (Mobile: Gill Printing, 1949).

8. Rayford, *Chasin' the Devil*, 15.

9. Jay Higginbotham, *Old Mobile: Fort Louis De La Louisiane, 1702–1711* (Mobile: Museum of the City of Mobile, 1977), 108.

10. Roberts, *Mardi Gras in Mobile*, 15 and 23.

11. Kinser argues that Gulf Coast Mardi Gras is not a French tradition, by identifying five elements that created US Carnival: "white plantation society's winter festivities, black society's need to adapt African customs in order to preserve them, the Gulf Coast's proximity to and influence by Caribbean festivities, its similar influence by the festive practices of Anglo-Americans migrating westward, and, cutting across all these factors, the Spanish and then American commercialization of leisure time." Yet it seems that only the "white plantation" and Anglo-American migration factors made it into the accounts of Mobile's Mardi Gras history. Kinser, *Carnival, American Style*, 21.

12. Higginbotham, *Mobile*, 187.

13. Higginbotham, *Mobile*, 187.

14. Rayford, *Chasin' the Devil*, 48.

15. James Gill notes in his investigation of New Orleans Mardi Gras krewes that by the mid-nineteenth century, New Orleans newspapers complained that ordinary folks' celebrations bothered the city's elites. Gill also shows how Comus (and other krewes/mystic societies) appropriated Creole masked balls, transforming them into an "emblem for an emerging elite determined to keep the rest of the population at once removed" while separating the new Carnival from the old celebrations "when street maskers were a motley of revelers more or less out of control." Gill, *Lords of Misrule*, 39, 46.

16. Steve Joynt, "How It All Started," in *The Art and Design of Mardi Gras*, by David Ernest Alsobrook, Judi Gulledge, Deborah Velders, Steve Joynt, Cartledge Weeden Blackwell III, Scotty E. Kirkland, and Karyn Zweifel (Mobile: Mobile Museum of Art, 2014), 12.

17. "Mobile Challenges New Orleans Claim: Alabama Does Not Concede Louisiana First Mardi Gras Fete," unidentified newspaper clipping, February 3, 1939, JFRL Mardi Gras Clippings: 1935–1939.

18. Pond, *Cowbellion*, 7.

19. Pond, *Cowbellion*, 8, 11.

20. Pond, *Cowbellion*, 111. In *Mardi Gras in Mobile*, L. Craig Roberts lists "sixty-two ball-only mystic societies formed between 1900 and the First World War." One of the

organizations listed for the year of 1906 was named KKK. It is unclear what the letters stood for, and the author does not provide any context for the information, but it is unlikely that the organization was not aware of the associations evoked by the acronym. Roberts, *Mardi Gras in Mobile*, 50.

21. Gill, *Lords of Misrule*, 86.
22. Pond, "Ritualized Construction," 1, 5.
23. Rayford, *Chasin' the Devil*, 63.
24. Rayford, *Chasin' the Devil*, 65.
25. Higginbotham, *Mobile*, 185. Kinser clearly articulates the connection between Mardi Gras and the Confederacy. See Kinser, *Carnival, American Style*.
26. Rayford, *Chasin' the Devil*, 72–73.
27. Higginbotham, *Mobile*, 188.
28. *Mobile Mask*'s Steve Joynt cites a document penned by Cain himself wherein he describes being in New Orleans during Mardi Gras and deciding that when he returned, "Mobile should have its own celebration." Joynt, "Changing His Story," 30. See also Dean, *Have a Good Time*.
29. Joynt, "How It All Started," 13. This is not to say that the alleged redface performance would not have been problematic as well. Elsewhere, musicologist Emily Ruth Allen and I unpacked the Confederate nostalgia and damaging parading indigeneity in Mobile's Mardi Gras pageantry analyzing specifically the Joe Cain celebrations. See Allen and Machado, "Mobile, Alabama's Joe Cain Day Procession."
30. Gill, *Lords of Misrule*, 58.
31. Kinser, *Carnival, American Style*, 99.
32. Gill, *Lords of Misrule*, 128.
33. Rayford, *Chasin' the Devil*, 51. See also Marler, *Merchants' Capital*.
34. As Kinser puts it, they "were ready to undo the pretensions of would-be aristocrats, but they also played their part in keeping black people in their place." Kinser, *Carnival, American Style*, 111.
35. See Hazel Carby, *Race Men* (Cambridge: Harvard University Press, 2001).
36. Rayford, *Chasin' the Devil*, 17.
37. Julian Lee Rayford, "Letter to Mobile Mayor Cecil F. Bates," CMMA, RG6, S10/B8, File 1310: Mardi Gras, 1916–1930. October 18, 1935.
38. Rayford, "Letter to Mobile Mayor."
39. Musicologist Emily Ruth Allen has analyzed the Confederate symbolism and manifestation of white supremacy in Joe Cain's procession pageantry, discussing "the racism of Joe Cain's sonic resonances." Emily Ruth Allen, "Parades in the Port City: Programming in Mobile, Alabama's Carnival," paper presented at the Society for Ethnomusicology's 65th Annual Meeting, October 30, 2020. See also Allen and Machado, "Mobile, Alabama's Joe Cain Day Procession."
40. Andrew Snyder, "'Carnaval em casa': Activist Inversions in Rio de Janeiro's Street Carnival during the COVID-19 Pandemic," *Journal of Festive Studies* 3 (2021): 17–46. See also Thomas Turino, *Music as Social Life: The Politics of Participation* (Chicago: University of Chicago Press, 2008).
41. Pierre Nora, "Between Memory and History."
42. Allen and Machado, "Mobile, Alabama's Joe Cain Procession," 109.

Chapter 2: Regulating, Controlling, and Sanctioning Revelry

1. Letter from Chairman of Deacons S.S. Cooksey and Pastor M. P. Harrisson (First Baptist Church of Mobile) to Mayor Lambert Mims, March 6, 1978, CMMA, RG6, S.24, B3. Cemeteries—Mobile Mardi Gras-Joe Cain Celebrations, 1978–1981.
2. Aurelie Godet, "Behind the Masks," *Journal of Festive Studies* 2 (2020): 13.
3. Santino, "From Carnivalesque to Ritualesque," 12.
4. Santino, "From Carnivalesque to Ritualesque," 4.
5. Santino, "From Carnivalesque to Ritualesque," 4.
6. See Jose Esteban Muñoz, *Disidentifications: Queers of Color and the Performance of Politics* (Minneapolis: University of Minnesota Press, 2015).
7. "Collection of the Ordinances Now in Force in the City of Mobile and Also the Various Acts of the Legislature Incorporating Said City," Mobile: The Office of Mercantile Advertiser, 1835, 33. Oliver N. Greene Jr. shows that already in 1781 New Orleans, the attorney general was recommending the prohibition of "all kinds of masking, the wearing of feathers, gathering at the local taverns and dancing by" Black people during the Carnival season. Oliver N. Greene, "The Aesthetic of Asé in the Black Masking Indians of New Orleans: Musical Africanisms and Orisa Manifestations in the Big Chief," *Fire!!!* 6, no. 2 (2020): 81. Keeping a "disorderly house" was the allegation for falsely convicting William Dorsey Swann in 1896. Often referred to as the "first drag queen," Swann was a formerly enslaved Black man who organized drag balls in Washington, DC. See Channing Gerard Joseph, "The First Drag Queen Was a Former Slave Who Fought for Queer Freedom a Century before Stonewall, *The Nation*, January 31, 2020, https://www.thenation.com/article/society/drag-queen-slave-ball/. Joseph is in the process of publishing a monograph about Swann entitled *House of Swann: Where Slaves Became Queen*.
8. Yet the document also reveals that downtown Mobile had a designated vice district where "houses of ill fame" were allowed to function in an attempt to contain deviant behavior and illicit pleasures. The area was located on "both sides of St. Michael westwardly from Lawrence to west side of Warren street, both sides of Cedar and Warren streets to north side of St. Louis street, and both sides of St. Louis from Cedar to Warren street." "The Charter and the Code of Ordinances of The City of Mobile." Mobile, AL: George Matzinger Printer, 1889. 51, 52, 119, 126 and 127, and 122.
9. *The Charter and the Code of Ordinances of the City of Mobile with Appendix*, 246, 247.
10. *The Commission Government Charter and the Code of Ordinances of the City of Mobile, Alabama*, prepared by Shelton H. Hendrix (Mobile: Authority of the Board of Commissioners of the City of Mobile, Alabama, 1934), 75.
11. *Code of Ordinances of the City of Mobile* (1934), 158.
12. *The Code of the City of Mobile, Alabama, 1955: The General Ordinances of the City. 1959 Supplement*, Fred G. Collins, City Attorney (Charlottesville, VA: Michie City Publications), 1960, 49.
13. John S. Sledge directly connects the prohibition of drumming, as well as other cultural expressions of Africans and Afro-descendants in colonial Mobile, to white fears, noting: "Nothing was more agitating to white town folk than the sight of a throng of black persons animated by a drum or more chilling to isolated and outnumbered plantation owners than the haunting, muffled sound of African beats in the humid night air. What if escaped slaves, living as maroons deep in the swamps, were able to call upon their brethren and convince them to rise up and kill their masters?" John S. Sledge, *The Mobile River* (Columbia:

University of South Carolina Press, 2015), 56. Katrina Dyonne Thompson associates the "outlawing of drums in many islands throughout the West Indies and areas of the New World" to "their role in communication and rebellion." Katrina Dyonne Thompson, *Ring Shout: The Racial Politics of Music and Dance in North American Slavery* (Urbana: University of Illinois Press, 2014), 68. On how the lack of access to drumming affected the development of the rituals and cultural practices of enslaved Africans and African Americans in the United States, see Sterling Stuckey, *Slave Culture: Nationalist Theory and the Foundations of Black America* (New York: Oxford University Press, 2014). For a look at the persecution of African and Afro-Brazilian religious and cultural practices, see João José Reis, *Divining Slavery and Freedom: The Story of Domingos Sodré, an African Priest in Nineteenth-Century Brazil* (New York: Cambridge University Press, 2015). See also Vincent Brown, *The Reaper's Garden: Death and Power in the World of Atlantic Slavery* (Cambridge: Harvard University Press, 2008); Dena J. Epstein, *Sinful Tunes and Spirituals: Black Folk Music to the Civil War* (Urbana: University of Illinois Press, 2003); Eileen Southern, *The Music of Black Americans: A History* (New York: W. W. Norton, 2006).

14. Rayford, *Chasin' the Devil*, 16.
15. Roberts, *Mardi Gras in Mobile*, 49.
16. Kinser, *Carnival American Style*, 24.
17. Gill, *Lords of Misrule*, 35.
18. "Press Offers $20 for Best Masker," unidentified newspaper clipping, February 28, 1930, JFRL Mardi Gras Clippings: 1930–1935.
19. "Prize Winner," unidentified newspaper clipping, March 3, 1930, JFRL Mardi Gras Clippings: 1930–1935.
20. "Characterizations by Mobile Masker Are Feature of Mardi Gras Parades," *Mobile Press Register*, February 17, 1946, JFRL Mardi Gras Clippings: 1945–1949.
21. "Characterizations by Mobile Masker."
22. "Characterizations by Mobile Masker."
23. "Stiff Competition Seen for Mardi Gras Maskers," *Mobile Press*, February 6, 1948, JFRL Mardi Gras Clippings: 1945–1949.
24. "Louis Diemert, Perennial King of Maskers, Breaks Tradition by Announcing 1948 Character," February 9, 1948, JFRL Mardi Gras Clippings: 1945–1949.
25. Libertee Belle, "Under the Bar Stool," *Alabama Forum* (March 1992), 14.
26. Interview with King Lawrence XV, recorded by Isabel Machado in Mobile, Alabama, on January 28, 2016, MGSCOH collection.
27. "Costume Wearers Encouraged by Mardi Gras Group," *Mobile Press Register*, 17 February 1953, JFRL Mardi Gras Clippings: 1950–1955.
28. See Allen and Machado, "Mobile, Alabama's Joe Cain Day Procession" for an analysis of those performances and their consequences. See also Katrin Sieg, *Ethnic Drag: Performing Race, Nation, Sexuality in West Germany* (Ann Arbor: University of Michigan Press, 2009).
29. *Mobile Press Register*, February 19, 1947, p. 6B, cols. 7–8, JFRL Mardi Gras Clippings: 1940–1949.
30. For more on the concept of ritualistic play and how it applies to Black Mobilians' celebrations, see Kern Jackson, "Going to the Boomalatta: Narrating Black Mardi Gras in Mobile, Alabama," *Tributaries*, no. 7 (2004), 38.
31. Letter from Margaret Arnold Schwartz to the *Mobile Press* editor, February 7, 1977, CMMA, RG6, S.24, B3, Mobile Mardi Gras 1977.

32. Letters to city commissioners about Joe Cain Day Celebration, CMMA, RG6, S.24, B3, Mobile Mardi Gras 1977.

33. Letters were sent to Alfred A. Atchinson, Julian Lee Rayford, Danny Treanor (WALA-TV Channel 10), retired police chief Ed. J. McLean, Jeff C. Mims Jr., Jimmie McWhorter, Martin Johnson (director of Social Security services), James B. "Red" Foster (fire inspector); George M. Callahan (data processing manager); Wayne Dean (community relations coordinator), CMMA, RG6, S.24, B3, Mobile Mardi Gras 1977.

34. From 1911 to 1985, a three-member city commission governed Mobile. The Commissioners took terms holding office of Mayor, and also received the title of President of the Commission.

35. Letter from Dr. Robert O. Harris III to Commissioner Lambert Mims, March 19, 1977, CMMA, RG6, S.24, B3, Mobile Mardi Gras 1977.

36. James B. Foster, "Travel On," Letters to the Editor, unidentified newspaper clipping, March 23, 1977, CMMA, RG6, S.24, B3, Mobile Mardi Gras 1977.

37. Report written by Julian Lee Rayford, Jimmy McWhorter, Wayne Dean, and James B. "Red" Foster, addressed to Chief Ed. J. McLean, chair of the Mardi Gras Special Events Committee and Members, July 1, 1977, CMMA, RG6, S.24, B3, Mobile Mardi Gras 1977.

38. Mardi Gras Committee Interim Report, July 11, 1977, CMMA, RG6, S.24, B3, Committees. In August they delivered another report to the Mobile City Commission, recommending the establishment of a permanent Events Committee that would generate "public interest and participation in Mobile's annual festival." Letter from Ed. J. McLean to Mobile's City Commissioners, October 21, 1977, CMMA, RG6, S.24, B3, Mobile Mardi Gras 1977.

39. "Delegation," Minutes of the meeting between members of the Mardi Gras Special Events Committee and the city's board of commissioners, held on August 18, 1977, CMMA, RG6, S.24, B3, Committees.

40. Letter from Sidney J. Gerhardt from Gerhardt Investment Group Mortgage Bankers to Mayor Lambert Mims, February 11, 1978, CMMA, RG6, S.24, B3, Joe Cain Celebration.

41. Letter and statement from D. H. W. Eddins to Commissioner Doyle, February 14, 1978, CMMA, RG6, S.24, B3, Joe Cain Celebration.

42. "Another Attack Leveled at Joe Cain Procession," untitled newspaper clipping, February 15, 1978, and "Minutes of Meeting of November 21, 1978, CMMA RG6, S.24, B3, Joe Cain Celebration.

43. Letter from Mrs. A. C. Redmond to The City Commissioners of Mobile, February 16, 1978, CMMA RG6, S.24, B3, Joe Cain Celebration.

44. Letter from the Mobile Historical Development Commission to the Mobile Board of City Commissioners, signed by Executive Director David L. Brown and President A. Meaher III, February 24, 1978, CMMA, RG6, S.24, B3, Joe Cain Celebration.

45. Letter and petition sent by Mary Louise (last name illegible) to Mayor Lambert Mims, February 28, 1978; "Petition against Joe Cain Celebration in Church Street Cemetery," CMMA, RG6, S. 24, B3, Joe Cain Celebration.

46. Statement Read by Brother Bill Whitfield, 04, 18, 1978, CMMA, RG6, S.24, B3, Mobile Mardi Gras Committee.

47. Letter from the advisory committee of the Society for the Restoration and Beautification of the Church Street Graveyard to Martin Johnson, January 25, 1979, CMMA RG6, S.24, B3, Mobile Mardi Gras—Joe Cain Celebration.

48. The Society for the Restoration and Beautification of the Church Street Graveyard, "Cain to Greet Bienville, L'Anglois," CMMA RG6, S.24, B3, Mobile Mardi Gras—Joe Cain Celebration.
49. "Cain to Greet Bienville, L'Anglois."
50. "No Graveyard Groovin' This Year," unidentified newspaper clipping, January 10, 1979, CMMA, RG6, S.24, B3, Joe Cain Celebration.
51. Letter from Pastor Charles W. Avery to city commissioners, May 7, 1979, CMMA, RG6, S.24, B3, Joe Cain Celebration.
52. Photograph of J. B. "Red" Foster, Governor George C. Wallace, and Bennet Wayne Dean Sr. holding the honorary plaque, September 12, 1978, CMMA, Mobile Mardi Gras Committees Folder: 1968–1981, RG6, S24, B3.
53. Visit Mobile, "Mobile Mardi Gras Fun Facts," May 11, 2021, https://www.mobile.org/blog/post/mobile-mardi-gras-fun-facts/?fbclid=IwAR1a8j6Z1GKLHUnbI15gTNnX4oIm5ezzonKUGFBf_QkZ1rLNMUYRVvHHKjo.

Chapter 3: Downtown

1. *This Is Mobile*, produced by Alex Kiker, posted October 29, 2017, https://www.youtube.com/watch?time_continue=172&v=2A4VKSfdPq4.
2. Alison Isenberg, *Downtown America: A History of the Place and the People Who Made It* (Chicago: University of Chicago Press, 2004), 5.
3. Isenberg, *Downtown America*, 6.
4. Ken Burns, *The War* (documentary series, PBS distribution, 2007).
5. Burns, *The War*, Episode 2: "When Things Get Tough."
6. Allen Cronenberg, "Mobile and World War II, 1940–1945," in *Mobile: The New History of Alabama's First City*, ed. Michael V. R. Thomason (Tuscaloosa: University of Alabama Press, 2012), 209. For more on the definition of Mobile as a "cotton city," see Amos, *Cotton City*.
7. The Alabama Drydock and Shipbuilding Company (ADDSCO) and Gulf Shipbuilding Company already existed in the WWI period but had "languished in the interwar era." Cronenberg, "Mobile and World War II," 214.
8. Cronenberg, "Mobile and World War II," 215; Kevern Verney, "'Every Man Should Try': John L. LeFlore and the National Association for the Advancement of Colored People in Alabama, 1919–1956," *Alabama Review* 66, no. 3 (July 2013): 195.
9. As Allen Cronenberg notes: "Mobile's black population grew from twenty-nine thousand in 1940 to forty-six thousand a decade later." Cronenberg, "Mobile and World War II," 215.
10. See Allan Bérubé, *Coming Out under Fire: The History of Gay Men and Women in World War Two* (New York: Free Press, 1990); Watkins, *Queering the Redneck Riviera*.
11. Burns, *The War*.
12. Seven thousand of the company's thirty thousand employees were African American, yet they were previously relegated to "low paid, unskilled labor." See Verney, "Every Man Should Try," 197; Melton McLaurin, "Mobile Blacks and World War II: The Development of a Political Consciousness," in Ted Carageorge, ed., *Gulf Coast Politics in the Twentieth Century* (Pensacola, FL: Historic Pensacola Preservation Board, 1973).

13. See Nahfiza Ahmed, "Race, Class and Citizenship: The Civil Rights Struggle in Mobile, Alabama, 1925–85" (PhD thesis, University of Leicester Department of Economic & Social History, 1999), 68; Verney, "Every Man Should Try."

14. City Planning Commission Mobile, Alabama, "Housing Market Analysis Mobile, Alabama: Part II Text and Charts" (August 1945), CMMA.

15. See Stuart Hall, Jessica Evans, and Sean Nixon, eds., *Representation: Cultural Representations and Signifying Practices* (Los Angeles: Sage, 2013).

16. Interview with Charles Torrey, recorded by Isabel Machado in Mobile, Alabama, August 12, 2014, MGSCOH collection. New Orleans experienced similar if not greater migration during this period. Hence, it is possible that the narrator's perception of the changes (or lack of changes) in the two cities is based not necessarily on the numbers of newcomers but rather in their society's attitudes toward them.

17. Interview with George Moore, recorded by Isabel Machado in Mobile, Alabama, February 10, 2016, MGSCOH collection.

18. Jack Bishop interview.

19. Letter from commissioner of public buildings Harry T. Hartwell to New Orleans mayor Robert S. Maestri, December 10, 1941, CMMA, RG6, S10, B8, File 1310, Mardi Gras 1931–1949.

20. Letter from New Orleans mayor Robert S. Maestri to commissioner of public buildings Harry T. Hartwell, December 13, 1941, CMMA, RG6, S10, B8, File 1310, Mardi Gras 1931–1949.

21. Letter from Mobile acting mayor Robin C. Herndon to Emperor Felix III, February 4, 1946, CMMA, RG6, S10, B8, File 1310, Mardi Gras 1931–1949.

22. Harvey H. Jackson III, "Mobile since 1945," in *Mobile: The New History of Alabama's First City. Tuscaloosa: University of Alabama Press, 2012*, ed. Michael V.R. Thomason (Tuscaloosa: University of Alabama Press, 2012), 277.

23. Jackson, "Mobile since 1945," 279.

24. "Confederate Band to Make Debut This Year in Mardi Gras Marches," *Mobile Register*, January 30, 1955, JFRL Mardi Gras Clippings: 1950–1955.

25. According to Isenberg, "The so-called Negro Main Street emerged when stores were pushed from their central downtown spots to fringe locations or to sites near black residential areas or institutions like colleges." Although it had some positive outcomes, this was not exactly a voluntary process. Isenberg, *Downtown America*, 113, 117.

26. Carter defined "Negro Main Street" as the "chief artery of business operated by and/or for" Black people, "formed as a group-oriented technique of urban adjustment," which assumed "its specific character under the impact of a continuously emphasized culturally permissive discrimination." Furthermore, to her, it was "an institution in American culture" that stood as "a symbol of . . . discrimination" and "a compensatory area of segregation." Wilmoth A. Carter. "Negro Main Street as a Symbol of Discrimination," *Phylon* 21, no. 3 (3rd qtr., 1960). See also Wilmoth Annette Carter, *The Urban Negro in the South* (New York: Vantage Press, 1961).

27. In the late 1980s, the street was finally renamed Dr. Martin Luther King, Jr. Avenue to correct the tragic irony of a street in an African American community named after Confederate president Jefferson Davis. To this day it is where all of Mobile's Black Mardi Gras parades start.

28. Paulette Davis-Horton, *Avenue . . . the Place, the People, the Memories, 1799–1986* (Mobile: Horton, 1991), 141, 143.

29. Linda and Bobby Dennison interview; Eric Finley interview; George Moore interview.

30. Eric Finley interview; Juanita and Palmer Richardson interview; Linda and Bobby Dennison interview.

31. See Jennifer Lynn Ritterhouse, *Growing Up Jim Crow: How Black and White Southern Children Learned Race* (Chapel Hill: University of North Carolina Press, 2006).

32. Kathie Hiers interview, recorded by Isabel Machado and Cari Searcy in Mobile, Alabama, on January 27, 2016; Suzanne Cleveland interview.

33. Juanita and Palmer Richardson interview.

34. Interview with Domingo Soto, recorded by Isabel Machado in Mobile, Alabama, on February 1, 2016, MGSCOH collection.

35. Isenberg, *Downtown America*, 212.

36. Jackson, "Mobile since 1945," 286. In 1962 downtown stores represented 40.3 percent of the sales in "shoppers-goods stores in Mobile County," down from 68.1 percent in 1948. Between 1958 and 1961, "downtown stores had a sharp $9,000,000 decline in sales," while "more than 741,000 square feet of new shoppers-goods store space was built outside of Downtown Mobile." See Hammer and Company Associates (for The Mobile City Planning Commission), "Downtown Mobile: An Analysis of Its Economic Potential," January 1963. CMMA, 37.

37. Jackson, "Mobile since 1945," 290. The theory (or gossip) in the city is that it was retaliation from President Lyndon B. Johnson for Mobile voting for the GOP candidate in the 1964 presidential elections. I also heard that it was because Mobilians did not reelect Congressman Boykin.

38. The study was conducted by the Southern Institute of Management based in Louisville, Kentucky, in conjunction with the American Institute of Management. The document explained: "Thirty percent of the jobs in the Mobile area are estimated to depend directly and indirectly upon the present employment level at Brookley Field alone." Hence, a drastic cut in Brookley jobs "would render a severe financial blow to the entire area. Businesses, churches, hospitals, schools, local governments, and individual citizens would suffer." The Southern Institute of Management, "The Mobile Metropolitan Area Audit, Preliminary Report No. 6: Armed Forces" (1960), CMMA, i–ii. A 1963 study also took notice of the "inherent instability in an economy that depends heavily upon substantial government employment." See Hammer and Company Associates (for The Mobile City Planning Commission), "Downtown Mobile: An Analysis of Its Economic Potential," January 1963, CMMA, 56.

39. The process of rehabilitation and redevelopment, which sought to identify Mobile's "blighted and deteriorated sections," had already been in place since the 1940s City Master Plan and was further developed in the Broad-Beauregard Redevelopment Project, which began in 1952. See The Mobile Urban Renewal Agency, "Church Street and Texas Street—a Downtown District and In-City Neighborhood: A General Neighborhood Renewal Plan" (1961), 1; and Mobile Housing Board, "Report on Urban Renewal Activities of Mobile Housing Board" (March 1968), 3. According to Jackson, "focusing its attention on the city's historic waterfront and older downtown residential neighborhoods, the board began clearing the land," destroying historic homes and buildings in its path. Jackson, "Mobile since 1945," 295.

40. Frederick Douglas Richardson, *The Genesis and Exodus of NOW* (Boynton Beach, FL: Futura Printing, 1996), 42.

41. "Ghost Town," paid advertisement by the Neighborhood Organized Workers, *Mobile Beacon*, May 31, 1969.

42. Richardson, *Genesis and Exodus of NOW*, 180, 181.
43. Davis-Horton, *Davis Avenue*, 222.
44. Malcolm Steiner and Michael P. Robinson, *Old Mobile Restaurants* (Mobile: Malcolm Steiner, 2009), 106.
45. A few years later, it moved to 155 Government.
46. George Chauncey Jr., "Christian Brotherhood or Sexual Perversion? Homosexual Identities and the Construction of Sexual Boundaries in the World War I Era," in *Hidden from History: Reclaiming the Gay and Lesbian Past*, ed. Martin Duberman, Martha Vinicius, and George Chauncey Jr., 294–317 (London: Penguin Books, 1991), 296.
47. Interview with Queen Richard IV, recorded by Isabel Machado in New Orleans on October 14, 2014.
48. King Lawrence XV interview; interview with Homer McClure, recorded by Isabel Machado in Mobile on January 26, 2016, MGSCOH collection.
49. Jack Bishop interview; Kathie Hiers interview; King Lawrence XV interview.
50. As Alison Isenberg notes, "those experiences and stories ranged from childhood adventures downtown to being denied service at lunch counters." Isenberg, *Downtown America*, 261.

Chapter 4: Official "Colored" Mardi Gras and Mobile's Black Liberation Struggle

1. Ricardo Woods, Mobile attorney, statement for the documentary *Mobile in Black and White*, directed by Robert Grey (U.S.A., 2014).
2. *The Order of Myths*, directed by Margaret Brown (Folly River Films, U.S.A., 2008).
3. See Kevin Kelly Gaines, *Uplifting the Race: Black Leadership, Politics, and Culture in the Twentieth Century* (Chapel Hill: University of North Carolina Press, 1996).
4. E. Frances White points out "the suppression of certain stories and the careful crafting of others" in the process of creating an African American counternarrative in reaction to racist discourses. White explains that although these narratives counteract "racist images of African Americans that circulate in hegemonic discourse," they can also suppress, police, and exclude certain experiences and stories by delineating the "boundaries of blackness." E. Frances White, *Dark Continent of Our Bodies: Black Feminism and the Politics of Respectability* (Philadelphia: Temple University Press, 2001), 5. See also Evelyn Higginbotham, "African-American Women's History and the Metalanguage of Race," *Signs* 17, no. 2 (1992): 251–74; Evelyn Brooks Higginbotham, *Righteous Discontent: The Women's Movement in the Black Baptist Church, 1880–1920* (Cambridge: Harvard University Press, 1994); and Hazel V. Carby, "Policing the Black Woman's Body in an Urban Context," *Critical Inquiry* 18, no. 4 (Summer 1992).
5. Roger D. Abrahams, "Conflict Displays in the Black Atlantic," in Santino, *Public Performances*, 53.
6. Miguel A. Valerio. "The Pardos' Triumph: The Use of Festival Material Culture for Socioracial Promotion in Eighteenth-Century Pernambuco," *Journal of Festive Studies* 3 (2021): 60–61. See also Valerio's investigation of festive Afro-Mexican kings in the sixteenth and seventeenth centuries: Miguel Valerio, *Sovereign Joy: Afro-Mexican Kings and Queens, 1539–1640* (Cambridge: Cambridge University Press, 2022).
7. Elijah Gaddis, "Processional Culture and Black Mobility in Maggie Washington's Wilmington," *Journal of Festive Studies* 3 (2021): 72–91.

8. "Mobile Carnival Museum History," http://www.mobilecarnivalmuseum.com/historical-timeline.

9. Rayford, *Chasin' the Devil*, 162.

10. Rayford, *Chasin' the Devil*, 163.

11. Rayford, *Chasin' the Devil*, 164.

12. I am borrowing here from Zandria F. Robinson's articulation of the idea of the North as a floating signifier in southern identity. Robinson, *This Ain't Chicago*, 192.

13. Lovett, Porter, and Tolbert, *Mardi Gras in Mobile*, 10.

14. The book consists mainly of the photos and names of all of the monarchs and their courts from 1940 to 1980. There are only eight short sections, no longer than a page each, with background information about Mobile, its Mardi Gras, Black Mardi Gras, and MAMGA's history more specifically. A couple of the sections are signed by Wayne Dean ("Mardi Gras and Economics" and "Float Building—An Unusual Occupation"), but it is unclear who wrote the sections mentioned here.

15. Davis-Horton, *Avenue*, 116. This was by no means an isolated incident. The Tuskegee Normal and Industrial Institute registered 116 lynchings in the state of Alabama from 1900 to 1920. The document, which opens by describing a lynching in Mobile from May 1835, mentions two cases of lynching in Prichard for the year of 1906. Richard Robinson and Henry Peters were lynched after being charged with rape. It is unclear if or how these are related with the ones described by Davis-Horton. In September 1907 Moses Dossett was also lynched after being charged of attempted rape in Prichard. In April 1908 Walter Clayton was lynched in Bay Minette after being charged with criminal assault. In January 1909 Dougla [sic], was lynched in Mobile after being charged with insulting a white woman. See the Tuskegee Normal and Industrial Institute, "Lynchings in Alabama," February 21, 1921, https://alabamamemory.as.ua.edu/source/lynching-in-alabama/.

16. Davis-Horton, *Avenue*, 116.

17. Davis-Horton, *Avenue*, 116.

18. Alderman document 1845, City of Mobile Aldermens Books, Book # 1843–47, CMMA.

19. "The O.O.D. Ball," February 1, 1894, *Mobile Daily Register*.

20. "The O.O.D.," February 3, 1894, *Mobile Daily Register*.

21. According to archivist Charles Torrey, while Banks was not identified as Creole in this document, he was identified as "mulatto" in the 1870 census for the Fourth Ward of the city of Mobile. To help this author, in November 2017 Charles Torrey created a document with all the information he could gather on the Order of Doves members. Charles Torrey, "Membership of the Order of Doves," November 2017. Document in the author's possession.

22. *George Matzenger's Mobile Directory for 1892*, vol. 27 (Mobile: George Matzenger Printer, 1892), 120, 335, 183, 150, 13, 229; and Torrey, "Membership."

23. The three Alabama militias composed of African American men were Birmingham's Magic City Guards, the Capital City Guards of Montgomery, and Mobile's Gilmer's Rifles, named after adjutant general James N. Gilmer. Beth Taylor Muskat, "Black Militias in Alabama," *Encyclopedia of Alabama*, March 7, 2007, last updated October 6, 2017, http://www.encyclopediaofalabama.org/article/h-1083. Beth Taylor Muskat notes that not many of these Black militias survived the turn of the twentieth century, crediting the success of Mobile's unit to Capt. Reuben Romulus Mims's "skills and diplomacy." Beth Taylor Muskat, "Mobile's Black Militia: Major R. R. Mims and Gilmer's Rifles," *Alabama Review* 57 (July 2004): 184. Mims had petitioned to start a "colored" militia in 1874, but his application was denied.

Creole cotton sampler William T. Foster applied again almost a decade later, and after an initial rejection, Adjutant General Gilmer accepted his petition.

24. Muskat, "Mobile's Black Militia," 192.

25. Ann Pond articulates the relationship between the white elite Mardi Gras organizations and the Freemasons. More study is needed to uncover if and how that was also the case for African American Mobilians. Pond, "Ritualized Construction."

26. Muskat, "Mobile's Black Militia," 186, 194, 185.

27. "Colored Mystics," *Mobile Daily Register*, February 24, 1897, JFRL Mardi Gras Clippings: 1890s. The same note also mentioned the K.O.I.'s first ball, which took place on March 1 at the hall of the Mill and Timber Laborers' Benevolent Association, providing further indication of the connection between early Black Mardi Gras and African American mutual aid societies. Unfortunately, the piece does not provide more information about that organization.

28. "The Order of Doves. Their Fourth Annual Ball a Grand Success," *Mobile Daily Register*, March 4, 1897, JFRL Mardi Gras Clippings: 1890s.

29. Davis-Horton, *Avenue*, 52.

30. Ahmed, "Race, Class and Citizenship," 51, 58.

31. Scotty Kirkland, "Community on Parade: The Mobile Area Mardi Gras Association's Diamond Anniversary," in *The Art and Design of Mardi Gras* by David Ernest Alsobrook, Judi Gulledge, Deborah Velders, Steve Joynt, Cartledge Weeden Blackwell III, Scotty E. Kirkland, and Karyn Zweifel (Mobile: Mobile Museum of Art, 2014), 35.

32. Shawn Bivens, *Mobile Alabama's People of Color: A Tricentennial History* (Victoria, BC: Trafford, 2004), 185, 194.

33. Kinser, *Carnival, American Style*, 272; Wayne Dean, *Mardi Gras: Mobile's Illogical Whoop-De-Doo* (Chicago: Adams Press, 1971), 103; Roberts, *Mardi Gras in Mobile*, 61. Emily Staples Hearin, *Let the Good Times Roll! Mobile, Mother of Mystics* (Mobile: E. S. Hearin & W. B. Taylor, 1996), 209.

34. See Jackson, "Going to the Boomalatta."

35. Dean, *Mardi Gras*, 103.

36. Davis-Horton, *Avenue*, 183.

37. "Best Parade in History Is Planned by Zulus," *Gulf Informer*, February 4, 1950.

38. "First Colored Mardi Gras Parade Scheduled Tuesday," and "King of Carnival Chosen," *Mobile Press and Register*, February 19, 1939.

39. The JFRL Mardi Gras Clippings sometimes contain notes about the identities of the people mentioned in the articles as well as the sources for that information. This clipping is from the 1935–1939 folder, and the document identifies the source for the information about Winston Allen's occupation as the 1939 Mobile City Directory, p. 37.

40. The newspaper spells his name as Manuel Carter, but in *Avenue*, Paulette Davis-Horton has it as Emanuel Carter. See Davis-Horton, *Avenue*, 177–78.

41. It also began at the Colored Community Center, heading east on St. Anthony to Hamilton, but then heading straight north to Davis Avenue, parading up to Lafayette, then back to Hamilton to make its way back to the Community Center. "First Colored Mardi Gras Parade Scheduled Tuesday," and "King of Carnival Chosen," *Mobile Press and Register*, February 19, 1939.

42. "Mobile Colored People Parade," *Mobile Press*, February 22, 1939.

43. See Davis-Horton, *Avenue*, 177 and Bivens, *Mobile Alabama's People of Color*, 193.

44. For more on how voluntary, mutual aid, fraternal and/or secret societies were involved in festivities in the Black Atlantic, see Roger D. Abrahams, "Conflict Displays in the Black Atlantic," in Santino, *Public Performances*.

45. Kirkland, "Community on Parade," 36.

46. "Parade and Dance Will Top Colored Carnival Program," *Mobile Press Register*, 1 February 1940, JFRL Mardi Gras Clippings: 1940–1949. Although the newspaper does not provide information about the other men on the ballot, it is possible that John Pope was J. C. Pope, the leader of the Excelsior Band.

47. Bivens, *Mobile Alabama's People of Color*, 155

48. Lovett, Porter, and Tolbert, *Mardi Gras in Mobile*, 13.

49. Roy Hoffman, "MAMGA Queen 1940 Looks Back at Age 90 on the Elegance and Festivity of First Black Mardi Gras," AL.com, February 19, 2012, https://www.al.com/entertainment/index.ssf/2012/02/mamga_queen_1940_looks_back_at.html.

50. Eric Finley interview. For an analysis of the role of debuts in Black communities and in the definition of respectful Black womanhood, see Robinson, *This Ain't Chicago*.

51. "Great Enthusiasm Shown for Carnival," *Mobile Press Forum Sun*, February 14, 1941, JFRL Mardi Gras Clippings: 1940–1949.

52. "Parade and Dance Will Top Colored Carnival Program," *Mobile Register*, February 1, 1940, JFRL Mardi Gras Clippings: 1940–1949. Information about the men's professional occupations from Davis-Horton, *Avenue*, 63, 69. "Colored Carnival Parade a Success," *Mobile Register*, February 1, 1940, JFRL Mardi Gras Clippings: 1940–1949.

53. The organization's official book, published in 1980, opens with a dedication to the "mother of us all." Lovett, Porter, and Tolbert, *Mardi Gras in Mobile*, iii.

54. Eric Finley interview.

55. Roberts, *Mardi Gras in Mobile*, 62.

56. Davis-Horton, *Avenue*, 128; "Final Rites Held," *Mobile Beacon-Alabama Citizen*, March 18, 1967, p. 11.

57. "Final Rites Held."

58. State of Alabama, "Certification of Incorporation of Colored Carnival Association," January 15, 1946. For more on African American communists in Alabama in the 1930s, see Robin D. G. Kelley, *Hammer and Hoe: Alabama Communists during the Great Depression* (Chapel Hill: University of North Carolina Press, 1990).

59. The New Orleans Zulu Social Aid and Pleasure Club began as a benevolent society in 1909 and was officially incorporated in 1916. Historian Committee, "History of the Zulu Social Aid & Pleasure Club," accessed July 29, 2018, http://www.kreweofzulu.com/history.

60. See Calvin Trillin, "The Zulus: New Orleans, Louisiana, 1964," in Calvin Trillin, *Jackson, 1964: And Other Dispatches from Fifty Years of Reporting on Race in America* (New York: Random House, 2016); Calvin Trillin, "The Zulus," *New Yorker*, July 20, 1964.

61. According to Kinser, "The NAACP, CORE, the main Christian churches, and many other organizations put pressure on The Zulus to abandon their parodic pleasures as undignified." Kinser, *Carnival, American Style*, 238.

62. "Colored Carnivalists Debate over Dignity vs. Burlesque," *Mobile Register*, February 15, 1947.

63. "Blast at Contribution to Mardi Gras as 'Undignified' Stirs King of Zulus," *New Orleans Times-Picayune*, February 15, 1947.

64. "2 Seek Post in Mardi Gras Election," *Gulf Informer*, February 11, 1950.

65. Rayford, *Chasin' the Devil*, 164, 165.

66. "Colored Event Depicts Explorers of America," *Mobile Register*, February 11, 1948.

67. Inaugurated in 2009, it is located in a small park "in the historic boundary between the white and black sections of town" called Unity Point Park. Journalist Matt Irvin describes the park's opening as a representation of Mobile officials' "hope to highlight the city's history of relative racial harmony and political unity," noting that "Mobile's progress toward desegregation came with less violence than occurred in Selma, Montgomery and Birmingham." Matt Irvin, "City to Unveil New Downtown Park Dedicated to Racial Unity," AL.com, August 22, 2009, http://blog.al.com/live/2009/08/city_to_unveil_new_downtown _pa.html. Scotty Kirkland, however, criticized the monument's "oversimplifying of Mobile's civil rights history," characterizing the narrative of "biracial cooperation" as "the very definition of a usable past" that "ultimately serves to obscure a much more complex racial history." He also criticizes the recurrent comparisons between Mobile and the "big three" (Selma, Montgomery, and Birmingham) as a means to minimize racial tensions in the city. Scotty E. Kirkland, "Insight: Oversimplifying Mobile's Civil Rights History," February 13, 2011, http://blog.al.com/press-register-commentary/2011/02/insight_oversimplifying_mobile.html.

68. Kenneth A. Robinson, *Port City Crusader: John LeFlore and the Non-Partisan Voters' League in Mobile, Alabama* (Mobile: Mod Mobilian Press, 2013), 24, 56, 17.

69. Cited in Verney, "Every Man Should Try," 189.

70. "Emancipation Program Set," *Mobile Register*, January 1, 1959; "Abernathy and Shuttlesworth: Non-Violence Workshop Here Fri.–Sat.," *Mobile Beacon*, March 19, 1960.

71. Although most Mobile writers praise Langan's liberal benevolence, Scotty Kirkland provides a more nuanced analysis of the politician, criticizing other scholarship's glossing over of his segregationist statements, noting he "was a more pragmatic gradualist than enlightened racial diplomat, especially in his early years in the commission." Scotty E. Kirkland, "Pink Sheets and Black Ballots: Politics and Civil Rights in Mobile, Alabama, 1945–1985" (master's thesis, University of South Alabama, 2009), 70.

72. The voting system developed by LeFlore and the NPVL worked through the use of "pink sheets," printed sample ballots containing the names of the candidates supported by these Black political leaders, which were distributed to the Black population and guided them on voting choices. This tactic created a significant voting bloc. See Kirkland, "Pink Sheets," and Ahmed, "Race, Class and Citizenship." If the NPVL's control over the Black vote meant bargaining power with whites, these pink ballots placed race men such as LeFlore in the role of gatekeepers who got to decide what was good for the "community." In this scenario Langan played the role of the benevolent white savior, who granted "good Blacks" certain rights if they stayed in line. In *Race Men* (1998), Hazel Carby provided a feminist interrogation of the construction of Black masculinity and how the Black male elite came to represent and speak for the "race." Carby looks at how the Black male intellectual challenged racial hegemony while creating assumptions about Black masculinity and gender that subordinated Black women. Hazel V. Carby, *Race Men* (Cambridge: Harvard University Press, 1998). For an analysis of masculinity and gender construction of Black men in the early twentieth century US, see Martin Anthony Summers, *Manliness and Its Discontents: The Black Middle Class and the Transformation of Masculinity, 1900–1930* (Chapel Hill: University of North Carolina Press, 2004). For the connection between masculinity and gender constructions and constructions of race and nation/citizenship, see Gail Baderman, *Manliness & Civilization: A Cultural History of Gender and Race in the United States, 1880–1917* (Chicago: University of Chicago Press, 1995).

73. Ahmed, "Race, Class and Citizenship," 146, 147, 231.

74. Burt Schorr, "Harmony in Mobile: An Alabama City Builds Racial Peace as Strife Increases Elsewhere," *Wall Street Journal*, July 18, 1963.

75. Schorr, "Harmony in Mobile."

76. Dorothy Williams, Jerry Pogue, and other activists started NOW as a grassroots organization in 1966, but it was rearticulated in 1968. According to Dalene M. Case, it "essentially became a new organization" under the leadership of Noble Beasley. See Delene M. Case, "Ain't Gonna Let Nobody Turn Me Around: The Black Freedom Struggle in Mobile, Alabama, 1902–1969" (MA thesis, University of South Alabama, 2004), 70.

77. Richardson, *Genesis and Exodus*, 4, 29.

78. Richardson, *Genesis and Exodus*, 30, 26.

79. Interview with Jerry Pogue, by Nahfiza Ahmed, July 26, 2001, Nahfiza Ahmed Oral History Collection, DLM, 6.

80. Interview with Joseph N. Langan, by Nahfiza Ahmed, July 25, 2001, Nahfiza Ahmed Oral History Collection, DLM, 12.

81. Robinson, *Port City Crusader*, 132. For a more in-depth look at the national context of the turning point in the Black liberation struggle, when younger activists began moving away from Dr. Martin Luther King Jr.'s nonviolence and toward Kwame Ture's Black Power, see Aram Goudsouzian, *Down to the Crossroads: Civil Rights, Black Power, and the Meredith March Against Fear* (New York: Farrar, Straus and Giroux, 2015).

82. See Nahfiza Ahmed, "The Neighborhood Organized Workers of Mobile Alabama: Black Power and Local Civil Rights Activism in the Deep South, 1968–1971," *Southern Historian* 20 (1999): 25–40; Kirkland, "Pink Sheets and Black Ballots; Richardson, *Genesis and Exodus*.

83. As Nahfiza Ahmed notes, while LeFlore tried to work within the legal system, "Beasley was influenced by SCLC's moral argument that such laws should be disobeyed until they were revoked." Ahmed, "Race, Class and Citizenship," 201.

84. Mayor Mims and the city commissioners tried to stop the event by refusing a permit for a rally at the municipal auditorium. FBI officers attended the meeting, and police escorted Ture throughout the visit. Richardson, *Genesis and Exodus*, 49.

85. Audrey Bridges, "2,000 Mobilians Rave over Speech by Stokely Carmichael," *Mobile Beacon*, August 3, 1968.

86. NOW, "NOW Outlines Position on Mardi Gras," *Mobile Beacon*, January 25, 1969.

87. Dr. W. L. Russell, "Carnival Assn. Halts Activities for '69," *Mobile Beacon*, January 25, 1969.

88. "Happenin' 'Round Town," *Mobile Beacon-Alabama Citizen*, March 9, 1968, p. 10.

89. Richardson, *Genesis and Exodus*, 81.

90. Scotty E. Kirkland, Neighborhood Organized Workers of Mobile (NOW), *Encyclopedia of Alabama*, August 10, 2015, http://www.encyclopediaofalabama.org/article/h-3104. See also Nahfiza Ahmed, "The Neighborhood Organized Workers of Mobile Alabama: Black Power and Local Civil Rights Activism in the Deep South, 1968–1971," *Southern Historian* 20 (1999): 25–40; Kirkland, "Pink Sheets and Black Ballots"; and Richardson, *Genesis and Exodus of NOW*. Beasley ended up spending almost three decades imprisoned for drug-related charges.

Chapter 5: Queering Mobile's Mardi Gras

1. Rhett's Butler, "Happenings in the Port City," *Alabama Forum*, May 1983, p. 3.

2. There have been earlier attempts to form gay carnival organizations in the city, but they did not last very long. Newer societies have also been created since.

3. As John Howard has shown, that decade marks the emergence of gay identity politics in the US South. Howard, *Men like That*.

4. Buring, *Lesbian and Gay Memphis*, 233.

5. See madison moore, *Fabulous: The Rise of the Beautiful Eccentric* (New Haven: Yale University Press, 2018); Katie Horowitz, *Drag, Interperformance, and the Trouble with Queerness* (London: Routledge, 2019); and Kemi Adeyemi, Kareem Khubchandani, and Ramón Rivera-Servera, eds., *Queer Nightlife* (Ann Arbor: University of Michigan Press, 2021).

6. Rayford, *Chasin' the Devil*, 126.

7. Rayford, *Chasin' the Devil*, 79.

8. "The City by Day," *Mobile Daily Register*, February 26, 1873, p. 1; "A Pink Domino Ball—Given by the Ladies at Colonel Kennerly's," *Daily Register*, January 1, 1899, p. 8. My thanks to Mobile independent historian Slade Watson for bringing these two stories to my attention.

9. "First Person Arrested," *Mobile Daily Item*, February 11, 1902.

10. While the definition of drag can be a contested terrain, I am relying here on the information provided by the narrator who brought this clipping to my attention. He personally knew one of the individuals in the photograph, who he described as a gay man who sometimes did drag. See Meredith Heller, *Queering Drag: Redefining the Discourse of Gender-Bending* (Bloomington: Indiana University Press, 2020).

11. "Southern 'Belles' Display Charms," *Mobile Register*, February 19, 1947, p. 8.

12. As these organizations did not leave much of an archive, we know about them now mostly via oral tradition. In *Queer Carnival* Amy L. Stone lists the names of the organizations as Apostles of Apollo and Order of Adonis. Stone also notes that the Krewe of Pan "held its first ball in a private home in 1968." Stone, *Queer Carnival*, 42.

13. Smith, *Unveiling the Muse*, 155.

14. King Lawrence XV interview.

15. His name will be omitted here in respect of his privacy, even though King Lawrence XV mentioned it on the record. Les Yeux, "The First Official Miss Gay Mobile Pageant," *Alabama Forum* 2, no. 7 (September 1982): 3.

16. Homer McClure interview

17. Queen Richard IV interview.

18. Yet, after almost three years of research, I was not able to find an older queer Black narrator willing to contribute to this project. Nan Alamilla Boyd has discussed difficulties in the collection of oral histories of people who have other social stigmas in addition to LGBTQIA+ identities. Nan Alamilla Boyd and Horacio N. Roque Ramírez, *Bodies of Evidence: The Practice of Queer Oral History* (New York: Oxford University Press, 2012).

19. John Alton Vaughan, "Neil-Al," October 5, 2015. This document is now part of the MGSCOH collection.

20. Janette Curry interview.

21. Vaughan, "Neil-Al."

22. William N. Eskridge Jr. shows how sodomy laws have been selectively enforced and used as a mechanism of social control. William N. Eskridge Jr., *Dishonorable Passions: Sodomy Laws in America, 1861–2003* (New York: Viking, 2008).

23. Jack Bishop interview.

24. Interview with Queen Vickie V, recorded by Isabel Machado, Mobile, Alabama, October 15, 2014, MGSCOH collection.

25. Queen Richard IV interview.

26. Jack Bishop interview.

27. A 1983 *Alabama Forum* column denounced the police harassment of "gays . . . blacks and other minorities" in Montgomery, claiming that law enforcement targeted gay establishments and might "create an incident" if they did not find one, confirming Officer Bishop's description of the police's attitude towards known queer establishments. "Gays Often Target of Police Harassment," *Alabama Forum*, May 1983, 11.

28. Kathie M. Hiers interview.

29. "By-Law of the Gulf Alliance for Equality." The document is part of a series of documents provided to the author by Janette Curry. Date and author not identified. The documents are now available in the Doy Leale McCall Rare Book and Manuscript Library and with the Invisible Histories Project.

30. Howard Philips Smith shows how that was the case for the origins of the Southern Decadence celebration in New Orleans, now known as "gay Mardi Gras." Howard Philips Smith and Frank Perez, *Southern Decadence in New Orleans* (Baton Rouge: Louisiana State University Press, 2018).

31. *G.A.E. Newsletter*, vol. 7, p. 5.

32. Facebook Messenger communication between the author and Domingo Soto from December 7, 2021. The text was edited for clarity by the author.

33. "Order of Osiris, 1981–2001," document in the author's possession. Mystic societies produce literature for new-member orientations. This particular document is from 2001, but passages from this official history can be found in earlier texts and articles.

34. *Alabama Forum*, July 1981, p. 8.

35. Les Yeux, "Forum Gossip—Bayside Briefs," *Alabama Forum*, January 1982, p. 6.

36. "Mobile Is Mardi Gras," *Alabama Forum*, February 1982, p. 1.

37. LGBTQIA+ scholarship has acknowledged different sources of heteronormativity defiance and community building. Allen Drexel identifies drag queens and gay balls as sites of "informal homosexual resistance," while other historians have looked at bar communities as a place of resistance. Allen Drexel, "Before Paris Burned: Race, Class, and Male Homosexuality on the Chicago South Side, 1935–1960," in Beemyn ed., *Creating a Place for Ourselves*.

38. Interview with L. Craig Roberts, recorded by Isabel Machado and Cari Searcy in Mobile, Alabama, on February 11, 2016. MGSCOH collection.

39. Interview with Ron Barrett, recorded by Isabel Machado in Mobile, Alabama, July 27, 2015. MGSCOH collection.

40. Unrecorded telephone conversation with Joey Potter, conducted by Isabel Machado, October 14, 2014.

41. Facebook Messenger conversation between the author and Queen Julie III. January 23, 2021.

42. King Lawrence XV interview.

43. Interview with Queen Janette XII, recorded by Isabel Machado and Cari Searcy in Mobile, Alabama, on February 13, 2016, MGSCOH collection.

44. Unrecoreded telephone conversation with Sherry Odom, conducted by Isabel Machado, 10 November 2014.

45. Les Yeux, "Osiris' *The Wiz* Grand Success in Mobile," *Alabama Forum*, July–August 1982.

46. Joey Potter, conversation, October 14, 2014.

47. Vaughan, "Neil-Al."

48. Queen Vickie V interview.

49. King Lawrence XV interview.

50. Horowitz, *Drag, Interperformance*. See also Roderick Ferguson, "Race-ing Homonormativity: Citizenship, Sociology, and Gay Identity," in *Black Queer Studies: A Critical Anthology*, ed. E. Patrick Johnson and Mae Henderson (Durham, NC: Duke University Press, 2005). For the specific experiences of Black gay men in rural Alabama, see Hoshall, "The Gay Side of Tuskegee: Separate but Equal in Black America" (parts 1 and 2), *Alabama Forum*, July/August and September issues.

51. Joey Potter, conversation, October 14, 2014.

52. Queen Richard IV interview.

53. Les Yeux, "The First Official Gay Mobile Pageant," *Alabama Forum* 2, no. 7 (September 1982): 1, 3.

54. "The First Annual Ball: The Order of Osiris," *Azalea City News and Review*, February 18, 1982.

55. All mystic society balls in Mobile are *costume du rigueur*. It means that women have to wear floor-length gowns, and men tails. Like other queer Mardi Gras mystic societies or krewes, Osiris kept that dress code but did not make it gender specific.

56. Interview with Queen Danielle II, recorded by Isabel Machado and Cari Searcy in Mobile, Alabama, on October 15, 2014.

57. Kathie Hiers interview.

58. She again served as captain of the XX ball.

59. Queen Janette interview.

60. Queen Richard interview.

61. Kathie Hiers interview.

Chapter 6: Carnivalesque Bodies

1. Richard Schechner, "Carnival (Theory) after Bakhtin," in *Carnival: Culture in Action: The Trinidad Experience*, ed. Milla Cozart Riggio (Abingdon: Routledge, 2004), 8, 10.

2. See Barbara Kirshenblatt-Gimblett and Brooks McNamara, "Processional Performance: An Introduction," *Drama Review* 29, no. 3 (Autumn 1985): 2–5; Santino, *Public Performances*; Victor Turner, "Introduction," in *Celebration: Studies in Festivity and Ritual*, ed. Victor Turner, 11–32 (Washington, DC: Smithsonian Institution Press, 1983); Dominic Bryan, "Parades, Flags, Carnivals and Riots: Public Space, Contestation and Transformation in Northern Ireland," *Peace and Conflict: Journal of Peace Psychology* 21, no. 4 (2015): 565–73; Lily Kong and Brenda S. A. Yeoh, "The Construction of National Identity through the Production of Ritual and Spectacle: An Analysis of National Day Parades in Singapore," *Political Geography* 16, no. 3 (1997): 213–39; Mary Ryan, "The American Parade: Representations of the Nineteenth-Century Social Order," in *The New Cultural History*, ed. Lynn Hunt, 131–53 (Berkeley: University of California Press, 2000).

3. The Athelstan Club is a men's club formed in December 1872, which derived from the Masonic Athelstan Lodge No. 369. One of its founders, Daniel E. Huger, was crowned Mobile's first Mardi Gras king earlier that same year. See Henry R. Luscher Jr., "Club History," accessed August 21, 2018, http://www.athelstanclub.org/subpage.asp?pageID=64.

4. As Pam R. Moore explains, "in polite society it's called the MAMGA parade. But, truly, growing up it was called the Black parade." For all the efforts of leaders from both the MCA and MAMGA to present a united front in promoting the idea of a single Mardi Gras, Mobilians often refer to the city's "Black" and "White" Mardi Gras as separate things.

5. Pam Richardson Moore interview, recorded by Isabel Machado in Mobile, Alabama, on February 2, 2016.

6. Peter G. Stillman and Adelaide H. Villmoare, "Democracy Despite Government: African American Parading and Democratic Theory," *New Political Science* 32, no. 4 (December 2010): 488.

7. Stillman and Villmoare, "Democracy Despite Government," 485, 486.

8. Stillman and Villmoare, 498.

9. "Colored Carnival Parade a Success," *Mobile Register*, February 1, 1940, JFRL Mardi Gras Clippings: 1940–1949.

10. MGSCOH interviews.

11. MGSCOH interviews.

12. DeFrantz and Gonzalez, *Black Performance Theory*, 9–10.

13. Mila Cozart Riggio, "Time Out or Time In? The Urban Dialectic of Carnival," in *Carnival: Culture in Action: The Trinidad Experience* (Abingdon: Routledge, 2004), 19.

14. Dirksen, *After the Dance*, 40.

15. See Jackson, "Going to the Boomalatta," and "Listening to the Wise Ones."

16. Jackson, "Going to the Boomalatta," 41.

17. Paula Amad, "Visual Riposte: Reconsidering the Return of the Gaze as Postcolonial Theory's Gift to Film Studies," in *Cinema Journal* 52, no. 3 (Spring 2013): 25–48. In an investigation of the "lexicons of desire" in hardcore porn, Jennifer C. Nash looks at race as an "erotic project" and understands performed Blackness as a site of both pain and pleasure, providing an interpretative model of representation that transcends this particular medium and subject. Jennifer C. Nash, *The Black Body in Ecstasy: Reading Race, Reading Pornography* (Durham, NC: Duke University Press, 2014), 1.

18. Grace Elizabeth Hale analyzes the performance of Blackness in the context of the construction of whiteness in the New South, investigating identity formation in the "imagining of a community" for southern whites through the "othering" of African Americans after emancipation. To Hale, African Americans performed their Blackness for whites as a coping mechanism. Although this is a compelling argument, it denies the possibility of *jouissance* in these performances. Grace Elizabeth Hale, *Making Whiteness: The Culture of Segregation in the South, 1890–1940* (New York: Vintage Books, 1999), 283. Other scholars, however, show how Black people "returned the gaze" and derived pleasure from racialized performances. Zandria F. Robinson, for instance, investigates how southern Blackness is "constructed, experienced, and performed," showing how Black southerners are able to "bracket" their traumatic past and invent new traditions. Robinson, *This Ain't Chicago*, 192, 118. E. Patrick Johnson gives another dimension to this discussion by showing how African American gay men in the US South drew upon the "performance of southernerness" in developing their identities. Johnson, *Sweet Tea*. See also Jayna Brown, *Babylon Girls: Black Women Performers and the Shaping of the Modern* (Durham, NC: Duke University Press, 2008); Shane Vogel, *The Scene of Harlem Cabaret: Race, Sexuality, Performance* (Chicago: University of Chicago Press, 2009); and James F. Wilson, *Bulldaggers, Pansies, and Chocolate Babies: Performance, Race, and Sexuality in the Harlem Renaissance* (Ann Arbor: University of Michigan Press, 2010).

19. Pamela Richardson Moore interview; Bobby Dennison and Linda Dennison interview; George Moore interview.

20. That is still the case, and not only during the Carnival season. For a deeper exploration of the concept of white spaces, see Elijah Anderson, "The White Space," *Sociology of Race and Ethnicity* 1, no. 1 (2015): 10–21.

21. Emily Ruth Allen further explores the origins and history of the Excelsior Band and finds another possible origin story. See Allen, "Brass B(r)ands."

22. As Davis-Horton notes, although the city's white and Black elites "did not mix and mingle . . . African-American bands and orchestras were frequently called upon to entertain at many white functions in Mobile." Davis-Horton, *Avenue*, 70, 150.

23. Jackson, "Going to the Boomalatta," 42.

24. Interview with Hosea London, recorded by Isabel Machado in Mobile, Alabama, on January 26, 2016, MGSCOH collection.

25. From 1998 to 2001, Kern Jackson conducted the Video Oral History Project of the City of Mobile's Tercentennial celebration. Interviewing people from traditional Black neighborhoods in Mobile, Jackson investigates how African Americans negotiated the rituals and norms of Mardi Gras in the context of the city's sociocultural changes. His work addresses the gap in other studies, which focused almost exclusively on white elites.

26. Jackson, "Listening to the Wise Ones," 115.

27. Davis-Horton, *Avenue*, 181.

28. George Moore interview.

29. Linda and Bobby Dennison interview.

30. Davis-Horton, *Avenue*, 181. Mobile historian Scotty Kirkland considers the float "a fanciful reminder of an old tradition from Mardi Gras along Davis Avenue" and describes the Mollies as "tricksters who stalked about the streets on parade days, often stealing the spotlight with ostentatious costumes: men dressed as women with outlandishly oversized proportions, or women pushing dogs in baby carriages and wailing for help from the amused crowd." Kirkland, "Community on Parade," 37.

31. Jackson, "Going to the Boomalatta," 56.

32. Cohen produced a fundamental analytic model that details "the relationship between deviance, defiance, and resistance" in African American politics. Cathy J. Cohen, "Deviance as Resistance: A New Research Agenda for the Study of Black Politics," *Du Bois Review: Social Science Research on Race* 1, no. 1 (2004): 30. See also Cathy J. Cohen, "Punks, Bulldaggers, and Welfare Queens: The Radical Potential of Queer Politics?," *GLQ* 3, no. 4 (May 1, 1997): 437–65.

33. Roy Hoffman, "In MAMGA Mardi Gras Parade, Mollies Are Fun Historical Figures from Community," AL.com, February 14, 2012, https://www.al.com/entertainment/index.ssf/2012/02/in_mamga_parade_mollies_based.html.

34. Jackson, "Going to the Boomlatta," 49.

35. Molly Cottontail was part of the cast of characters in the Disney comic strip *Uncle Remus and His Tales of Bre'er Rabbit* (1945–1972), created to promote their controversial 1946 feature *Song of the South*. See Allan Holtz, *American Newspaper Comics: An Encyclopedic Reference Guide* (Ann Arbor: University of Michigan Press, 2012); Dave Strickler, *Syndicated Comic Strips and Artists, 1924–1995: The Complete Index* (Cambria, CA: Comics Access, 1995).

36. In 1785 Francis Grose defined a Molly as "an effeminate fellow, a sodomite." Francis Grose, *A Classical Dictionary of the Vulgar Tongue* (London: S. Hopper, 1785), https://archive.org/details/b28761900x/page/n3. See also Randolph Trumbach, *Sex and the Gender Revolution: Volume One, Heterosexuality and the Third Gender in Enlightenment London* (Chicago: University of Chicago Press, 1998); Martin Duberman, Martha Vicinus, and George Chauncey, eds., *Hidden from History: Reclaiming the Gay and Lesbian Past* (London: Penguin Books, 1991); Rictor Norton, *Mother Clap's Molly House: The Gay Subculture in*

England, 1700–1830 (London: Gay Men's Press, 1992); Marlon B. Ross, *Sissy Insurgencies: A Racial Anatomy of Unfit Manliness* (Durham NC Duke University Press, 2022).

37. See Nadia Davids, "'It Is Us': An Exploration of 'Race' and Place in the Cape Town Minstrel Carnival," *TDR (1988–)* 57, no. 2 (2013): 86–101; Bett Pacey, "The Emergence and Recognition of *Moffies* as Popular Entertainers in the Cape Minstrel Carnival," *SATJ: South African Theatre Journal* 27, no. 2 (January 2014): 111–24; Amanda Lock Swarr, "Moffies, Artists, and Queens," *Journal of Homosexuality* 46, no. 3–4 (2004): 73–89.

38. Lyle Saxon, Edward Dreyer, and Robert Tallant, *Gumbo Ya-Ya: A Collection of Louisiana Folk Tales* (Boston: Houghton Mifflin, 1945), 77.

39. See Angela Y. Davis, *Women, Race & Class* (New York: Random House, 1981); Danielle L. McGuire, *At the Dark End of the Street: Black Women, Rape, and Resistance—a New History of the Civil Rights Movement from Rosa Parks to the Rise of Black Power* (New York: Vintage Books, 2011); Crystal N. Feimster, *Southern Horrors: Women and the Politics of Rape and Lynching* (Cambridge: Harvard University Press, 2009).

40. Jerry T. Watkins III, *Hot Times on the Gay Gulf Coast: Queer Networks and Cruising through North Florida's Spaces, 1945–1965* (PhD diss., Kings College London, 2013), 184.

41. Linda and Bobby Dennison interview.

42. Hoffman, "In MAMGA Mardi Gras Parade."

43. Hoffman, "In MAMGA Mardi Gras Parade."

44. Eric Finley, George Moore, Palmer Richardson interviews.

45. Jackson, "Going to the Boomalatta," 45.

46. Jackson, "Going to the Boomalatta," 47.

47. Jackson, "Going to the Boomalatta," 47, 48, 53.

48. La Fountain-Stokes, *Translocas*, 14.

49. Dirksen, *After the Dance*, 46.

50. Cohen, "Deviance as Resistance," 31. When discussing constructions of Blackness and gender, Cohen refers specifically to Evelyn Higginbotham's work. Higginbotham, *Righteous Discontent*. See also Hazel V. Carby, "Policing the Black Woman's Body in an Urban Context," *Critical Inquiry* 18, no. 4 (1992): 738–55.

51. Cohen, "Deviance as Resistance," 37.

Chapter 7: Plus Ça Change?

1. Paul R. Cherney (coordinator), *Civic Index Review: Milestones in Community Development, Mobile, Alabama, 1960–1994*" (Mobile: Mobile United, 1995), 1.

2. Cherney, *Civic Index Review*, 2, 75.

3. Cherney, *Civic Index Review*, 47.

4. Cherney, *Civic Index Review*, 40.

5. Cited in Keith Nicholls, "Politics and Civil Rights in Post–World War II Mobile," in Thomason, ed., *Mobile*, 268.

6. Ahmed, "Race, Class and Citizenship," 219.

7. As Kirkland notes, during "the decade-long legal battle over the case, Mobile experienced two of its most brutal acts of racial violence in over a century, which had a direct impact on the outcome of the case." Kirkland, "Pink Sheets and Black Ballots," 203.

8. Kevin Lee, "How a Detective Who Was Blamed for One Lynching Solved Another," *Daily Beast*, March 21, 2021. https://www.thedailybeast.com/how-a-detective-who-was-blamed-for-one-lynching-solved-another.

9. Kirkland, "Pink Sheets and Black Ballots," 166, 167.

10. Kirkland, "Pink Sheets and Black Ballots," 169–70. According to Keith Nichols, "without doubt this situation contributed to the racially charged atmosphere in which the *Bolden* case was heard." Nicholls, "Politics and Civil Rights," 268.

11. Kirkland, "Pink Sheets and Black Ballots," 175–76.

12. Kirkland, "Pink Sheets and Black Ballots," 183.

13. Laurence Leamer, *The Lynching: The Epic Courtroom Battle That Brought Down the Klan* (New York: William Morrow, 2016), 5, 6.

14. Kirkland, "Pink Sheets and Black Ballots," 186.

15. Kirkland, "Pink Sheets and Black Ballots," 190–91.

16. Leamer, *The Lynching*, 11.

17. Leamer, *The Lynching*, 27.

18. Scotty Kirkland, excerpt from chapter 9, "Sad History," from the forthcoming book "Jordan's Stormy Banks: Politics and Race in Twentieth-Century Mobile, Alabama."

19. Kirkland, "Sad History."

20. Claire Matturro, "Photographs of United Klans of America march in Mobile, Alabama Collection," part of the Alabama Photographs and Pictures Collection, Alabama Department of Archives & History.

21. Kirkland, excerpt from chapter 9.

22. The line between protest and celebration is, of course, often ill defined and porous. See Santino, "From Carnivalesque to Ritualesque," and Isabel Machado, "Introduction: On the Materiality of Festivity," *Journal of Festive Studies* 3 (2021): 1–13.

23. Cherney, *Civic Index Review*, 57.

24. Homer McClure interview.

25. Cherney, *Civic Index Review*, 54.

26. Christopher Harress, "'We Are about Love': Story Hour Thrusts Mobile's Drag Queens into Spotlight," AL.com, September 7, 2018 (last updated: March 7, 2019, https://www.al.com/news/2018/09/we_are_about_love_story_hour_t.html.

27. Queen Richard IV interview.

28. See Neil Miller, *Out of the Past: Gay and Lesbian History from 1869 to the Present* (New York: Alyson Books, 2006); Lillian Faderman, *The Gay Revolution: The Story of the Struggle* (New York: Simon & Schuster, 2016).

29. L. Craig Roberts interview.

30. "Directory," *Alabama Forum*, July–August 1989, p. 2.

31. Queen Janette XII interview.

32. Kathie Hiers interview.

33. "Order of Osiris, 1981–2001." On their nineteenth anniversary, they moved to an even bigger location: the Arthur Outlaw Riverside Convention Center.

34. Different people remember different dates. Yet it is most likely that it took place in 1987, their sixth ball, since Queen Richard IV, who remembers quite vividly having to make the decision of not cancelling the ball despite the threat, was the captain that year. Queen Richard IV, interview.

35. The state's most important lesbian/gay publication, the *Alabama Forum*, however, provided enthusiastic coverage of the ball, as well as other Osiris activities.

36. "The First Annual Ball: The Order of Osiris."

37. Susie Spear Cloos (Susie's Parlor), "Splendor, Diversity, Mark Ball," *Mobile Register*, February 8, 1998, 1A.

38. Spear Cloos, "Splendor."

39. Susie Spear Cloos (Susie's Parlor), "Cavaliers Plan to Rock and Roll with Fabulous Bands," *Mobile Register*, January 24, 2002.

40. The Masked Observer, "Kings Rule at Osiris," *Mobile Register*, February 15, 2001, 1A.

41. Pan and Phoenix are also LGBTQIA+ mystic societies.

42. Katelyn Gardner, "Insider's Look at Mardi Gras: Alternative Lifestyle Organizations," *Lagniappe*, January 24, 2013.

43. Howard Philips Smith discussed what he perceived was lost when gay Mardi Gras was accepted into the mainstream in New Orleans. Smith, *Unveiling the Muse*.

44. Kirkland, "Community on Parade."

45. Jackson, "Going to the Boomalatta," 58, 59.

46. Linda and Bobby Dennison interview.

47. Kirkland, "Community on Parade," 37, 38.

48. This idea of Black US Americans' two-ness, or double-consciousness, was of course already expressed by W. E. B. Du Bois in 1903. W. E. B. Du Bois, *The Souls of Black Folk* (New York: Barnes & Noble Classics, 2003).

49. For more on the history of the *Clotilde* and Africatown, see Sylviane A. Diouf, *Dreams of Africa in Alabama: The Slave Ship "Clotilda" and the Story of the Last Africans Brought to America* (Oxford: Oxford University Press, 2009); Zora Neale Hurston, *Barracoon: The Story of the Last "Black Cargo"* (New York: Harper Collins, 2018).

50. Domingo Soto interview.

51. Pam R. Moore interview

52. Conde Explorers: Making Mardi Gras History in Mobile, https://www.condeexplorers.org/about-us/.

53. Kirkland, "Pink Sheets and Black Ballots," 203.

54. Eric Finley interview.

55. Eric Finley interview.

56. SoKold Ent, "Mardi Gras Song 2 Major Twinz," March 25, 2011, https://www.youtube.com/watch?v=-34INx_Puf8.

Conclusion

1. Stuart Hall, "Cultural Identity and Diaspora," in *Theorizing Diaspora: A Reader*, ed. Jana Evans Braziel and Anita Mannur (Malden, MA: Blackwell, 2003), 236.

2. The description is from the show's official website: http://www.oxygen.com/the-prancing-elites-project/about.

3. The film begins with Labeija's voiceover narration: "I remember my dad say: You have three strikes against you in this world. Every Black man has two—that they're just black and they're male. But you're Black and you're male and you're gay." Jennie Livingston, dir., *Paris Is Burning* (New York: Off White Productions, 1990).

4. The Mobile Mask, Facebook post, April 23, 2015. The Mobile Mask's Facebook page has since been deactivated and substituted by @MrsMobileMask.

5. moore, *Fabulous*, vii.

6. For more on the MWOC, see Stone, *Queer Carnival*.

7. https://www.cainsmerrywidows.org/.

8. http://www.mistressesofjoecain.com/history-2/.

9. Nick Shantasio, interview with Nick Shantazio and Stephen Gaudet, recorded by Isabel Machado in Mobile, Alabama, on March 5, 2017, MGSCOH collection.

10. Stephen Gaudet, interview with Nick Shantazio and Stephen Gaudet.

11. Gaudet and Shantazio interview.

12. Michael Dumas, "New Mardi Gras Crewe, Order of Many Faces, Will Debut in 2016 and Be Open to All," AL.com, posted September 5, 2015, last updated, January 13, 2019, https://www.al.com/news/mobile/2015/09/new_mardi_gras_crewe_order_of.html.

13. Amanda Holpuch, "Same-Sex Marriage to Begin in Alabama as Federal Court Affirms End of Ban," *The Guardian*, February 3, 2015, https://www.theguardian.com/society/2015/feb/03/same-sex-marriage-begins-alabama-appeals-court-affirms-ruling.

14. On the commodification of drag, see Horowitz, *Drag, Interperformance*; Selby Wynn Schwartz, *The Bodies of Others: Drag Dances and Their Afterlives* (Ann Arbor: University of Michigan Press, 2019); LaFontaine-Stokes, *Translocas*; Adeyemi, Khubchandani, Rivera-Servera, eds., *Queer Nightlife*.

15. Harress, "We Are about Love."

16. Tatiana Fogelman, "Straights in a Gay Bar: Negotiating Boundaries through Time-Space, in *Geographies of Sexualities: Theory, Practices and Politics*, ed. Jason Lim and Kath Browne (London: Routledge, 2016): 137–50; Jaime Hartless, "Questionably Queer: Understanding Straight Presence in the Post-Gay Bar," *Journal of Homosexuality* 66, no. 8 (2016): 1035–57.

17. See Marcus Anthony Hunter and Zandria F. Robinson, *Chocolate Cities: The Black Map of American Life* (Oakland: University of California Press, 2018).

18. *Montgomery Advertiser*, "2020 Decennial Census: How Many People Live in Mobile City, Alabama," https://data.montgomeryadvertiser.com/census/total-population/total-population-change/mobile-city-alabama/160-0150000/.

BIBLIOGRAPHY

Archival Sources

City of Mobile Municipal Archives, Mobile, AL (CMMA)

Records of the Board of Commissioners of the City of Mobile, 1911–85
Office Files of Commissioner Robert B. Doyle, Jr. 1967–84
Sergeant's Dockets, 1935–51
City of Mobile Aldermen's books
Code of Ordinances of the City of Mobile
City Directories
Joe Cain Celebration documents

The Amistad Research Center, New Orleans, LA (ARC)

Inez Adams papers, 1914–66
Alabama Forum (Birmingham, AL, United States)

The Jack Friend Research Library, History Museum of Mobile, Mobile, AL (JFRL)

Mardi Gras Clippings, 1890–1999

Charles Torrey's Private Archive

The Order of Osiris Papers

The Local History & Genealogy, Mobile Public Library, Mobile, AL (LHGL)

Various periodicals

The Doy Leale Mccall Rare Book and Manuscript Library, University of South Alabama, Mobile, AL (DLM)

The Nahfiza Ahmed Oral History Collection
Photographs
Mardi Gras and Social Change Oral Histories

University Libraries, The University of Alabama

Alabama Forum Newspaper Archive

Periodicals

Alabama Forum
AL.com
Azalea City News and Review
Bayou La Batre Trawler
Lagniappe Weekly
Mobile Beacon
Mobile Daily Item
Mobile Daily Register
Mobile Mask: The Revelers Guide to Mardi Gras
Mobile Press
Mobile Press and Register
Mobile Press Register
Mobile Register
Montgomery Advertiser
New Orleans Times-Picayune
Press Forum Sun
Wall Street Journal

Published Reports

The Charter and the Code of Ordinances of the City of Mobile with Appendix. Prepared by Saffold Bernew, Attorney-at-Law. Mobile: Commercial Printing, 1897.
The Charter and the Code of Ordinances of the City of Mobile. Mobile: George Matzenger Printer, 1889.
Cherney, Paul R. (coordinator). *Civic Index Review: Milestones in Community Development, Mobile, Alabama, 1960–1994.* Mobile: Mobile United, 1995.
City Planning Commission Mobile, Alabama. "Housing Market Analysis Mobile, Alabama: Part II Text and Charts" (August 1945).
The Code of the City of Mobile, Alabama, 1955: The General Ordinances of the City. 1959 Supplement. Fred G. Collins, City Attorney. Charlottesville, VA: Michie City Publications, 1960.
Collection of the Ordinances Now in Force in the City of Mobile and Also the Various Acts of the Legislature Incorporating Said City." Mobile: Office of the Mercantile Advertiser, 1835.

The Commission Government Charter and the Code of Ordinances of the City of Mobile, Alabama. Prepared by Shelton H. Hendrix. Mobile: Authority of the Board of Commissioners of the City of Mobile, Alabama, 1934.
George Matzenger's Mobile Directory for 1892. Vol. 27. Mobile: George Matzenger Printer, 1892.
Hammer and Company Associates (for The Mobile City Planning Commission). "Downtown Mobile: An Analysis of Its Economic Potential" (January 1963).
Mobile Housing Board. "Report on Urban Renewal Activities of Mobile Housing Board" (March 1968).
The Mobile Urban Renewal Agency. "Church Street and Texas Street—A Downtown District and In-City Neighborhood: A General Neighborhood Renewal Plan" (1961).
The Southern Institute of Management. "The Mobile Metropolitan Area Audit. Preliminary Report No. 6: Armed Forces" (1960).
State of Alabama. "Certification of Incorporation of Colored Carnival Association" (January 15, 1946).

Audio-Visual

Botstein, Sarah, Geoffrey C. Ward, Ken Burns, Lynn Novick, Keith David, Tom Hanks, Josh Lucas, et al. *The War*. OKS Print. [United States]: PBS Home Video, 2007.
Brown, Margaret, dir. *The Order of Myths*. New York: Cinema Guild, 2008.
Embry, Laura, and Carolyn Sherer, dirs. *Alabama Bound*. Birmingham: Living in Limbo Inc. Productions, 2017.
Grey, Robert, dir. *Mobile in Black and White*. Mobile: Spectral Grey Productions, 2014. https://cultureunplugged.com/documentary/watch-online/play/52025/Mobile-in-Black-and-White
Kiker, Alex. *This Is Mobile*. YouTube video, 3:14 minutes. October 29, 2017. https://www.youtube.com/watch?time_continue=172&v=2A4VKSfdPq4.
Livingston, Jennie, dir. 1990. *Paris Is Burning*. New York: Off White Productions, 1990.
Visit Mobile. *Born to Celebrate*. YouTube video. 1:31 minutes. Nov 18, 2015. https://www.youtube.com/watch?v=IohsMHfMZqw.

Websites and Social Media

Cain's Merry Widows. https://www.cainsmerrywidows.org/.
Conde Explorers. https://www.condeexplorers.org/about-us/.
Historian Committee, "History of the Zulu Social Aid & Pleasure Club." http://www.kreweofzulu.com/history.
Henry R. Luscher Jr. "Club History." http://www.athelstanclub.org/subpage.asp?pageID=64.
"Mistresses History." http://www.mistressesofjoecain.com/history-2/.
"Mobile Carnival Museum History." http://www.mobilecarnivalmuseum.com/historical-timeline.
The Mobile Mask. Facebook post, uploaded April 23, 2015, https://www.facebook.com/mobilemask/photos/a.365507873464804.106040.357389564276635/1098085106873740/?type=1&theater.
Mobile Museum of Art. "The Art and Design of Mardi Gras." http://www.mobilemuseumofart.com/exhibitions/art-design-mardi-gras.

Mobtown Merch. https://mobtownmerch.com/products/official-mobile-mardi-gras-flag-3×5.
Sweet Home Alabama Facebook page. "Mobile's Mardi Gras in Times Square," Facebook post, uploaded June 15, 2017, https://www.facebook.com/AlabamaTravel/videos/vb.85442653844/10154833390873845/?type=2&theater.
OMG 1903. https://omg1703.com/.

Secondary Sources

Abu-Lughod, Lila. "Writing against Culture." In *Anthropology in Theory: Issues in Epistemology*, edited by Henrietta Moore and Todd Sanders, 466–79. Oxford: Blackwell, 2006.
Adeyemi, Kemi, Kareem Khubchandani, and Ramón Rivera-Servera, eds. *Queer Nightlife*. Ann Arbor: University of Michigan Press, 2021.
Ahmed, Nahfiza. "The Neighborhood Organized Workers of Mobile Alabama: Black Power and Local Civil Rights Activism in the Deep South, 1968–1971." *Southern Historian* 20 (1999): 25–40.
Ahmed, Nahfiza. "Race, Class and Citizenship: The Civil Rights Struggle in Mobile, Alabama, 1925–85." PhD thesis, University of Leicester Department of Economic & Social History, 1999.
Allen, Emily Ruth. "Brass B(r)ands in Mobile, Alabama's Mardi Gras." PhD diss., Florida State University, 2019.
Allen, Emily Ruth, and Isabel Machado. "Mobile, Alabama's Joe Cain Procession: A Confederate Memorial or The People's Parade?" *Journal of Festive Studies* 3, no. 1 (2021): 92–120.
Alsobrook, David Ernest, Judi Gulledge, Deborah Velders, Steve Joynt, Cartledge Weeden Blackwell III, Scotty E. Kirkland, and Karyn Zweifel. *The Art and Design of Mardi Gras*. Mobile: Mobile Museum of Art, 2014.
Amad, Paula. "Visual Riposte: Reconsidering the Return of the Gaze as Postcolonial Theory's Gift to Film Studies." *Cinema Journal* 52, no. 3 (Spring 2013): 25–48.
Amos, Harriet E. *Cotton City: Urban Development in Antebellum Mobile*. Tuscaloosa: University of Alabama Press, 1985.
Anderson, Elijah. "The White Space." *Sociology of Race and Ethnicity* 1, no. 1 (2015): 10–21.
Ashley, Bob, Ben Taylor, and Joanne Hollows. *Food and Cultural Studies*. London: Routledge, 2002.
Atkins, Jennifer. *New Orleans Carnival Balls: The Secret Side of Mardi Gras, 1870–1920*. Baton Rouge: Louisiana State University Press, 2017.
Baderman, Gail. *Manliness & Civilization: A Cultural History of Gender and Race in the United States, 1880–1917*. Chicago: University of Chicago Press, 1995.
Bakhtin, Mikhail. *The Dialogic Imagination: Four Essays*. Austin: University of Texas Press, 1981.
Bakhtin, Mikhail. *Rabelais and His World*. Bloomington: Indiana University Press, 1984.
Battistella, Edwin L. *The Logic of Markedness*. New York: Oxford University Press, 1996.
Beemyn, Brett, ed. *Creating a Place for Ourselves: Lesbian, Gay and Bisexual Community Histories*. New York: Routledge, 1997.
Bell, David, and Gill Valentine. *Mapping Desire: Geographies of Sexualities*. Abingdon: Routledge, 2006.

Bérubé, Allan. *Coming Out under Fire: The History of Gay Men and Women in World War Two*. New York: Free Press, 1990.
Bivens, Shawn. *Mobile Alabama's People of Color: A Tricentennial History*. Victoria, BC: Trafford, 2004.
Boyd, Nan Alamilla. *Bodies of Evidence: The Practice of Queer Oral History*. Oxford: Oxford University Press, 2012.
Boyd, Nan Alamilla, and Horacio Roque Ramírez. "Who Is the Subject? Queer Theory Meets Oral History." *Journal of the History of Sexuality* 17, no. 2 (May 2008): 179–89.
Boyd, Nan Alamilla. *Wide-Open Town: A History of Queer San Francisco to 1965*. Berkeley: University of California Press, 2003.
Brasseaux, Carl A. *Creoles of Color in the Bayou Country*. Jackson: University Press of Mississippi, 1996.
Brook, Daniel. *The Accident of Color: A Story of Race in Reconstruction*. New York: W. W. Norton, 2020.
Brown, Jayna. *Babylon Girls: Black Women Performers and the Shaping of the Modern*. Durham, NC: Duke University Press, 2008.
Brown, Vincent. *The Reaper's Garden: Death and Power in the World of Atlantic Slavery*. Cambridge: Harvard University Press, 2008.
Bryan, Dominic. "Parades, Flags, Carnivals and Riots: Public Space, Contestation and Transformation in Northern Ireland." *Peace and Conflict: Journal of Peace Psychology* 21, no. 4 (2015): 565–73
Buring, Daneel. *Lesbian and Gay Memphis: Building Community behind the Magnolia Curtain*. New York: Garland, 1997.
Burke, Peter. *Popular Culture in Early Modern Europe*. New York: Harper & Row, 1978.
Caillois, Roger. *L'homme et le sacré*. Paris: Presses universitaires de France, 1939.
Cannadine, David. "The Context, Performance and Meaning of Ritual: The British Monarchy and the 'Invention of Tradition,' c. 1820–1977." In *The Invention of Tradition*, edited by Eric Hobsbawm and Terence Ranger, 101–64. Cambridge: Cambridge University Press, 1983.
Capelleveen, Remco van. "West Indian Carnival in Brooklyn." In *Feasts and Celebrations in North American Ethnic Communities*, edited by Ramón A. Gutiérrez and Geneviève Fabre, 159–71. Albuquerque: University of New Mexico Press, 1995.
Capó, Julio. *Welcome to Fairyland: Queer Miami before 1940*. Chapel Hill: University of North Carolina Press, 2017.
Carageorge, Ted, ed. *Gulf Coast Politics in the Twentieth Century: Proceedings of the Gulf Coast History and Humanities Conference*. Pensacola, FL: Historic Pensacola Preservation Board, 1973.
Carby, Hazel V. "Policing the Black Woman's Body in an Urban Context." *Critical Inquiry* 18, no. 4 (Summer 1992): 738–55.
Carby, Hazel V. *Race Men*. Cambridge: Harvard University Press, 1998.
Carter, Wilmoth Annette. "Negro Main Street as a Symbol of Discrimination." *Phylon* 21, no. 3 (3rd qtr. 1960): 234–42.
Carter, Wilmoth Annette. *The Urban Negro in the South*. New York: Vantage Press, 1961.
Case, Delene M. "Ain't Gonna Let Nobody Turn Me Around: The Black Freedom Struggle in Mobile, Alabama, 1902–1969." MA thesis, University of South Alabama, 2004.
Chaudron, Louis de Vendel. *Mobile Mystics and the Story of Mardi Gras Societies*. Mobile: Bienville Historical Society, 1910.

Chauncey, George Jr. "Christian Brotherhood or Sexual Perversion? Homosexual Identities and the Construction of Sexual Boundaries in the World War I Era." In *Hidden from History: Reclaiming the Gay and Lesbian Past*, ed. Martin Duberman, Martha Vinicius, and George Chauncey Jr., 294–317. London: Penguin Books, 1991.

Chauncey, George. *Gay New York: Gender, Urban Culture, and the Making of the Gay Male World, 1890–1940*. New York: Basic Books, 1994.

Chomsky, Noam, and Morris Halle. *The Sound Pattern of English*. New York: Harper & Row, 1968.

Cixous, Hélène. "Sorties." Translated by Ann Liddle. In *Modern Criticism and Theory: A Reader*, edited by David Lodge, 287–93. London: Longman, 1988.

Cobb, James C. *Away Down South: A History of Southern Identity*. New York: Oxford University Press, 2005.

Coffey, Michele Grigsby. "The State of Louisiana v. Charles Guerand: Interracial Sexual Mores, Rape Rhetoric, and Respectability in 1930s New Orleans." *Louisiana History: The Journal of the Louisiana Historical Association* 54, no. 1 (Winter 2013): 47–93.

Cohen, Cathy J. "Deviance as Resistance: A New Research Agenda for the Study of Black Politics." *Du Bois Review: Social Science Research on Race* 1, no. 1 (2004): 27–45.

Cohen, Cathy J. "Punks, Bulldaggers, and Welfare Queens: The Radical Potential of Queer Politics?" *GLQ* 3, no. 4 (May 1, 1997): 437–65.

Colomina, Beatriz. *Sexuality & Space*. New York: Princeton Architectural Press, 1992.

Cox, Aimee Meredith. *Shapeshifters: Black Girls and the Choreography of Citizenship*. Durham, NC: Duke University Press, 2015.

Cox, Karen L. *Dixie's Daughters: The United Daughters of the Confederacy and the Preservation of Confederate Culture*. Gainesville: University Press of Florida, 2004.

Craighead, Erwin. *Mobile: Fact and Tradition, Noteworthy People and Events*. Mobile: Powers Printing, 1930.

Crenshaw, Kimberlé. "Demarginalizing the Intersection of Race and Sex: A Black Feminist Critique of Antidiscrimination Doctrine, Feminist Theory and Antiracist Politics." *University of Chicago Legal Forum* 1989, no. 1 (1989): 139–67.

Cunha, Maria Clementina Pereira. *Ecos da folia: Uma história social do carnaval carioca entre 1880 e 1920*. São Paulo: Companhia das Letras, 2001.

DaMatta, Roberto. *Carnivals, Rogues and Heroes: An interpretation of the Brazilian Dilemma*. Notre Dame: University of Notre Dame Press, 1991.

Danow, David K. *The Spirit of Carnival: Magical Realism and the Grotesque*. Lexington: University Press of Kentucky, 1995.

Davis, Angela Y. *Women, Race & Class*. New York: Random House, 1981.

Davis, Susan G. *Parades and Power: Street Theatre in Nineteenth-Century Philadelphia*. Berkeley: University of California Press, 1988.

Davis, Natalie Zemon. *Society and Culture in Early Modern France*. Stanford, CA: Stanford University Press, 1965.

Davis-Horton, Paulette. *Avenue . . . the Place, the People, the Memories, 1799–1986*. Mobile: Horton, 1991.

Dean, Bennett Wayne. *Mardi Gras: Mobile's Illogical Whoop-De-Doo*. Chicago: Adams Press, 1971.

Dean, Bennett Wayne. *Have a Good Time but Don't Get Bad!* Mobile: Joe Cain Marching Society, 2019.

D'Emilio, John. *Sexual Politics, Sexual Communities: The Making of a Homosexual Minority in the United States, 1940–1970*. Chicago: University of Chicago Press, 1983.

DeFrantz, Thomas F., and Anita Gonzalez, eds. *Black Performance Theory*. Durham, NC: Duke University Press, 2014.

Degler, Carl N. *Neither Black nor White: Slavery and Race Relations in Brazil and the United States*. New York: Macmillan, 1971.

Derrida, Jacques. *On Grammatology*. Baltimore: Johns Hopkins University Press, 1976.

Dews, Carlos L., and Carolyn Leste Law. *Out in the South*. Philadelphia: Temple University Press, 2001.

Diard, Francois Ludgére. *The Tree: Being the Strange Case of Charles R. S. Boyington*. Mobile: Gill Printing Company, 1949.

Diouf, Sylviane A. *Dreams of Africa in Alabama: The Slave Ship "Clotilda" and the Story of the Last Africans Brought to America*. Oxford: Oxford University Press, 2009.

Dirksen, Rebecca. *After the Dance, the Drums Are Heavy: Carnival, Politics, and Musical Engagement in Haiti*. New York: Oxford University Press, 2020.

Domínguez, Virginia R. *White by Definition: Social Classification in Creole Louisiana*. New Brunswick, NJ: Rutgers University Press, 1986.

Duberman, Martin, Martha Vicinus, and George Chauncey, eds. *Hidden from History: Reclaiming the Gay and Lesbian Past*. London: Penguin Books, 1991.

Du Bois, W. E. B. *The Souls of Black Folk*. New York: Barns & Noble Classics, 2003.

Dusselier, Jane. "Understandings of Food as Culture." *Environmental History* 14, no. 2 (2009): 331–38.

Eagleton, Terry. *Walter Benjamin, or Towards a Revolutionary Criticism*. New York: Verso Books, 2009.

Eco, Umberto, Thomas Albert Sebeok, Vjačeslav Vsevolodovič Ivanov, and Monica Rector. *Carnival!* Berlin: Mouton, 1984.

Ehrenreich, Barbara. *Dancing in the Streets: A History of Collective Joy*. London: Granta Books, 2008.

Eligon, John. "A Debate over Identity and Race Asks, Are African-Americans 'Black' or 'black'?" *New York Times*, June 26, 2020.

Epstein, Dena J. *Sinful Tunes and Spirituals: Black Folk Music to the Civil War*. Urbana: University of Illinois Press, 2003.

Escott, Paul D., and Sally G. MacMillen. *Major Problems in the History of the American South: Documents and Essays, Vol. II: The New South*. Lexington, MA: Heath, 2012.

Eskridge, William N. Jr. *Dishonorable Passions: Sodomy Laws in America, 1861–2003*. New York: Viking, 2008.

Faderman, Lillian. *The Gay Revolution: The Story of the Struggle*. New York: Simon & Schuster, 2016.

Feimster, Crystal N. *Southern Horrors: Women and the Politics of Rape and Lynching*. Cambridge: Harvard University Press, 2009.

Fleetwood, Nicole R. *Troubling Vision: Performance, Visuality, and Blackness*. Chicago: University of Chicago Press, 2011.

Fogelman, Tatiana. "Straights in a Gay Bar: Negotiating Boundaries through Time-Space." In *Geographies of Sexualities: Theory, Practices and Politics*, edited by Jason Lim and Kath Browne (London: Routledge, 2016): 137–50.

Fraser, Nancy. "Rethinking the Public Sphere: A Contribution to the Critique of Actually Existing Democracy." *Social Text*, no. 25/26 (1990): 56–80.

Freyre, Gilberto, and Mário Souto Maior. "Carnaval: De onde veio? Como era? Como evoluiu?" *História* (São Paulo), no. 9 (February 1974): 81–91.

Gaddis, Elijah. "Processional Culture and Black Mobility in Maggie Washington's Wilmington." *Journal of Festive Studies* 3 (2021): 72–91.

Gaines, Kevin Kelly. *Uplifting the Race: Black Leadership, Politics, and Culture in the Twentieth Century*. Chapel Hill: University of North Carolina Press, 1996.

Gates, Henry Louis. "The 'Blackness of Blackness': A Critique of the Sign and the Signifying Monkey." *Critical Inquiry* 9, no. 4 (June 1983): 685–723.

Gates, Henry Louis. *The Signifying Monkey: A Theory of Afro-American Literary Criticism*. New York: Oxford University Press, 1988.

Gerber, Cheryl. *Cherchez la femme: New Orleans Women*. Jackson: University Press of Mississippi, 2020.

Gill, James. *Lords of Misrule: Mardi Gras and the Politics of Race in New Orleans*. Jackson: University Press of Mississippi, 1997.

Godet, Aurélie. "Behind the Masks." *Journal of Festive Studies* 2 (2020): 1–31.

Gontijo, Fabiano. *O Rei Momo e o Arco-Íris: Homossexualidade e Carnaval no Rio de Janeiro*. Rio de Janeiro: Garamond Universitária, 2009.

Goudsouzian, Aram. *Down to the Crossroads: Civil Rights, Black Power, and the Meredith March Against Fear*. New York: Farrar, Straus and Giroux, 2015.

Grabher, Barbara. "Somewhere over the Rainbow: Investigating Festival Decorations in the LGBT50 Celebration of Hull, UK City of Culture 2017." *Journal of Festive Studies* 3 (2021): 156–64.

Green, Garth L., and Philip W. Scher. *Trinidad Carnival: The Cultural Politics of a Transnational Festival*. Bloomington: Indiana University Press, 2007.

Greene, Oliver N. "The Aesthetic of Asé in the Black Masking Indians of New Orleans: Musical Africanisms and Orisa Manifestations in the Big Chief." *Fire!!!* 6, no. 2 (2020): 73–127.

Griffin, Larry J. "Southern Distinctiveness, Yet Again, or, Why America Still Needs the South." *Southern Cultures* 6, no. 3 (Fall 2000): 47–72.

Grose, Francis. *A Classical Dictionary of the Vulgar Tongue*. London: S. Hopper, 1785.

Gutiérrez, Ramón A., and Geneviève Fabre. *Feasts and Celebrations in North American Ethnic Communities*. Albuquerque: University of New Mexico Press, 1995.

Hale, Grace Elizabeth. *Making Whiteness: The Culture of Segregation in the South, 1890–1940*. New York: Vintage Books, 1999.

Hall, Stuart, Jessica Evans, and Sean Nixon, eds. *Representation: Cultural Representations and Signifying Practices*. Los Angeles: Sage, 2013.

Hall, Stuart. "Cultural Identity and Diaspora." In *Theorizing Diaspora: A Reader* edited by Jana Evans Braziel and Anita Mannur, 23346. Malden, MA: Blackwell Pub., 2003.

Hanhardt, Christina B. *Safe Space: Gay Neighborhood History and the Politics of Violence*. Durham, NC: Duke University Press, 2013.

Hardy, Arthur. *Mardi Gras in New Orleans: An Illustrated History*. 4th ed. New Orleans: Arthur Hardy Enterprises, 2009.

Harker, Jaime. *The Lesbian South: Southern Feminists, the Women in Print Movement, and the Queer Literary Canon*. Chapel Hill: University of North Carolina Press, 2018.

Hartless, Jaime. 2019. "Questionably Queer: Understanding Straight Presence in the Post-Gay Bar." *Journal of Homosexuality* 66, no. 8: 1035–57.

Haspelmath, Martin. "Against Markedness (And What to Replace It With)." *Journal of Linguistics* 42, no. 1 (March 2006): 25–70.

Hearin, Emily Staples. *Let the Good Times Roll! Mobile, Mother of Mystics*. Mobile: E. S. Hearin & W. B. Taylor, 1996.
Hearin, Emily Staples, and Kathryn Taylor DeCelle. *Queens of Mobile Mardi Gras, 1893–1986*. Mobile: Museum of the City of Mobile, 1986.
Heers, Jacques. *Fêtes des fous et carnavals*. Paris: Hachette Littératures, 2007.
heinz, matthew. *Entering Transmasculinity: The Inevitability of Discourse*. Bristol, UK: Intellect Books, 2016.
Heller. Meredith. *Queering Drag: Redefining the Discourse of Gender-Bending*. Bloomington: Indiana University Press, 2020.
Higginbotham, Evelyn Brooks. "African-American Women's History and the Metalanguage of Race." *Signs* 17, no. 2 (1992): 251–74.
Higginbotham, Evelyn Brooks. *Righteous Discontent: The Women's Movement in the Black Baptist Church, 1880–1920*. Cambridge: Harvard University Press, 1994.
Higginbotham, Jay. *Mobile: City by the Bay*. Mobile: Mobile Junior Chamber of Commerce, 1999.
Higginbotham, Jay. *Old Mobile: Fort Louis De La Louisiane, 1702–1711*. Mobile: Museum of the City of Mobile, 1977.
Hirsch, Arnold R., and Joseph Logsdon. *Creole New Orleans: Race and Americanization*. Baton Rouge: Louisiana State University Press, 1992.
Hobsbawm, Eric, and Terence Ranger. *The Invention of Tradition*. Cambridge: Cambridge University Press, 1983.
Holtz, Allan. *American Newspaper Comics: An Encyclopedic Reference Guide*. Ann Arbor: University of Michigan Press, 2012.
Horowitz, Katie. *Drag, Interperformance, and the Trouble with Queerness*. London: Routledge, 2019.
Howard, John, ed. *Carrying On in the Lesbian and Gay South*. New York: New York University Press, 1997.
Howard, John. *Men like That: A Southern Queer History*. Chicago: University of Chicago Press, 1999.
Hunt, Lynn. *The New Cultural History*. Berkeley: University of California Press, 2000.
Hunter, Marcus Anthony, and Zandria F. Robinson. *Chocolate Cities: The Black Map of American Life*. Oakland: University of California Press, 2018.
Hurston, Zora Neale. *Barracoon: The Story of the Last "Black Cargo."* New York: Harper Collins, 2018.
Isenberg, Alison. *Downtown America: A History of the Place and the People Who Made It*. Chicago: University of Chicago Press, 2004.
Jackson, Kern. "Going to the Boomalatta: Narrating Black Mardi Gras in Mobile, Alabama." *Tributaries*, no. 7 (2004): 38–74.
Jackson, Kern. "Listening to the Wise Ones: Personal Narrative as a Window into Traditional Black Neighborhoods in Mobile, AL." PhD diss., Indiana University, 2004.
Jansson, David R. "Internal Orientalism in America: W. J. Cash's *The Mind of the South* and the Spatial Construction of American National Identity." *Political Geography* 22 (March 2003): 293–316.
Johnson, E. Patrick. *Appropriating Blackness: Performance and the Politics of Authenticity*. Durham, NC: Duke University Press, 2003.

Johnson, E. Patrick. *Black. Queer. Southern. Women: An Oral History*. Chapel Hill: University of North Carolina Press, 2018.

Johnson, E. Patrick. *Sweet Tea: Black Gay Men in the South*. Chapel Hill: University of North Carolina Press, 2014.

Jones, Amelia. *In Between Subjects: A Critical Genealogy of Queer Performance*. New York: Routledge, 2021.

Joseph, Channing Gerard. "The First Drag Queen Was a Former Slave Who Fought for Queer Freedom a Century before Stonewall." *The Nation*, January 31, 2020.

Joynt, Steve. "How It All Started." In *The Art and Design of Mardi Gras*, by David Ernest Alsobrook, Judi Gulledge, Deborah Velders, Steve Joynt, Cartledge Weeden Blackwell III, Scotty E. Kirkland, and Karyn Zweifel, 11–22. Mobile: Mobile Museum of Art, 2014.

Joynt, Steve. "Changing His Story." *Mobile Mask* (2015): 28–33.

Kein, Sybil. *Creole: The History and Legacy of Louisiana's Free People of Color*. Baton Rouge: Louisiana State University Press, 2000.

Kelley, Robin D. G. *Hammer and Hoe: Alabama Communists during the Great Depression*. Chapel Hill: University of North Carolina Press, 1990.

Kennedy, Elizabeth Lapovsky, and Madeline D. Davis. *Boots of Leather, Slippers of Gold: The History of a Lesbian Community*. New York: Routledge, 1993.

Kinser, Samuel. *Carnival, American Style: Mardi Gras at New Orleans and Mobile*. Chicago: University of Chicago Press, 1990.

Kirkland, Scotty E. Excerpt from chapter 9, "Sad History," from "Jordan's Stormy Banks: Politics and Race in Twentieth-Century Mobile, Alabama" (unpublished manuscript).

Kirkland, Scotty E. "John Langan." *Encyclopedia of Alabama*. August 10, 2015. http://www.encyclopediaofalabama.org/article/h-2979.

Kirkland, Scotty E. "Neighborhood Organized Workers of Mobile (NOW)." *Encyclopedia of Alabama*, August 10, 2015, http://www.encyclopediaofalabama.org/article/h-3104.

Kirkland, Scotty E. "Pink Sheets and Black Ballots: Politics and Civil Rights in Mobile, Alabama, 1945–1985." Master's thesis, University of South Alabama, 2009.

Kirkland, Scotty. "Community on Parade: The Mobile Area Mardi Gras Association's Diamond Anniversary." In *The Art and Design of Mardi Gras*, by David Ernest Alsobrook, Judi Gulledge, Deborah Velders, Steve Joynt, Cartledge Weeden Blackwell III, Scotty E. Kirkland, and Karyn Zweifel, 35–44. Mobile: Mobile Museum of Art, 2014.

Kirshenblatt-Gimblett, Barbara and Brooks McNamara. "Processional Performance: An Introduction," *Drama Review* 29, no. 3 (Autumn 1985): 2–5.

Kong, Lily, and Brenda S. A. Yeoh. "The Construction of National Identity through the Production of Ritual and Spectacle: An Analysis of National Day Parades in Singapore." *Political Geography* 16, no. 3 (1997): 213–39.

Krauthamer, Barbara. *Black Slaves, Indian Masters: Slavery, Emancipation, and Citizenship in the Native American South*. Chapel Hill: University of North Carolina Press, 2015.

Kruse, Kevin Michael. *White Flight: Atlanta and the Making of Modern Conservatism*. Princeton: Princeton University Press, 2005.

Laborde, Errol. *Krewe: The Early New Orleans Carnival, Comus to Zulu*. New Orleans: Carnival Press, 2007.

Ladurie, Emmanuel Le Roy. *Carnival in Romans*. New York: Braziliar, 1979.

La Fountain-Stokes, Lawrence. *Translocas: The Politics of Puerto Rican Drag and Trans Performance*. Ann Arbor: University of Michigan Press, 2021.

Lassiter, Matthew D. *The Silent Majority: Suburban Politics in the Sunbelt South*. Princeton: Princeton University Press, 2006.

Leamer, Laurence. *The Lynching: The Epic Courtroom Battle That Brought Down the Klan*. New York: William Morrow, 2016.

Lee, Kevin. "How a Detective Who Was Blamed for One Lynching Solved Another." *Daily Beast*, March 21, 2021.

Lévi-Strauss, Claude. *Le cru et le cuit*. Paris: Pilon, 1964.

Lief, Shane, and John McCusker. *Jockomo: The Native Roots of Mardi Gras Indians*. Jackson: University Press of Mississippi, 2019.

Lorini, Alessandra. "Public Rituals and the Culture Making of the New York African American Community." In *Feasts and Celebrations in North American Ethnic Communities*, edited by Ramón A. Gutiérrez and Geneviève Fabre, 29–46. Albuquerque: University of New Mexico Press, 1995.

Lovett, William J., Charles W. Porter, and Jean Tolbert. *Mardi Gras in Mobile: A Chronicle of Black Participation*. Mobile: Mobile Area Mardi Gras Association, 1980.

Lynn, Sharon, and Robert James. *All about Mardi Gras*. Abilene, TX: County Road, 2012.

Machado, Isabel. "Introduction: On the Materiality of Festivity." *Journal of Festive Studies* 3 (2021): 1–13.

Machado, Isabel. "Never Too Big, Never Too Much: How the Order of Osiris Helped Build a Visible LGBTQ Community in Mobile, Alabama." *Oral History* 46, no. 1 (March 2018).

Marinucci, Mimi. *Feminism Is Queer: The Intimate Connection between Queer and Feminist Theory*. London: Zed Books, 2010.

Marler, Scott P. *The Merchants' Capital: New Orleans and the Political Economy of the Nineteenth-Century South*. Cambridge: Cambridge University Press, 2013.

Marshall, Margaret M. "The Creole of Mon Louis Island, Alabama, and the Louisiana Connection." *Journal of Pidgin and Creole Languages* 6, no. 1 (1991): 73–87.

Maurantonio, Nicole. *Confederate Exceptionalism: Civil War Myth and Memory in the Twenty-First Century*. Lawrence: University Press of Kansas, 2019.

McGuire, Danielle L. *At the Dark End of the Street: Black Women, Rape, and Resistance: A New History of the Civil Rights Movement from Rosa Parks to the Rise of Black Power*. New York: Vintage Books, 2011.

McLaurin, Melton. "Mobile Blacks and World War II: The Development of a Political Consciousness." In *Gulf Coast Politics in the Twentieth Century*, edited by Ted Carageorge, 47–56. Pensacola, FL: Historic Pensacola Preservation Board, 1973

McMillan, Uri. *Embodied Avatars: Genealogies of Black Feminist Art and Performance*. New York: New York University Press, 2015.

Mercer, Korbena. *Welcome to the Jungle: New Positions in Black Cultural Studies*. New York: Routledge, 1994.

Miguez, Paulo. "Muitos (outros) carnavais." *Revista Observatório Itaú Cultural*, no. 14 (May 2013).

Miller, Neil. *Out of the Past: Gay and Lesbian History from 1869 to the Present*. New York, NY: Alyson Books, 2006.

Mitchell, Reid. *All on a Mardi Gras Day: Episodes in the History of New Orleans Carnival*. Cambridge: Harvard University Press, 1995.

Moore, Henrietta. "Divided We Stand": Sex, Gender, and Sexual Difference." *Feminist Review* no. 47 (Summer, 1994): 78–95.
moore, madison. *Fabulous: The Rise of the Beautiful Eccentric*. New Haven Yale University Press 2018.
Morais, Eneida de. *História do carnaval carioca*. Rio de Janeiro: Editôra Civilização Brasileira, 1958.
Muñoz, José Esteban. *Disidentifications: Queers of Color and the Performance of Politics*. Minneapolis: University of Minnesota Press, 2015.
Murphy, Kevin P., Jennifer L. Pierce, and Jason Ruiz. "What Makes Queer Oral History Different." *Oral History Review* 43, no. 1 (2016): 1–24.
Muskat, Beth Taylor. "Black Militias in Alabama." *Encyclopedia of Alabama*. March 7, 2007. Last updated October 6, 2017. http://www.encyclopediaofalabama.org/article/h-1083.
Muskat, Beth Taylor. "Mobile's Black Militia: Major R. R. Mims and Gilmer's Rifles." *Alabama Review* 57 (July 2004): 183–205.
Nash, Jennifer C. *The Black Body in Ecstasy: Reading Race, Reading Pornography*. Durham, NC: Duke University Press, 2014.
Nora, Pierre. "Between Memory and History: Les Lieux de Mémoire." Special issue "Memory and Counter-Memory." *Representations*, no. 26 (Spring 1989): 8–9.
Nora, Pierre. *Realms of Memory*. New York: Columbia University Press, 1996.
Norton, Rictor. *Mother Clap's Molly House: The Gay Subculture in England, 1700–1830*. London: Gay Men's Press, 1992.
Pond, Anne Janine. *Cowbellion: The Antebellum Gulf Coast and the Birth of America's Mardi Gras*. N.p.: self-published, Lulu.com, 2015.
Pond, Anne Janine. "The Ritualized Construction of Status: The Men Who Made Mardi Gras, 1830–1900." PhD diss., University of Southern Mississippi, 2006.
Queiroz, Maria Isaura Pereira de. *Carnaval brasileiro: O vivido e o mito*. São Paulo: Brasiliense, 1992.
Rao, Rahul. *Out of Time: The Queer Politics of Postcoloniality*. New York: Oxford University Press, 2020.
Rayford, Julian Lee. *Chasin' the Devil Round a Stump*. Mobile: American Print, 1962.
Reis, João José. *Divining Slavery and Freedom: The Story of Domingos Sodré, an African Priest in Nineteenth-Century Brazil*. New York: Cambridge University Press, 2015.
Reis, João José. *Ganhadores: A greve negra de 1857 na Bahia*. São Paulo: Companhia das Letras, 2019.
Rhett's Butler (pseud.). "Happenings in the Port City." *Alabama Forum*, May 1983, 3.
Ribeiro, Djamila. *Quem tem medo do feminismo negro?* São Paulo: Companhia das Letras, 2018.
Ribeiro, Djamila. *Lugar de Fala*. São Paulo: Editora Jandaíra, 2020.
Richardson, Fredrick Douglas. *The Genesis and Exodus of NOW*. Boynton Beach, FL: Futura Printing, 1996.
Riggio, Milla Cozart. *Carnival: Culture in Action: The Trinidad Experience*. Abingdon: Routledge, 2004.
Ritterhouse, Jennifer Lynn. *Growing Up Jim Crow: How Black and White Southern Children Learned Race*. Chapel Hill: University of North Carolina Press, 2006.
Roach, Joseph. *Cities of the Dead: Circum-Atlantic Performance*. New York: Columbia University Press, 1996.

Roberts, L. Craig. *Mardi Gras in Mobile*. Charleston, SC: History Press, 2015.
Robinson, Kenneth A. *Port City Crusader: John LeFlore and the Non-Partisan Voters' League in Mobile, Alabama*. Mobile: Mod Mobilian Press, 2013.
Robinson, Zandria F. *This Ain't Chicago: Race, Class, and Regional Identity in the Post-Soul South*. Chapel Hill: University of North Carolina Press, 2014.
Rosenthal, Gregory Samantha. *Living Queer History: Remembrance and Belonging in a Southern City*. Chapel Hill: University of North Carolina Press, 2021.
Ross, Marlon B. *Sissy Insurgencies: A Racial Anatomy of Unfit Manliness*. Durham: Duke University Press, 2022.
Rutherford, Jonathan. *Identity: Community, Culture, Difference*. London: Lawrence & Wishart, 1990.
Ryan, Mary. "The American Parade: Representations of the Nineteenth-Century Social Order." In *The New Cultural History*, ed. Lynn Hunt, 131–53. Berkeley: University of California Press, 2000.
Santino, Jack, ed. *Public Performances: Studies in the Carnivalesque and Ritualesque*. Logan: Utah State University Press, 2017.
Santino, Jack. "From Carnivalesque to Ritualesque: Public Ritual and the Theater of the Street," in *Public Performances: Studies in the Carnivalesque and Ritualesque*, ed. Jack Santino, 3–15. Logan: Utah State University Press, 2017.
Saxon, Lyle Edward Dreyer, and Robert Tallant. *Gumbo Ya-Ya: A Collection of Louisiana Folk Tales*. Boston: Houghton Mifflin, 1945.
Schechner, Richard. "Carnival (Theory) after Bakhtin." In *Carnival: Culture in Action: The Trinidad Experience*, edited by Milla Cozart Riggio, 3–12. Abingdon: Routledge, 2004.
Schindler, Henri. *Mardi Gras: New Orleans*. Paris: Flammarion, 1997.
Schwartz, Selby Wynn. *The Bodies of Others: Drag Dances and Their Afterlives*. Ann Arbor: University of Michigan Press, 2019.
Scott, Joan W. "Gender: A Useful Category of Historical Analysis." *American Historical Review* 91, no. 5 (1986): 1053–75.
Sears, James T. *Lonely Hunters: An Oral History of Lesbian and Gay Southern Life, 1948–1968*. Boulder: Westview Press, 1997.
Sears, James T. *Rebels, Rubyfruit, and Rhinestones: Queering Space in the Stonewall South*. New Brunswick, N.J.: Rutgers University Press, 2001.
Self, Robert O. *American Babylon: Race and the Struggle for Postwar Oakland*. Princeton: Princeton University Press, 2003.
Sergidou, Katerina. "'Living like Queens.'" *Journal of Festive Studies* 2 (2020): 153–178.
Sheftel, Anna, and Stacey Zembrzycki. "Who's Afraid of Oral History? Fifty Years of Debates and Anxiety about Ethics." *Oral History Review* 43, no. 2 (September 2016): 338–66.
Shilling, Chris. "The Body and Difference." In *Identity and Difference*, ed. Kathryn Woodward (London: Sage, 1997): 63–120.
Sledge, John S. *The Mobile River*. Columbia: University of South Carolina Press, 2015.
Smith, Howard Philips. *Unveiling the Muse: The Lost History of Gay Carnival in New Orleans*. Jackson: University Press of Mississippi, 2017.
Smith, Howard Philips, and Frank Perez. *Southern Decadence in New Orleans*. Baton Rouge: Louisiana State University Press, 2018.
Snyder, Andrew. "'Carnaval em casa:' Activist Inversions in Rio de Janeiro's Street Carnival during the COVID-19 Pandemic." *Journal of Festive Studies* 3 (2021): 17–46.

Souther, J. Mark. *New Orleans on Parade: Tourism and the Transformation of the Crescent City*. Baton Rouge: Louisiana State University Press, 2006.
Southern, Eileen. *The Music of Black Americans: A History*. New York: W. W. Norton, 2006.
Southern Poverty Law Center. "Alabama's Shame: HB 56 and the War on Immigrants." splcenter.org, January 31, 2012, https://www.splcenter.org/20120131/alabamas-shame-hb-56-and-war-immigrants.
Spielmann, Ellen. *Teorías y formas de análisis de las relaciones entre globalidad y localidad en América latina (1982–2005)*. Berlin: Wissenschaftlicher Verlag Berlin, 2007.
Stanonis, Anthony J. *Creating the Big Easy: New Orleans and the Emergence of Modern Tourism, 1918–1945*. Athens: University of Georgia Press, 2006.
Steiner, Malcolm, and Michael P. Robinson. *Old Mobile Restaurants*. Mobile: Malcolm Steiner, 2009.
Stephens, Michelle Ann. *Skin Acts: Race, Psychoanalysis, and the Black Male Performer*. Durham, NC: Duke University Press, 2014.
Stillman, Peter G., and Adelaide H. Villmoare. "Democracy Despite Government: African American Parading and Democratic Theory." *New Political Science* 32, no. 4 (December 2010): 485–99.
Stone, Amy L. "Making an Inclusive Collective Party or Building LGBTQ+ Community? Tensions In LGBTQ Festival Events in American Mardi Gras." *Journal of Policy Research in Tourism, Leisure and Events*. Published online on March 4, 2022. doi: 10.1080/19407963.2022.2046012.
Stone, Amy L. *Queer Carnival: Festivals and Mardi Gras in the South*. New York: New York University Press, 2022.
Strickler, Dave. *Syndicated Comic Strips and Artists, 1924–1995: The Complete Index*. Cambria, CA: Comics Access, 1995.
Stuckey, Sterling. *Slave Culture: Nationalist Theory and the Foundations of Black America*. New York: Oxford University Press, 2014.
Sugrue, Thomas J. *The Origins of the Urban Crisis: Race and Inequality in Postwar Detroit*. Princeton: Princeton University Press, 2005.
Summers, Martin Anthony. *Manliness and Its Discontents: The Black Middle Class and the Transformation of Masculinity, 1900–1930*. Chapel Hill: University of North Carolina Press, 2004.
Swarr, Amanda Lock. "Moffies, Artists, and Queens." *Journal of Homosexuality* 46, no. 3–4, (2004): 73–89
Tannen, Deborah. "Marked Women, Unmarked Men." *New York Times Magazine* (June 20, 1993.
Thomason, Michael V. R., ed. *Mobile: The New History of Alabama's First City*. Tuscaloosa: University of Alabama Press, 2012.
Thompson, Brock. *The Un-Natural State: Arkansas and the Queer South*. Fayetteville: University of Arkansas Press, 2010.
Thompson, Katrina Dyonne. *Ring Shout: The Racial Politics of Music and Dance in North American Slavery*. Urbana: University of Illinois Press, 2014.
Trillin, Calvin. *Jackson, 1964: And Other Dispatches from Fifty Years of Reporting on Race in America*. New York: Random House, 2016.
Trillin, Calvin. "The Zulus." *New Yorker*, July 20, 1964.
Trumbach, Randolph. *Sex and the Gender Revolution: Volume 1, Heterosexuality and the Third Gender in Enlightenment London*. Chicago: University of Chicago Press, 1998.

Turino, Thomas. *Music as Social Life: The Politics of Participation*. Chicago: University of Chicago Press, 2008.
Turner, Richard Brent. *Jazz Religion, the Second Line, and Black New Orleans*. Bloomington: Indiana University Press, 2009.
Turner, Victor. "Introduction." In *Celebration: Studies in Festivity and Ritual*, edited by Victor Turner, 11–32. Washington, DC: Smithsonian Institution Press, 1983
Valerio, Miguel A. "The Pardos' Triumph: The Use of Festival Material Culture for Socioracial Promotion in Eighteenth-Century Pernambuco." *Journal of Festive Studies* 3 (2021): 47–71.
Valerio, Miguel A. *Sovereign Joy: Afro-Mexican Kings and Queens, 1539–1640*. Cambridge: Cambridge University Press, 2022.
Vaz, Kim Marie. *The "Baby Dolls": Breaking the Race and Gender Barriers of the New Orleans Mardi Gras Tradition*. Baton Rouge: Louisiana State University Press, 2013.
Verney, Kevern. "'Every Man Should Try': John L. LeFlore and the National Association for the Advancement of Colored People in Alabama, 1919–1956." *Alabama Review* 66, no. 3 (July 2013): 186–210.
Vogel, Shane. *The Scene of Harlem Cabaret: Race, Sexuality, Performance*. Chicago: University of Chicago Press, 2009.
Wade, Leslie A. *Downtown Mardi Gras: New Carnival Practices in Post-Katrina New Orleans*. 2019.
Ware, Carolyn. *Cajun Women and Mardi Gras: Reading the Rules Backward*. Urbana: University of Illinois Press, 2007.
Warner, Michael. "Publics and Counterpublics (Abbreviated Version)." *Quarterly Journal of Speech* 88, no. 4 (November 2002): 413–25.
Warner, Michael. *Publics and Counterpublics*. New York: Zone Books, 2014.
Watkins, Jerry T. III. "Hot Times on the Gay Gulf Coast: Queer Networks and Cruising through North Florida's Spaces, 1945–1965." Thesis, Kings College London, 2013.
Watkins, Jerry T. III. *Queering the Redneck Riviera: Sexuality and the Rise of Florida Tourism*. Gainesville: University Press of Florida, 2018.
Waugh, Linda. "Marked and Unmarked: A Choice between Unequals in Semiotic Structure." *Semiotica* 38 (1982): 299–318.
Waugh, Linda R., Morris Malle, and Roman Jakobson. *Russian and Slavic Grammar: Studies 1931–1981*. Berlin: Mouton, 1984.
White, E. Frances. *Dark Continent of Our Bodies: Black Feminism and the Politics of Respectability*. Philadelphia: Temple University Press, 2001.
Wilson, James F. *Bulldaggers, Pansies, and Chocolate Babies: Performance, Race, and Sexuality in the Harlem Renaissance*. Ann Arbor: University of Michigan Press, 2010.
Wirth, Thomas H. *Gay Rebel of the Harlem Renaissance: Selections from the Work of Richard Bruce Nugent*. Durham, NC: Duke University Press, 2002.
Woodward, Kathryn, ed. *Identity and Difference*. London: Sage, 2014.
Young, Harvey. *Embodying Black Experience: Stillness, Critical Memory, and the Black Body*. Ann Arbor: University of Michigan Press, 2010.

INDEX

References to figures are in **bold**.

Aaron, Hank, 85
Abernathy, Rev. Ralph D., 94
activism: African American, 76, 81; LGBTQIA+, 101, 109–12. *See also* GAE; NOW
ADDSCO (Alabama Dry Dock and Shipbuilding Company), 54
Africatown (Plateau/Magazine Point), 146, 163, 212n49
AIDS (Acquired Immune Deficiency Syndrome). *See* HIV/AIDS
AIDS Alabama, 156, 157, 179
Alabama Civic Affairs Association, 94
Alabama Forum, 39, 101, 104, 112, 115, 156, 158
Alabama House of Representatives, 94
Alabama State Teacher's College, 84, 85, 97
Alabama Tourism Department, 17
Aldridge, Neil, 70, 112, 115, **116**, **117**, 118, **119**, 120, **121**, 156
Allen, Winston (King Tuttle), 83, 84, 201n39
Argo, Larry, 112
Ash Wednesday, 7, 43, 100
Atkinson, Budgie, 112. *See also* Queen Budgie I
Azalea City News and Review, 120, 158

balls: cross-dressing in, **102**, 103; gay Mardi Gras societies, 103; Mystic Womyn of Color, 168; nineteenth-century African American, 79, 80, 81, 83; prohibition for Black people, 11, 32, 79; twentieth-century African American, 86, 91, **174**; white elites, 18, 172. *See also* Osiris Ball
Banks, Willis, 80
Barret, Ron, 114, 181
bars: community building in, 110, 113, 115, 169; gay/lesbian, 65, 69–71, 106–10, 113, 115, 123, 173; Greek, 69; police harassment and raids in, 107–9
Barton Academy, 133
Baton Rouge, Louisiana, 103, 143
Battle, Lya (Queen), **89**
Baumhauer, Charles A., 84
B-Bob's (LGBTQIA+ club), xviii, 173
Beasley, Noble, 97, 99
Besteda, Samuel, 77, 84
Betbeze, Yolande, 38
Bienville, Jean Baptiste Lemoyne, 20, 46, 93
Bienville Square, 3, 45, 46, 107, 129, 151
Birmingham, Alabama, 64, 79, 100, 157
birthplace of Mardi Gras, 10, 12, 17, 20, 25, 36, 48, 165. *See also* Mother of Mystics; original Mardi Gras
Bishop, Jack, xiii, 3, 56, 70, 107, 108, 178
Black militias, 80, 200n23

Black mutual aid organizations, 77, 84
Black women, 84, 87, 88, 141, 143
blackface (costuming as African Americans), 24, 26, 27, 37, 40, 64, 91, 147
Bobbie Lord (drag performer), 107
Boeuf Gras, 21, 26, 112
Bolden, Willey, 150
Bolden v. City of Mobile, 150–52, 154
Boykin, Frank, 28, 54
Brenda Dee (drag performer), 107
Brookley Army Air Field (Brookley Field), 54, 56, 65, 198n38
Brown, Margaret, 75, 162. See also *Order of Myths, The*
Brown v. Board of Education, 58

Cain, Joe (Joseph Stillwell), 10, 19, 24, 25, **26**, 29, 30, 44, 45, 46, 48. *See also* Joe Cain Day; Joe Cain Procession
Carmichael, Stokely (Kwame Ture), 97
Carnaval (Brazil), 10
Carnival American Style, 20
carnivalesque, 12, 31, 32, 77, 83, 110, **145**, 146, 147
Carter, Emanuel, 84, 201n40
Carter, Wilmoth A., 59
Central High School, 67; band, 138, **138**, 176
Champagne Munroe (drag performer), **173**
Chasin' the Devil Round a Stump, 19–20, 28, 77
Church Street Cemetery, xvii, 30, 41, 44, 45
City Codes of Ordinance, xix, 31–35
City Planning Commission of Mobile, 55
civil rights movement, 82; activism, 65–67, 81, 93–97, 150; Mobile leaders, 54. *See also* John LeFlore; NOW; NPVL
Civil War (US), 10, 24, 26, 48, 54, 112
Cleveland, Suzanne, xii, 3, **42**, 63, 181
Clotilda (ship), 162
Club 55 (brothel), 69
Club Park Avenue (gay club), 123
Cohen, Cathy, 142, 148, 209n32
Colored Carnival Association. *See* MCCA
Comic Cowboys, 27, 101, 102, 172
Compton Cafeteria riot, 108
Conception Street, 65, 71, 106, 155. *See also* Fruit Loop

Confederacy (US): battle flag, 7; culture, 9; mythology and nostalgia, 18, 19, 24–27, 30, 47, 58, 63
Conti Street, 21, 69, 71. *See also* Fruit Loop
costuming contests, 36–40, 83. *See also* blackface; redface
Cowbellion de Rakin Society, 21–23, 27
Creole Fire Company, 135
Creoles, xix, 81, 183n6
cross-dressing, xx, 143, 147; in Mardi Gras societies, 101, **102**, 103; prohibition of, 11, 33, 39. *See also* drag; Mollies
Curry, Janette. *See* Queen Janette XII

Dauphin Street, 21, 50, 60, 62, 80, 102, 108, 152, 155, 156, 171
David's (gay bar), 112, **113**, 115
Davis Avenue (Dr. Martin Luther King Jr. Ave.): Black Mardi Gras in, 40, 77, 82–84, 129–30, **132**, 133, 138, 145; as commercial and social hub for African Americans, 59–61, 94; decline of, 67; memories of, 59–60, 130–31, 133; and origins of NOW, 66; represented in MAMGA float, 160, 161
Davis-Horton, Paulette, 59, 67, 79, 84, 138, 141
Dean, Wayne (Bennet Wayne Dean Sr.), xi, 30, 41, 42, 46, 47, 82
Dees, Morris, 152
Dennison, Bobby, xiii, 11, 62, 131, 134, 138–41, 160, 177
Dennison, Linda, xiii, 60, 62, 131, 133, 135, 143, 160, 179
desegregation. *See* integration
Diamond, Glen, 151
Diemert, Louis ("The Man of Many Faces"), 36–40, 171
Dobson, Roland, 103
Donald, Beulah Mae, 152
Donald, Michael Anthony, 149–54, 163, 164
drag: in Mardi Gras costuming, 35–40, 102, 103, 125, 143, **145**; queens, 70, 104, 107, 115, 120, 156, **173**; shows, xviii, 68, 107, 110, 173. *See also* cross-dressing
Dragon's Social Club, 84; ball, **174**

Ehlen, Jerry, 173
Elks Lodge, 85
Emperor Felix, **5**, 33, 57
Epiphany (Twelfth Night), 20, 21
Excelsior Band, 43, 84, 135, 137, 138

fabulousness, politics of (madison moore), 168
Fair Employment Practices Commission (FEPC), 54
Finklea, James, 160
Finley, Dora, 144
Finley, Eric Franklin, xiii, 3, 60, 61, 85, 87, 130, 133, 164, 165, 178
Finley, James, 99
Fireside Lounge (gay bar), 123
flambeau/flambeaux, 4, 134, 135, **137**
Flaming Thesbians, 110
Flipside (gay bar), 155
Fort Whiting Armory, 118
Foster, J. B. "Red," 30, 41, 42, 43, 46, **47**
Franklin, James A., 84, 165
Freakers Ball, 110, **111**
French Quarter (gay bar), 69, 106, 113
Fruit Loop, xviii, 5, 68–71, 105–6, 109, 110, 126, 129, 154–55, 169, 173, 185n7

Gabriel's (gay bar), 169
GAE (Gulf Alliance for Equality), 109, 110
Gaudet, Stephen, xiii, 169, 171, 180
gay, as umbrella term, xx
Gay Pride, 110
Genesis and Exodus of NOW, The, 95
Gentlemen of Pleasure Social Club, 84, 93
Gilliard, Robert, 154
Gilmer Rifles, 80
Glover-Evans, Frederica, 87, 88
Godwin, Edna (Queen), **89**
Golden Rod Social Club, 68
Gomez, Francisco, Jr., 80
Government Street, 42, 45, 68, 69, 71, 102, 106, 131. *See also* Fruit Loop
Grace's (lesbian bar), 107
Greek immigrants, 68, 69
Gulf Alliance for Equality. *See* GAE
Gulf Informer, 82, **89**

Hagan, Leo (King), **89**
Hampton, Diane, 110, 123, 156
Hays, Bennie Jack, 151, 152
Hays, Henry, 152
Henderson, Morgan, 80
Herman, Alexander (Alex), 84, 87
Hiers, Kathie, xii, xiii, 63, 70, 109, 110, 120, 123, 126, 157, 179
Higginbotham, Jay, 20–22, 25, 26
HIV/AIDS: epidemic, 120, 149, 154, 155; fundraising for, 115; role of lesbian women in activism and care, 156, 157
Hobsbawm, Eric, 9
Holy Dayworth (drag performer), 70
homosexuality, illegality of, 11, 107

Infant Mystics, 33, 40, 125, **136**, **137**
integration, 5, 7, 54, 65, 67, 95, 110, 164, 203n67
intersectionality, xxi, xxii, 9, 81, 141, 189n27
invented traditions, 6–11, 19, 26, 41, 43, 46, 47, 72, 83, 112, 127, 128, 148

Jackson, Kern, x, 134, 135, 137, 141, 142, 146, 147, 148, 160
Jackson, Rev. Jesse, 152
Jackson, Thomas R. W., 80
Jenkins, Aline Necella, 85
Jim Crow, 81, 87, 134, 164
Joe Cain Day, 19, 30, 39, 40, 41–49, 100, 115, 168, **170**, 171, **174**
Joe Cain procession, 30, 31, 40, 41, 42, 43, 45, 46, 168, 171
Joe Cain Society. *See* Society for the Restoration and Beautification of Church Street Graveyard Inc.
Joe Cain's Merry Mistresses, 168
Joe Cain's Merry Widows, 168
Joe Cain's Secret Misters, xviii, 168–71, **174**, 175
Johnson, Rev. Clinton, 154
Jones, James A., 151
Jones, Samuel Leon (Sam), 164, 172
Jones, Vivian (Queen), **89**
Joynt, Steve, xi, 22, 167

King, Martin Luther, Jr., 94, 96, **97**
King Charles XXIV (Charles Torrey), xi, 56, 179, 200n21
King Elexis, 87, **89**
King Jan I, 120, **121**
King Lawrence XV, xiii, 39, 71, 103, 104, 114, 118, 179
Kinser, Samuel, 20, 21, 35; *Carnival American Style*, 20
Kirkland, Scotty, xi, 151, 152
KKK, 34, 143, 151, 152, **153**
Knights of May Zulu Club, 82, 84, 92
Knights of Revelry, 33, 37
Knowles, James "Tiger," 152
Krafft, Michael, 21–23, 36, 112
Krewe of Elks, 84, 92
Krewe of Pan, 103
Krewe of Phoenix, 159
Ku Klux Klan. *See* KKK

LaBeija, Lady, 166–67
Langan, Joseph (Joe), 93, 94, 96, 154, 203n71
Lauren Mitchell (drag performer), **173**
League of White Supremacy, 54
Leavens, Frank, 80
LeFlore, John, 54, 93–96
lesbians: bars catering to, 106–7; Mardi Gras experiences, 120; prejudice against in gay organizations, 123; role in HIV/AIDS activism and care, 156, 157
Levi, Dave, 101
London, Hosea, xiii, 137, 178
Lost Cause, 7, 10, 19, 25, 30, 47, 49, 165
Lost Cause Minstrels, 25, 26
Lovett, William J., Jr., 78
Lucky Lady (strip club), 65, 69
Lumpkins, Wayne Cheaere (King), **90**
Lundi Gras (Mardi Gras Monday), 129, 130, 159, 171, **172**
lynching, 149, 151, 152, 163, 200n15

MAMGA (Mobile Area Mardi Gras Association), xxi, 78, 84, 85, **86**, 87, 98, 99, 130, 141, 142, 144, 149, 159, 160, **161**, **162**, 163, 164, 165, 172. *See also* MCCA (Mobile Colored Carnival Association)
Mammoth Parade, 130, 141, 149, 159
Mardi Gras in Mobile: A Chronicle of Black Participation, 78
Mardi Gras Special Events Committee, 41, 42, 43, 45, 46
markedness, definition of, 7–9
masking: in African American Mardi Gras, 130, 141, 146, 160; in LGBTQIA+ organizations, 115, 124; ordinances, 33, 34, 103; prohibition, 34–36; public masking, 23, 36, 40, 43, 77, 102, 103, **104**; in white "unmarked" organizations, 22, **102**, **136**. *See also* costume contests; Mollies
Matturro, Claire, **153**, 154
May, Augustine S., 82. *See also* Knights of May Zulu Club
MCA (Mobile Carnival Association), 76, 92, 93, 104, 130, 164, 172
MCCA (Mobile Colored Carnival Association), xxi, 76, 78, 84, 85, 86, 87, 88, **89**, **90**, 93, 94, **132**; dispute with NOW, 98, 99; feud with New Orleans' Zulus, 91, 92
McClure, Homer, xiii, 70, 104, 154, 178
McKeand, Kim, xiii, 172, 173
McKinnis, J. T., 84
McLean, Ed J., 41, 43
Meaher, Timothy, 162
Mims, Lambert, 45, 96
Mims, Reuben Romulus, 80
Miss Betty, 106, 107
Miss Cie (drag performer), xii, xiii, xviii, **119**, 156
Miss Gay Mobile Pageant, 106, 178
Miss Mazie Savage (drag performer), 107
Miss Venus Shante DaVis (drag performer), xviii, **173**
Mistick Krewe of Comus, 22, 27
MLK Business and Civic Organization, 159, 171, **172**
MLK Monday Mystics, 159, 171, **172**
Mobile AIDS Buddy Program, 156
Mobile AIDS Support Services (MASS), 155, 156

Mobile Area Mardi Gras Association. *See* MAMGA
Mobile Beacon, 66, 67, 97, 98
Mobile Carnival Association. *See* MCA
Mobile City Commission, 41, 43, 45, 94, 150, 164
Mobile Colored Carnival Association. *See* MCCA
Mobile Historic Development Commission, 41, 45
Mobile Housing Board, 66
Mobile Mardi Gras Museum, 7, 21, 34, 77, 144, 159
Mobile Mask, 22, 167
Mobile Urban Renewal Agency, 66
Mollies, 92, 141–48; float, 141, **142**, 160, **162**
Moore, George, xiii, 56, 60, 129, 135, 138, 145, 178
Morgan, Ruby, 83
Mother of Mystics, 18, 20–25, 37, 112. *See also* birthplace of Mardi Gras; original Mardi Gras
Mystic Womyn of Color, 168

NAACP (National Association for the Advancement of Colored People), 85, 93, 95, 152
Neighborhood Organized Workers. *See* NOW
New Orleans: Black Mardi Gras, 35, 78, 82, 91, 129; gay and lesbian experiences in, 39, 107; gay Mardi Gras, 103, 106; Mobile Mardi Gras rivalry, 10, 17, 18, 22–23, 28–29, 44, 78, 82, 91–92, 112; Mobile's position in relation to, 6, 56; *Times-Picayune*, 91; white Mardi Gras, 24, 27, 32, 37, 128. *See also* Zulu Social Aid and Pleasure Club
Nicholas, Florina, 79
Non-Partisan Voters' League of Mobile. *See* NPVL
Northside Merchants, 159, 171, **172**
NOW (Neighborhood Organized Workers), 66, **67**, 76, 95–99

NPVL (Non-Partisan Voters' League of Mobile), 93–95, 203n72. *See also* LeFlore, John

Odom, Sherry, xii, xiii, 115, **116**, 123, 181
Operation Ghost Town, 66, **67**
Order of Doves: nineteenth century, 77, 79, 80; twenty-first century, 171
Order of Many Faces, 171
Order of Myths (Mardi Gras society), 33, 159, 162–64
Order of Myths, The (documentary film), 75, 149
Order of Osiris, 100, 103, 104, 110, 112–25, 149, 158–59. *See also* Osiris ball
Order of Pan, 159
original Mardi Gras, 17, 18, 48, 164. *See also* birthplace of Mardi Gras; Mother of Mystics
Osiris ball, 100, 110, 112, 114, 115, **117**, 118–25, 149, 157–59

Paris Is Burning (documentary film), 166–67
People's Parade. *See* Joe Cain procession
Pogue, Jerry, 95, **97**
Pond, Ann J., xi, 23, 24
Pope, J. Alexander, 135
population: African American, 81, 164, 173; changing demographics, 173, 175; WWII boom, 54, 57
Potter, Joey, xii, xiii, 110, **113**, 115, **116**, 118, **121**, **122**, 178
Prancing Elites, 166, **167**, 168
Prancing Elites Project, The (reality TV show), 166, 168
Princess Lounge and Restaurant (Princess House), 68, 70, 106
public performances, 30, 147; African American, 76, 91, 92, 135, 141; deviant, 148; gendered, 101; regulation of, 32, 35
publics and counter-publics, 4, 129, 185n7

Queen Budgie I, 120, **121**. *See also* Atkinson, Budgie
Queen Danielle II, xii, **119**, 120, 121, 123, 180

Queen Eva, 102
Queen Vickie V (John G. Uptagrafft), xiii, 108, **117**, 118, 181
Queen Janette XII (Janette Curry), xiii, 107, 110, 114, 123, 156, 180
Queen Julie III (Julie Dunlap), xii, xiii, 114, 123, 179
Queen Richard IV (Richard Rain Perez), xii, xiii, 69, 105, 108, 118, 124, 125, 156, 180
queens: of African American Mardi Gras societies, 75, 77, 85–87, **89**, **90**, 91, 92, 162, 163; drag, 70, 104, 107, 115; Louis Diemert as Elizabeth II, 37, **38**; of the Order of Osiris, 105, **117**, 120, **121**, 123–25; of white Mardi Gras societies, 75, 137, 162, 163, 172; Zulu, 82, 83
queer, definitions and language choices, xix, xx
queer spaces, xx, 68–69, 109, 113, 118, 126, 173

racial uplift, 76, 86, 88, 92, 93, 160
Rayford, Julian Lee: on Black participation in Mardi Gras, 28, 77, 78, 92; on gender segregation in Mardi Gras, 101, **102**; and Joe Cain celebrations, 41, 42; and Joe Cain's mythmaking, 19, 22, 24, 25, 29, 30; on masking ban, 34, 35. See also *Chasin' the Devil Round a Stump*
Reconstruction: end of, 80; resentment, 25, 26, 27, 49; second, 10, 29
redface (costuming as Native Americans), 7, 10, 25, 26, 43, 102
respectability politics, 11, 12, 76, 87, 91, 134, 142, 144, 148
Richardson, Fredrick Douglas, 66, 95, 172
Richardson, Juanita, xiii, 64, 179
Richardson, Palmer, xiii, 11, 62, 131, 133, 146, 180
Richardson Moore, Pam (Pamela), xiii, 129, 134, 163, 180, 207n4
ritualistic play (Kern Jackson), 40, 146, 194n30
Roberts, L. Craig, xiii, 20, 34–35, 71, 114, 156, 179
RuPaul's Drag Race, 173

Russell, Loretta (Queen), **90**
Russell, Wilborn L., 28, 84, **86**, 91, 92, 94, 98, 144

SCLC (Southern Christian Leadership Conference), 94, 97, 204n83
Searcy, Cari, xiii, 173, 179, 180
segregation: downtown Mobile, 59, 61; experiences of, 3, **53**, **55**, 62–64, 95, 137; in Mardi Gras, 11–13, 28, 58, 75, 98, 129, 131, 134
Shantazio, Nick, xiii, 169, **170**, 171, 180
Shelton, Robert, 151, 152
Shuttlesworth, Rev. Fred, 94
Slacabamorinico, Chief, **27**, 30, 41–43. *See also* Joe Cain
slavery, 22, 23, 27, 35, 75, 77, 162, 163
Smart and Thrifty Ladies Social Club, 84, 88
Smith, Hilliard (King), **89**
Society for the Restoration and Beautification of Church Street Graveyard Inc., 44–46
Society Lounge (gay/lesbian bar), 106, 107, 110, 113
Soto, Domingo, xii, xiii, 65, 111–12, 163, 177
Southern Christian Leadership Conference. *See* SCLC
Southern Poverty Law Center (SPCL), 152
Stein & Still (bar), 65, 69
Stonewall riots, 100, 108

tableau/tableaux, **102**, 120, 158, 159
Tee Jays (gay/lesbian bar), 106, 107
Terrie Roberts (drag performer), 104, 107
Thompson, Tommy S., Jr. (King), **90**
tourism, 7, 44, 135, 171
Trinidad Carnival, 127
Tunstall, Charles, 154
Ture, Kwame (Stokely Carmichael), 97
Tuskegee Institute, 84, 87, 88
Twelfth Night. *See* Epiphany

UKA (United Klans of America), 151, 152, **153**, 154
University of South Alabama, 110, 120

urban renewal, 5, 52, 66, 67, 72
Utopia Social Club, 84–87, 92

Vaughan, John Alton (Al), xii, xiii, 106, 115, **117**, 178

Wallace, George, 46, **47**
War, The (documentary), 52, 54
Warren Street Baptist Church, 97
Washington, Samuel S. H., 80
Watson, Irmatean, 154
White Citizens Council, 65
white gaze, 134, 135, 140, 141, 146, 160
white supremacy: League of, 54; in Mardi Gras mythology, xviii, 6, 18, 24, 27, 163, 165; in Mobile's social structure, 55, 72, 76, 79, 127; violence, 54, 96, 150, 152
white women, 4, 9, 19, 58
Williams, Dorothy, 96
Williams, Hershel, 87
women: participation in LGBTQIA+ Mardi Gras, 112, 120, 123, 158; resistance to participation in LGBTQIA+ Mardi Gras, 123. *See also* Black women; lesbians; white women
Women's Space (feminist collective), 110
World War II, 52–57, 68, 94

YMCA, 68; "colored," 84

Zulu Social Aid and Pleasure Club, 82; feud with MCCA, 91–92

ABOUT THE AUTHOR

Photo by Daniel Caja Rubio

Isabel Machado is a cultural historian who specializes in the fields of gender and sexuality studies and celebration studies, currently focusing on carnivals and drag competitions. She has published articles in *Oral History*, *Journal of Festive Studies*, *O olho da história*, and *Study the South*.